LAST CHANCE HIGH

LAST CHANCE HIGH

How Girls and Boys
Drop In and Out of
Alternative Schools

Deirdre M. Kelly

Foreword by Jeannie Oakes

YALE UNIVERSITY PRESS
NEW HAVEN AND LONDON

Set in Baskerville and Gill Sans types by Maple-Vail Composition Services, Binghamton, New York. Printed in the United States of America by Edwards Brothers, Ann Arbor, Michigan.

Library of Congress Cataloging-in-Publication Data

Kelly, Deirdre M.
Last chance high : how girls and boys drop in and out of alternative schools / Deirdre M. Kelly ; foreword by Jeannie Oakes.
p.   cm.
Includes bibliographical references and index.
ISBN 0-300-05272-3
1. Evening and continuation schools—United States.   2. Dropouts—United States—Attitudes.   3. Sex differences in education—United States.   4. Educational sociology—United States.
LC5551.K44 1993
373.12'913'0973—dc20   92-41978 CIP

A catalogue record for this book is available from the British Library.
The paper in this book meets the guidelines for permanence and durability of the Committee on Production Guidelines for Book Longevity of the Council on Library Resources.

10 9 8 7 6 5 4 3 2 1

TO DAVE

CONTENTS

TABLES AND FIGURES

FOREWORD

Jeannie Oakes

For a century American schools have been buffeted by competing, even contradictory, ideas and interests. Perhaps most powerful are the tensions that arise from the nation's wish to be simultaneously an egalitarian community and a competitive meritocracy. These cultural tensions manifest themselves in the demand for a universal system of schooling that provides both a common education and the means for individuals to attain very different opportunities and rewards as adults. In part to resolve the obvious conflicts between these values and expectations, American schools have adopted an ideology and a structure of equal, but differentiated, opportunities in a common school. The ideal has been for all American youth to attend the common schools wherein they acquire the social and civic virtues necessary for democratic life. At the same time, the schools provide different instructional programs tailored to different students' needs; in senior high schools these programs range from rigorous academic curricula to programs stressing life skills and vocational training. The combination of common and differentiated school experiences has generally been viewed as educationally appropriate and socially just, given the diversity of American teenagers' abilities, interests, and motivations. Thus, an *equal* educational opportunity in American schools has been construed as that which best matches individual students' current competencies and best prepares them for their probable adult lives. With participation in (or dropping out of) various programs driven by individual choice and merit, the comprehensive high school—so the logic of American schooling goes—can provide fairly for the common good and for individual attainment.

Deirdre M. Kelly's study of two continuation high schools joins a growing body of work showing that this schooling solution is at best a naive and at worst a pernicious prescription, very likely to perpetuate social, political, and economic inequalities. In both form and substance, Kelly's two schools expose the underbelly of our idealistic claims about American schools. That Beacon and La Fuente exist at all illuminates the broken promise of comprehensive high schools to accommodate all young Americans. That both these schools and the students they serve are stigmatized as misfits exposes the hierarchical nature of differentiation in American schools. "Alternative" opportunities—particularly those provided as second chances—are viewed as second rate, and participating in them is regarded as a remedy for individual rather than institutional failings. Moreover, these two schools expose the artifice of meritocratic placements. Although most Beacon and La Fuente students were there because of their poor academic achievement or destructive school-related behaviors, some chose to attend these schools, and these students demonstrate how choice and merit are powerfully conditioned by race, class, and gender.

Kelly's work tells an intriguing story of schools whose explicit charge was to provide students at risk with an alternative to the comprehensive high school—an ostensibly benign, just, and appropriate (if extreme) form of differentiation. But, juxtaposing the image of this "safety net" for students with that of a "safety valve," Kelly provides a rich portrayal of schools whose implicit mandate was to relieve the comprehensive high schools of students who defied academic and social norms.

Beacon and La Fuente exist to be educational institutions where the failures of "regular" schools could succeed, where potential dropouts would stay in school, and where pregnant and parenting girls could safely complete their schooling. In fact, these schools had abundant failures and dropouts, and many girls were doubly stigmatized by their nontraditional choices and their schools. Some Beacon and La Fuente students were looking for a second chance, some were being pushed through school despite their disinterest in regular schooling, and many were on their way out of school altogether. All were disengaged. Within the two schools, however, the forms and consequences of disengagement play out differently. Using the lens of gender, Kelly examines the hierarchies that characterize the peer and organizational cultures inside continuation schools as well as between them and "regular" high schools. Girls come to Beacon and La Fuente for different reasons than boys, and once there, girls' experiences are shaped by low expectations, little serious attention, and traditional gender stereotypes. Although girls are more likely than boys to complete school, the consequences of marginalized schooling are different and more momentous for them.

Kelly's analysis brings home two central lessons about schooling and schooling research. First, school reformers and school researchers miss the central point when they view reform as primarily a technical matter. In the case of continuation schools, when the differentiated high school did not meet the needs of the most deviant students (first because they held jobs, later because they were maladjusted or "different"), reformers invented a more refined type of differentiation. Flexible, shortened schedules, an easier version of the traditional curriculum, individualized learning, counseling services, and small class sizes housed in separate settings were conceived to accommodate marginal students' special needs. These schools prided themselves, often with good cause, as being more caring, more innovative, and more relevant than regular schools. But on close examination we find that continuation schools largely parody the regularities of comprehensive high schools. Continuation schools bring into sharp relief the chameleon-like nature (to borrow Kelly's words) of reform: Eager to please their constituents and to "do better," schools and schooling researchers earnestly scrutinize and refine schooling technologies and create the illusion of change. At the same time, the deep structure of schools—firmly rooted beliefs about the nature of knowledge and learning, the purposes of education, and students' intellectual capacities, as well as the politically charged intersections of race, social class, gender, schooling, and life chances—go unquestioned and unchanged.

By placing basic descriptive statistics in the context of rich and thick descriptions of the meanings students assign to their day-to-day experiences, Kelly brings to life her account of disengagement in continuation high schools. She captures the complexity of these students and their schools with interpretive case-study methods that enable her to examine the process, context, and consequences of disengagement at first hand, inside the schools where it occurs. Herein lies the second important lesson of this work. Deirdre Kelly demonstrates that it is not simply the differentiated organizational structure of schooling that makes continuation high schools problematic; neither is it simply the culture of failure and deviance that characterizes these schools. Rather, it is the powerful combination of this structure and culture and individuals' efforts to act sensibly within them that illustrate how the good intentions of reformers go awry. Kelly's methods enable her to document and account for the interactive nature of disengagement—that is, the way structures and cultures trigger responses in students and how those responses, in turn, sometimes alter, but mostly cement, those structures and cultures. By doing so, Kelly reveals how these interactions reflect normative and political concerns as well as technical matters; she documents how both students and faculty respond in ways that are consistent with their existing knowledge, beliefs, and practices, and in ways governed by what they consider politically possible in the schooling context. In the end, Kelly's analysis of continuation high schools reminds us that serious efforts to understand and solve fundamental schooling problems like disengagement and dropping out must render problematic the values and politics that undergird schooling as well as its organizational structures and pedagogical techniques. These are lessons reformers and researchers would do well to learn.

PREFACE

High school is like a soap opera. You totally get stressed out cuz
you can't handle it. You've got to treat your boyfriend one way,
your friends another way, your parents another way, your
teachers one way. You've gotta separate all those things, and
you've gotta think about what you wanna do, and you get confused.
—Kris, age sixteen

At a time when the high school as an institution is under great scrutiny
and a fever of restructuring has taken hold of administrators, educators,
and businesspeople, a distinct world within this larger schooling environment has gone strangely unnoticed and its purpose and future un-
debated. It is the hidden world of continuation high schools. These
schools, variously called alternative, opportunity, and second-chance, make
up the nation's longest running, most widespread dropout-prevention
program, yet surprisingly little is known about what actually goes on
inside them.

Why is it critical to learn more about continuation schools? First,
although they are a safety net for some students, they are more often
an arena for the final stage of dropping out. In California, where this
form of alternative education was pioneered and flourishes today, about
one-fifth of all dropouts and pushouts leave via continuation schools (Calif.
Legislature, 1985: 40). In recent years only 10 percent of continuation
students in California have received a diploma or the equivalent (Stern
et al., 1985: 44). The two schools featured most prominently in this book,
Beacon and La Fuente (pseudonyms), show dismal rates of completion.

Comprehensive high schools send disengaging students to continuation, thus masking their own true dropout and pushout rates. Using
continuation programs as a safety valve, many districts continue to col-

lect attendance monies for students even when they are highly disengaged from the schooling enterprise.

The continuation school is also worth studying because it tells us a lot about the educational mainstream, although it is out of this mainstream. In California continuation schools have expanded in number from 13 before 1965 to 425 today. They serve more than 115,000 students—nearly one-tenth of California's high school student population and about one-fifth of eleventh- and twelfth-graders (Weber, 1972; Calif. Legislature, 1985; Calif. State Dept. of Education, 1987). Nationwide, an estimated four million students attend public alternative schools, of which continuation schools comprise the single largest category (Young, 1990: 19–21). With so many young people going through alternative programs, questions arise about why the "regular" schools are not working for so many.

What are continuation schools doing right, and what does this mean for restructuring the mainstream? High school reformers propose a number of features that characterize many continuation programs: small size (for example, by dividing comprehensive schools into houses or creating schools within schools), personalized learning, student involvement in decision making, innovative learning techniques, community involvement. What might be good for potential dropouts may work best for the bulk of high school students. In the case of the continuation school, however, its position as stepchild of public education limits its effectiveness in engaging students most alienated by academic learning. My study of this institution's history reveals that, like the lower tracks within the comprehensive high school, it too readily becomes a dumping ground for rebels and the academically underprepared. Unfortunately, educational policymakers have been content to provide a "second chance" to those not well served by the mainstream without necessarily demanding that it be a better chance. Indeed, continuation schools often offer diluted academic preparation and become stigmatized as second rate.

Within this hidden world, I focused the lens of gender, an analytical tool used in dropout research much less often than ethnicity and class. Among working-class and low-income students and across racial and ethnic groups, I found that girls and boys often disengage for different reasons, in different ways, and with different consequences. These differences are revealed in the metaphors students use to describe their schooling experiences. The soap opera analogy, a favorite among girls, points up the importance they place upon relationships. The opening quotation highlights that getting along with teachers and family members, maintaining close friendships, and going steady can conflict and create stress as girls like Kris weigh the value of striving for school success. As in the soap operas, girls tend to prefer talk as a means of coping with such conflict.

Disengaging boys, by contrast, are more likely to compare high school to prison where principals are wardens and teachers, guards; these boys often cope with their mandatory confinement by flaunting the rules and fighting with teachers and peers—a direct action approach more likely featured in cop shows than soap operas.

In daytime television serials, early pregnancy, illness, divorce, criminal activity, drug abuse, affairs, domestic violence—problems girls on the margin experience in their own lives and at school—are prime subject matter. Many educators consider such issues "personal," unfortunate distractions from the formal curriculum. The high schools' failure to acknowledge and make connections to students' soap opera–like experiences contributes to the disengagement process.

I chose to use the term *disengagement* instead of dropout or pushout, although these latter terms retain some usefulness in denoting endpoints in a long, often tortuous process. The binary concept of dropout/ stayin does not adequately capture the number of paths through high school and the fluidity among them or the myriad levels and ways students engage. Disengaging students may take an equivalency or GED test, enter independent or home study or adult education programs, drift through remedial classes and work study, or transfer to a continuation program. One student may just squeak by academically but attend classes regularly in order to see friends and enthusiastically participate in sports and other extracurricular activities. Another may ace standardized tests even while skipping school to avoid confrontation with teachers over unfinished homework or with peers who resent nonconformity.

In examining gender relations within an arena of disengagement— where, as one boy told me, "misfits rule"—the importance of peer groups emerged again and again. While many dropout studies focus on teacher-student relations or family background, I found in the continuation school that groups of disengaging peers warranted close scrutiny because they helped define alternative models of success that diverged for boys and girls. They influenced whether or not students bonded to the continuation school and how. And peer groups gave a few the power to challenge gender stereotypes, but more often maintained traditional class- and ethnic-shaped gender identities. This and other elements of the hidden curriculum, together with the formal curriculum, reinforced the different and more severely negative consequences of disengagement for girls.

To explore these issues, I spent more than a year in two continuation schools and a month in a third, observing these programs and interviewing in depth nearly a hundred students and dozens of teachers and administrators. Until recently, I was a consultant to California's High School Task Force, which had been charged with developing an action plan for restructuring secondary schooling statewide. Task Force members have been especially perplexed about what to do to aid what some have bluntly called "the bottom 40 percent," students expected to leave school without graduating and noncollege-bound youth who corporate employers say are unprepared for entry-level jobs. Concerns about the class and racial implications of proposed reforms are close to the surface. To date, however, a concern for gender equity has been invisible.

I hope to show that if we continue to ignore gender, as virtually all the influential reports on education reform issued in the 1980s did, our understanding of this "bottom 40 percent" will be seriously skewed. Continuation schools provide a crucial window for seeing how young people slip in and out of the educational system, in ways patterned by relations not only of class and ethnicity but of gender as well.

David Tyack, Martin Carnoy, and Myra Strober read an early version of the entire manuscript, and I would like to thank them for their advice and encouragement. Dave Beers allowed me to test my ideas out on him repeatedly and provided editorial guidance and invaluable support and inspiration when I needed them most. A Spencer Foundation fellowship supported me financially during the early writing. Kelly Warner helped me generate the statistics used in the study. JoAnn Johnson transcribed taped interviews with speed and precision after my arms gave out. Phyllis Bravinder, Jean Gonick, Dan Hubig, Marion Kelly, Sue Kolodin, and members of the Beers, Kelly, and Wade families helped me maintain my sense of humor and sanity along the way. Nelly Stromquist, Chiqui Ramirez, Leslie Roman, and Josette McGregor read individual chapters and provided me with useful suggestions. Gladys Topkis of Yale University Press thankfully saw potential in the early version of the manuscript. Finally, I would like to express my gratitude to the students, teachers, administrators, and support staff who participated in the study and unfortunately must remain anonymous. Without their cooperation, this research would not have been possible.

ABBREVIATIONS

APP   Attendance, Productivity, and Punctuality; a program designed to monitor a student's progress

CHSPE   California High School Proficiency Exam; with parent's or guardian's permission, a person can take this test at age sixteen

CSBE   California State Board of Education

CSDE   California State Department of Education

GED   General Educational Development; normally a person must be at least eighteen to take these tests

ISP   Independent Studies Program

ROC   Regional Occupational Center; a student must be sixteen or a junior to attend

ROP   Regional Occupational Program; same as ROC but classes are usually held at the regular high school

SAM   School-Age Mothers

I

OVERVIEW

High school is like being pregnant for twelve years. When you're pregnant you wait and wait until the moment is right. Each trimester of the pregnancy seems forever, as for school, a grade level means eternity. When you're pregnant there's lesser things you do, as for school, there's no party. You wait for the end of being pregnant. You wait for 220 credits [and your diploma].
—Cecilia, age sixteen, a recent mother and continuation student

I think school is like the circus. The principal is the ringmaster and the teachers are the trainers. We, the students, are the animals. Sometimes I think we're pretty much animals with invisible cages called morals. Of course we can leave school at any time, but you must suffer the consequences—just as a lion could lose it and attack its master, the lion would get severely punished. The animals listen to the trainers, and the trainers listen to the ringmaster, and the ringmaster runs the show. There would be no circus if it weren't for the animals! But still, even as the stars of the show, they pay heavy consequences for screwing up.

Without students there would be no school. But they still treat us like dirt.
—Todd, age seventeen, continuation student

High school is like a soap opera, a war zone, and a crack house blended all into one. There are all kinds of people; all different types. There is always some people who hate another group of people, people who talk about others behind their back, and people who plan to take revenge on others. There are "couples" who are either always fighting or always "making out" or both

1

at the same time. These people are the ones that make high school seem like a soap opera.

Then there are those who are fight-happy. They love to fight others and get a thrill when they kick other people's asses. These people make high school a war zone.

Finally, there are the people who take drugs, and don't care about anything, and don't know anything because they are too stoned to notice that life is passing them by. These people are the ones who make school seem like a crack house.

If I had been born a man, I would view high school differently. Guys really don't pay attention to "couples" unless they have a girlfriend of their own. So if I was a guy, I probably wouldn't care about people who were couples. Plus, if I was a guy, I'd probably be fight-happy.

Altogether, high school is a place where no one wants to be, but everyone has to go. I wish everyone could get along, then maybe I'd really like high school.

—Amber, age sixteen, continuation student

These are voices from the hidden world of the continuation high school. The inhabitants of this world are difficult to classify. In the state of California, about 45 percent of the continuation students are female, 55 percent male; these proportions seem to hold true nationally, as well (Duke and Muzio, 1978: 469–70).[1] The racial, ethnic, and class composition of continuation schools varies depending on the community, but alternative school evaluations and reports often include little or no information on the background characteristics of students (Duke and Muzio, 1978: 469). In urban areas, typically well over half the students are African-American and Latino, although whites make up 60 percent of students enrolled across California. Arnove and Strout (1980: 463), who observed alternative schools for disruptive youth in twelve urban areas across the United States, concluded that such programs "may become enclaves for black, Latino, native American, and poor white students." A case study of one district in Washington state "confirmed that at-risk options serve a student clientele that is, if not minority, disproportionately poor" (Young, 1990: 122). In wealthy suburbs, continuation programs often take on the character of free schools; they serve primarily

---

1. Foley and McConnaughy (1982: 63) surveyed eight of New York City's ten public alternative high schools and found that, on average, about half of the students were female and the other half were male. This masked some differences, however; three schools had twice as many girls as boys, while two schools had twice as many boys as girls.

middle-class white youths who have basic academic skills but are "turned off" by conventional schooling practices. In high density, low-income communities, continuation schools can become warehouses for academically underprepared sons and daughters of working-class families or single parents receiving welfare.

Given this diversity, generalizing about the students is hazardous, but as the excerpts that open this chapter show, they tend to be more plainspoken and oppositional than the typical high school student. "I like these kids," one continuation teacher told me. "At the first place I taught, students would take everything I said as the truth. Here, they're more skeptical, more of a challenge." This quality, valued in certain contexts (say, in honors classes, where teachers often delight in students who question conventional wisdom), created trouble in others. Unwillingness to conform to the "good student" mold brings many a student to the doors of continuation school.

Joan, a gifted mimic, relived a trip to the vice principal's office for chronically missing her early morning classes at the comprehensive high school. In an interview she recalled Mr. Lucca's words:

"You don't like this school very much, do you? You don't like to get up in the morning, do you?" That's what he starts off like, then his voice gets louder. [Joan pauses for effect, then pounds her fist on the desk.] "Do you hang around on The Strip? I mean, who are your friends, really? What kind of things do you do? I mean, is it because of a boyfriend? Drugs? Is there something going on here? I mean, do you party all night and you just can't get up in the morning? Is that what it is?"

And you are sitting there and you're like, "No."

And he'd go, "Well, I just don't understand." And he starts banging again. "I just don't understand what could be going on in your mind. Now would you like to tell me what's going through your mind, when you're sitting at home during first and second period? Why don't you just drop out of school if that's what you want? Why are you wasting my time?"

And then I'd just sit there. I was the type, I'd come straight out and just go, "I don't have an excuse for you. I was sleeping. I just felt like sleeping. That's all I can say. I just don't like coming to school." Which I think just infuriated him more cuz he would start yelling.

Joan's story is common among continuation students and represents a power struggle between pupil and school authorities. During a role play on how to avoid conflict with teachers over tardiness, continuation students saw little difference between "brownnosing" and diplomacy. When the counselor leading the session suggested that students try to change themselves and the way they looked at the situation, Tom interpreted this to mean, "I flex to please the teacher." He rejected the counselor's idea that a "win-win" scenario was possible.

Most continuation students have disengaged from school, but they do so at different levels of intensity and for different reasons. Some took a vacation from their studies, distracted by a new car or a boy- or girlfriend. "As far as classes went, I participated and tried. I did everything I was scheduled and supposed to do. But it just all went downhill, down the highway to the beach, as soon as I got that car," recounted Bob. Others never really liked school, and a few are on a collision course with disaster.

"We're not getting kids who are filtered in here," a teacher reminded me. "We're getting anywhere from behavior problems to academic problems. So in other words, we have a mishmash of students with all different needs." Because they do not have the same needs, the students, not surprisingly, experience continuation school differently. Kris lived with her boyfriend and needed a compressed school day in order to work. She also liked the continuation school because "teachers aren't commanders; they're friends. They let you learn at your own pace. A lot of people say, 'Beacon is for losers.' I don't think so. We're just people who aren't satisfied with the regular school."

Jim, sent to La Fuente against his will for poor attendance at the comprehensive high school, had little good to say about his time at continuation:

> Here, you just go to school on time and do what they tell you
> to do, but at [comprehensive high] they really go into details;
> they give you a subject and explain it all the way. Here, they
> don't care if you do it good or bad. As long as you do it, they
> give you points for it.

In between Kris and Jim were those who agreed with Matt that, whether continuation or comprehensive: "School is school."

Not all continuation students have been or are in special education classes. In fact, most are of average ability, and a fair number—roughly equivalent to their distribution in the general school population—have been identified as "mentally gifted" (Osborne and Byrnes, 1990). Not all continuation students are juvenile delinquents, gang members, or drug addicts, contrary to popular mythology. In the schools I came to know, about one in ten had been or was on probation, usually for being drunk and disorderly, smoking marijuana, or petty theft.

WHERE ARE THE GIRLS?

How does the process of disengagement from school differ for girls and boys within the continuation high school? Again contrary to conventional wisdom, girls now fail to graduate from high school at almost the same rate as boys,[2] and for girls the adverse employment consequences

---

2. At the national level, girls have dropped out of high school at nearly the rate of boys for the past two decades (Markey, 1988: 37). Before that, girls enrolled in and graduated from high school in larger numbers than boys (U.S. Bureau of the Census, 1978: 379).

Dropout statistics vary widely depending on, among other things, the source of the data, the definition of dropout, and the method of calculating the rate (see Rumberger, 1987, for a discussion of these issues). Today two of the most widely cited sources of national dropout data are the U.S. Census and the "High School and Beyond" study. The Census Bureau calculates the dropout rate as the proportion of a given age cohort that is not enrolled in school and has not completed high school. Rumberger analyzed census data for October 1986 by ethnicity and sex and concluded: "In general, dropout rates are similar for males and females" (forthcoming: 7). Among persons aged twenty-five and older, for example, 26 percent of white females and 25 percent of white males had not completed high school; the figures for persons of Mexican origin were 57 percent for females and 56 percent for males. Among eighteen- to nineteen-year-olds, 11 percent of white females, 13 percent of white males, 35 percent of Mexican-origin females, and 32 percent of Mexican-origin males were dropouts in 1986 (ibid.: table 1).

"High School and Beyond," a large longitudinal survey begun by the National Center for Education Statistics in 1980, includes a group of tenth-graders whose educational progress has been tracked at two-year intervals. At the end of what would have been their senior year (spring 1982), 14 percent of white males, 13 percent of white females, 21 percent of African-American males, 14 percent of African-American females, and 19 percent each of Hispanic males and females had failed to graduate from high school (Barro and Kolstad, 1987: table 4.1). (The High School and Beyond study understates dropout rates because students who dropped out before the spring of their sophomore year were not included in the baseline survey.)

Subsequent follow-up surveys using High School and Beyond data have shown that a sizable proportion of dropouts return to school and obtain a diploma or, more often, a GED. For example, Kolstad and Kaufman (1989) found, using the 1986 follow-up survey results, that 44 percent of the dropouts had completed high school or the equivalent. Overall, slightly more males than females had obtained a diploma or GED (45 vs. 43 percent); the difference was more pronounced among Hispanics, particularly for those passing the GED: 40 percent of males vs. 27 percent of females had completed high school or the equivalent (ibid.: table 1).

are significantly greater (Markey, 1988). Because women are in a different, often subordinate, position within major social, political, and economic institutions, girls may disengage from school for different reasons, in different ways, with different consequences. This study aims to explore these potential differences as well as similarities.

Historically, research and public policy agendas have given girl truants and dropouts a much lower priority. First, most researchers have been men who may have felt they could gain easier access to male dropouts. Second, from the time when educational reformers and others in society first came to see dropouts as a serious problem, at the turn of the century, schools have been criticized as overly feminine organizations that have pushed out boys—working-class boys especially—at a higher rate than girls (Tyack and Hansot, 1990).

Third, researchers and policymakers have assumed that boys alone were future breadwinners; a high male dropout rate suggested a potential shortage of productive labor. Further, unemployed boys seemed prone to acts of delinquency that threatened private property (for example, burglary) and the social order (for example, gang violence); in contrast, girl dropouts were more likely to stay at home to help with family tasks and thus were less publicly visible as potential delinquents.

Fourth, scholars have tended to conceptualize the reasons for dropout as school-related rather than personal or family-related. In doing so, they have inadvertently directed attention away from the interaction between institutions. Do girls leave school because of early pregnancy, or is early pregnancy a means of escape from an institution—the school—that has failed to offer them a sense of purpose and competence? Researchers have implicitly assumed that school has had little influence on girls' decisions to leave early to get married or have a baby.

To date, much of the research on students who fail to complete high school can be divided into two imperfect schools of thought. The dominant school—which fits within the status-attainment and social-psychology traditions—conceives of early school leaving as dropping out. Researchers who use this framework favor correlation models in which students' behavior, performance in school, psychological states, and family background are independent variables (for example, Ekstrom et al., 1986). This approach generally casts dropping out as an individual act, signifying individual, or perhaps family or cultural, failure.

The other school of thought conceives of noncompleters as pushouts. Such researchers see the variables emphasized by the status-attainment school as symptoms, not causes. They focus on unequal economic, political, and social structures and certain schooling practices, like tracking and expulsion, that serve to stigmatize, discourage, and exclude certain children. Researchers using this model have tended to document the inequities in the economic and political system and to have then postulated that pushouts are a product of the reproduction of the capitalist order (for example, Bowles and Gintis, 1976). Viewed through this lens, how the educational system sorts working-class and ethnic minority children into the lowest places in a labor force stratified by class, ethnicity, and gender and why the pushouts comply is relatively unproblematic.

The few ethnographies or qualitative research studies done on dropouts or pushouts have highlighted student perspectives and the immediate context within which these were shaped (Wax, 1970; Haro, 1979; Olsen, 1982; Fine, 1986; Hess et al., 1986). Several of these have focused on a particular ethnic group, but none that I am aware of has made gender its major focus.

In the dropout-pushout literature, gender has either been ignored or, like ethnicity and class, treated as a demographic variable (that is, sex, the biological division into female and male); recent exceptions have focused on the experiences of female dropouts (Earle and Roach, 1987; Zane, 1988; Fine and Zane, 1989). The correlational approach has indicated broad dimensions of the problem, such as early pregnancy for girls, without pinpointing the human processes involved. Typically, attempts to explain why certain subgroups drop out at disproportionately high rates do not go much beyond post-hoc references to sex-role socialization (for example, Poole and Low, 1982); adults in positions of hierarchical authority over children, such as parents and teachers, pass on their prejudices, values, and habits to the next generation.

In contrast, the influence of peers on the disengagement process, while recognized as important in the dropout literature, has been little studied. Eventual dropouts and pushouts tend to have friends who are likewise disengaging from school (Ekstrom et al., 1986: 56). Yet scholars have neglected the diverse situational meanings of gender, class, and ethnicity produced by such friendship and peer groups.

Some ethnographic work has drawn attention to the critical influence of peers on the success of certain class and ethnic groups in school generally. Willis (1977), for example, studied a group of white, working-class "lads" who rejected as feminine the school ideology of individualism, conformity, and academic credentials. For the lads, manual labor came to symbolize a kind of masculinity and opposition to authority. Willis focused his analysis on boys, however, and did not discuss gender as it interacts with class and ethnicity, nor did he detail the school setting by analyzing the organizational influences on the formation of the lads' class, ethnic, and gender identities.

FROM FACTORY TO SOAP OPERA

When businesspeople, scholars, and educators discuss how to improve education, they often implicitly equate schools with factories. In this model, the goals are economic efficiency and improving aggregate output, as measured by test scores and other indicators of student quality. The analogy is not lost on students, who more often see themselves as workers than as products. "High school is like having a job and your units are the pay," wrote Irene, adding: "Some get promoted, others don't." Roberto, facing the strong possibility of unemployment, stretched the metaphor still further. "School," he explained, "is like a job without pay. You sit there and bust your ass just to get a diploma which won't even get you a decent job any more."

The metaphor of the school-as-factory where children are processed (educated) and approved (awarded a diploma) is familiar to anyone who has spent time in classrooms. A very different metaphor of high school arose from my discussions with continuation students—the soap opera. In this drama, girls' societal scripts differ from those of boys; like age, ethnicity, and class, gender status carries with it certain expectations. These structural forces influence individuals as they improvise with peers on societal scripts and create personal ones, experimenting with actions and attitudes and refining strategies for coping within institutions such as the high school (Davies, 1984). For those marginalized by institutional practices like tracking, academic failure, in-grade retention, and standardized tests as well as curriculum and instruction, the drama becomes painful and tiresome. Such students seek out alternative, more sustaining roles. In disengaging from school, girls often turn to relationships that can lead to pregnancy and marriage, boys to jobs.

The dramas observed here unfold within the continuation high school setting, although the students on center stage reflect on parts played within the conventional school setting as well. Although the heart of my analysis concerns the improvising by individuals within certain youth subcultures and against other subcultures, their actions and attitudes cannot be fully understood without a discussion of the basic plot (the givens of history) and the mise-en-scène (the institutionalized setting).

In chapter 2, I provide a history of the continuation school as a way of exploring the social and political meanings attached to the category *dropout* as well as of analyzing what groups have pushed for and benefited from the maintenance of an organization designed to serve mainstream school "misfits." Chapter 3 argues that the stigma attached to the continuation school and its students, reinforced by institutional practices (namely, districtwide use of the program as a disciplinary threat) and grounded in the day-to-day routines of comprehensive and continuation administrators, teachers, and students, persists and limits reengagement.

The next four chapters more closely examine how gender interacts with school-based practices and organizational factors and how student cultures operate for both boys and girls to produce dropouts and push-outs. Chapter 4 focuses on the symptoms and signs of disengagement, while chapter 5 discusses the causes and timing of disengagement by gender. Chapter 6 explores the gender implications of the continuation school's formal and hidden curricula (including the critical role played by peer groups in maintaining traditional gender identities) and how these tend to reinforce the different and more negative consequences of disengagement for girls. Finally, chapter 7 shows that girls were marginally more successful at reengaging (as measured by the dropout and graduation rates at Beacon and La Fuente) and analyzes the various reasons for this, highlighting distinctive organizational features of the continuation school as well as peer influences.

In blending these four different levels of analysis (individual, peer-group, organizational, and historical-structural), I have tried to address one of the most intractable problems in social theory: how to conceptualize the relationship between choice and coercion, between individual agency and structural constraint (Giddens, 1979). This tension underlies the debate over whether disengaging students should be seen as dropouts or pushouts, whether students choose to transfer to continuation schools or are coerced into them, and whether some girls de-emphasize academic success in favor of family out of preference or because they are sex-role-socialized.

ENTERING THE HIDDEN WORLD

Before entering graduate school, I lived and worked in the cities where La Fuente and Beacon continuation schools are located. My last employer was a community-based organization that provided job training and other services to low-income people. As the grant writer for a project serving ethnic-minority single mothers, I recorded abbreviated life histories of participants, all of whom had been on welfare and most of whom had dropped out of high school. With hindsight, the mostly middle-aged women regretted their decision to drop out of school. Blanca, age thirty-five, told me:

> Boy, if I was back to seventeen or eighteen years old, I would have stayed in school, graduated, and studied all I could because you never know what's going to turn out. Like I never

expected to have handicapped children, then having to cope with them myself afterwards [after her divorce].

Yet they were unclear on why they felt differently about school at the time of departure; elsewhere they spoke enthusiastically of working in local canneries, earning good pay, and helping their families financially. Their stories sparked my interest in studying the disengagement process among girls who were still struggling in school. I wondered how their experiences might differ from those of disengaging boys and among themselves, especially in light of dramatic changes in the community. The fast-growth economy had helped spawn housing developments and industrial parks where orchards stood twenty years before. Jobs had attracted large numbers of immigrants, and an insufficient supply of housing to meet the needs of low- and middle-income families had created familiar urban problems. The once-promising high-technology economy, intertwined with and buffeted by volatile world markets, now seemed increasingly polarized into the haves and have-nots.

The year before beginning the fieldwork, I assisted with two dropout studies in three districts. The first was a collaborative project in Beacon and La Fuente districts aimed at developing a system for tracking dropouts through high school to produce more accurate longitudinal dropout rates. A mid-sized, suburban, centrally administered district, Beacon Unified's enrollment shrank by half in the 1970s and early 1980s, but it remained solvent through school closings and teacher layoffs. As the student population declined, its ethnic composition shifted so that minorities became the near majority (primarily Asian- and Mexican-American).[3] La Fuente District, spanning a suburban-style barrio and pockets of wealth, served primarily low-income ethnic minorities. It had twice the student enrollment of Beacon and faced financial trouble as well as employee unrest.

Administrators in both districts suggested I work with teachers at the continuation high schools to deepen my understanding of the dropout problem as it manifested itself locally. Meanwhile, in the Willows District, I was investigating whether or not the recent implementation of a court-ordered desegregation plan had increased the number of students dropping out or being pushed out, and I discovered that the continuation school was one place students disgruntled with busing and ethnic tension went.

---

3. White and middle-class flight does not explain the changes in the ethnic composition of Beacon's student population. Instead, whites as a group were older and having fewer children than the new Asian-immigrant and more established Mexican-American groups.

Somewhat fortuitously, then, I had gained access to three different continuation schools in three districts. As a pilot for my research, the principals agreed to let me observe classes and talk to students and teachers, both alone and in groups. At Beacon, my suggestion to involve students formally in the collaborative dropout-reduction project met with enthusiasm. Teachers recruited twelve volunteers, with whom I met alone for eight two-hour group discussions. They agreed to serve as an advisory group and help survey their classmates. The advisory group helped me identify student concerns and ways of wording particular interview questions. After the interview schedule was complete, I trained them with the help of a video camera to do interviewing. In all, the students interviewed a stratified random sample of thirty-six of their peers and helped me analyze some preliminary findings. On the basis of the fact that three-fourths of those surveyed said they would prefer to be interviewed one-on-one rather than in a group, I decided to make individual rather than focus-group interviews the heart of my research.

At the end of the 1987–88 school year, I received permission to conduct my fieldwork at Beacon and La Fuente; logistically, I did not feel I could adequately cover three sites, and Beacon and La Fuente seemed to contrast most. I continued to collaborate with student and teacher volunteers on dropout-prevention projects. The Beacon survey revealed that the transition from junior to senior high had been particularly difficult. Acting on this, a number of students, teachers, administrators, and I developed a group called Student-to-Student. Thirteen students were trained as peer counselors and spent time at two junior high schools talking to small groups of students about their own schooling experiences and answering questions.

At La Fuente, the principal wanted me to work with the orientation and student activities teachers. I led group discussions as a regular part of the three-week orientation cycle. In addition, student council members decided that fighting on campus was a problem and, under my guidance, surveyed the school to determine the causes.

A MINI-TRADITIONAL SCHOOL AND A HYBRID ALTERNATIVE

Both La Fuente and Beacon were established in the mid-1960s, in response to a state requirement that all school systems provide continuation or equivalent education for youths suspended long-term or face financial penalties. At the beginning, district administrators meant La Fuente and Beacon to serve pushouts, students considered troublemakers. For this reason, surveillance was and is at a premium.

No fancy facade, mascot, or playing field announces the presence of these or most other continuation schools. Few people know they even exist. Although students are closely watched inside the continuation gates, they are largely hidden from the outside community.

Beacon and La Fuente at a Glance

Beacon	La Fuente
128 pupils	343 pupils
55% white	20% white
individualized	traditional
suburban	urban

La Fuente is surrounded by a six-foot-high wire fence, with fifteen portable classrooms, a library, a multi-use room, and an administrative complex forming a circle around a yard of asphalt and grass. "There's no place they can't see us," Carmen, a school-age mother, said. Students who tried to jump the fence were easily stopped by the plainclothes officer assigned full-time to the campus or by La Fuente's informal enforcer, Mr. Zuniga. During my first week at the school, Mr. Zuniga stopped me as I walked across the yard during class time, demanding to search my backpack. I explained that I was not a student but someone with permission to observe. The experience helped me empathize with Alva, whom I later overheard complaining about her treatment: "We're not prisoners. We're La Fuente students!"

Beacon's surveillance methods were more friendly. The school is not fenced in, but all rooms face in toward a courtyard and feature tinted windows that allow staff members to look out without being seen. Teachers and administrators considered this "visual control" critical to maintaining discipline. One can leave the campus only by passing by the office or around back and through the one-exit parking lot. On rare days when students did not return to classes promptly after lunch, the secretary or principal would flick the lights on and off and admonish them over the intercom. One afternoon, as I chatted with teachers in the faculty lounge, Mr. Ullmann and Ms. Prack spotted two of their counselees through the windows overlooking the parking lot. Together they dashed out in time to smile and wave at the students as they hopped into a pickup truck. The boys paused and then, apparently hoping to avoid punishment later, returned to class.

Continuation education usually involves a flexible and reduced school schedule, individualized instruction, extra counseling, small class size, open-entry/open-exit (students can enter and graduate from the program throughout the year), and a curricular emphasis on personal growth and vocational and academic goals. Because of these and other features, continuation education, which has been around since the turn of the century, can be seen as a forerunner of the 1970s alternative school movement. Like many alternative schools, Beacon and La Fuente lacked systematic guiding philosophies and were unstable (Deal and Nolan, 1978: 6–7). As Deal predicted, both schools evolved into more stable forms: La Fuente became more traditional while Beacon, once threatened with closure during a budget crunch, developed into a hybrid most closely resembling the "negotiation" school, itself largely a mixture of traditional and "do your own thing" models (8–16).

Although La Fuente was small and had retained its variable credit system, classes (with the exception of those taught by the only original teacher left on the staff) were not individualized. The school's last two principals had been hired with a mandate to improve its dumping-ground reputation. Both men wanted to do away with what were derisively referred to as "packets," sets of work sheets, activities, and readings that students completed at their own pace. Teachers interviewed said students did not learn this way; they argued that the packets were punitive, boring—which created discipline problems—and not conducive to learning group skills such as participating in discussion. Equally important, teachers had not been trained to use this approach and felt it left them without a teaching role. Argued one, "Teachers go batty, too, just day by day handing out a work sheet or packet." Most teachers lectured or had students read aloud from texts and complete written exercises, emphasizing existing knowledge in graded tests.

In the La Fuente classrooms, teachers made instructional decisions and established norms for behavior. Schoolwide, administrators made decisions and resolved conflicts. The counselor's time was consumed by class scheduling and disciplinary action rather than personal counseling. A few teachers informally attended to what the principal called students' "special needs" in group discussions and during one of their two prep periods, but most others agreed with him that the school had previously neglected "cognitive needs" and that personal problems were best dealt with by trained counselors.

Beacon had been better able to resist reverting to a mini-comprehensive (that is, traditional) school for several reasons. First, the school opened with a clear commitment to counseling and self-paced learning. Originally, all four teachers were also credentialed counselors, and two were still at Beacon (a third substituted regularly) during my field research. Second, at a critical phase, Beacon attracted a principal committed to alternative education, and under his nine-year tenure, the school earned the reputation as a continuation model. Third, school board members and central office administrators supported Beacon despite some early public opposition, fanned by real estate interests worried about the potentially negative effects of a stigmatized educational program on property values.

At the time of this study, Beacon students, after their skill levels were evaluated, worked individually on a variety of activities negotiated with a teacher. Each student contracted with up to six teachers to achieve certain competencies within a set time frame. Usually, students could choose from among a variety of texts and other learning materials. In contrast with a past tendency to let students initiate learning activities, teachers emphasized what students needed to learn within the framework of discipline-based courses required by the district of all high school students. In response to a recent accreditation evaluation and district concerns, some teachers offered group instruction (usually lectures combined with discussion and group activities and projects) once a week. Instead of administering tests, teachers graded students individually on the quality and quantity of work done; failure was not considered possible.

Beacon students worked around large tables and could use one another as resources; at La Fuente, students sat at individual desks arranged in traditional rows and talking was discouraged. In contrast to a more traditional school, Beacon tried to minimize rules and pressures and had previously allowed cigarette smoking on campus. School staff at Beacon sought student advice on how to deal with infractions of existing rules through an advisory group. Within the classroom, most teachers negotiated informal norms with students and used a variety of strategies for resolving conflict.

Although historically Beacon has been more successful than La Fuente at retaining and graduating students, the levels of academic preparation of the respective student bodies have been roughly comparable, if passage rates of district competencies are valid indicators. Both feature tidy campuses with portable classrooms surrounding well-maintained grounds. La Fuente is a more ethnically diverse environment in terms of its teaching staff and student body. It is also larger because it houses both a SAM program and an independent studies program, which enrolled about two hundred additional students.

Table 1 summarizes information about the two sites and provides a comparison with the latest California data on continuation education programs along a number of dimensions.

TABLE I

Comparison of Beacon and La Fuente, 1988–89, with All California Continuation Programs, 1986–87

Characteristic	Beacon '88–89	La Fuente '88–89	California '86–87
Community profile	Middle income with pockets of poverty; ethnic mix but majority white	Low income; majority minority, particularly Mexican origin	41% small city 29% rural 16% urban 14% suburban
History and reputation, including no. of 18 state-set Performance Achievement Requirements (PARs) met	Founded 1966; has ranked among top continuation programs in CA; met or exceeded 11 out of 18 PARs in '86–87	Founded 1965; bad reputation, recent efforts to raise standards; met or exceeded 1 out of 18 PARs in '86–87	Part-time education law passed 1919; strengthened by 1965 law
Transfer procedures	100% voluntary; 2 feeder schools	50% voluntary; 10 feeder schools	82% voluntary
Cumulative enrollment	216 pupils	748 pupils	103,980 pupils
Average school size	128 pupils	343 pupils	122 pupils
Student:staff ratio	13:1 full-time, certificated	17:1 full-time, certificated	17:1 full-time, certificated
Student body			
% Female	42%	46%	44%
% Ethnic Minority	45%	80%	40%
% Latino	34%	54%	26%
% Black	3%	14%	10%

TABLE 1 (*Continued*)

Characteristic	Beacon '88–89	La Fuente '88–89	California '86–87
Teaching staff			
% Female	44%	61%	unavailable
% Ethnic Minority	0%	61%	unavailable
% Latino	0%	28%	unavailable
% Black	0%	33%	unavailable
Counseling	6 teacher-counselors	.5 for schools; 1 for SAM	unavailable
Pregnant minors	no program	on-site program 17% of enrollment	at 77/449 sites
Pupils passing district exams			
Reading	79%	59%	66%
Computation	59%	58%	56%
Writing	54%	79%	55%

Sources: CSDE, 1988; CSDE, unpublished data, 1989.

IN THE EYES OF THE BEHOLDER:
HELPER, HIPPIE, STONER, SPY

I enjoyed relatively warm relationships with the teachers and students who worked directly with me on the collaborative project. I helped teachers by leading discussions, reading essays, organizing outings, running errands. I worked with students to run the student store and organize social activities, tutored those who needed extra help, listened to personal problems, and informally advised them on college and work plans. These activities seemed to dispel the inevitable awkwardness created by having a stranger, without a defined role, observing among them.

Initially, a few teachers seemed wary of me, perhaps suspecting I might be informally evaluating them for the administration. To most, I appeared relatively young, reserved, helpful, nonthreatening, and neutral (perhaps naive) with respect to internal politics. I was occasionally mistaken for a student by new or visiting school people. Fortunately, at both schools the teachers I worked with closely on the collaborative project were generally well liked by fellow teachers, administrators, and students.

The first and sometimes lasting impression many students had of me was that of a "hippie" because of the way I presented myself: long, straight, unstyled hair; neat, but casual dress (typically jeans, tennis shoes, and a blouse); no makeup; straight talking with occasional '60s slang; knowledgeable about rock music; and slightly "weird" because I wore no wedding ring, had kept my maiden name, and preferred that students address me by my first name. As with school staff, students felt I looked younger than I was. One boy asked if I was a new classmate, and when I explained I was a researcher, he exclaimed: "I was gonna say, 'You must have really messed up bad!' "

In a sense, these perceptions of me, combined with my "helper" role, eased student fears that I was a "narc." A number of students tended to divide the adult world into "business types" (conformists) and "hippies" (nonconformists), and given this dichotomy, the fact that I was seen as a hippie meant that more students identified with me than not. I did have to battle a cynicism among students, particularly the boys, about research. They justifiably complained that little seemed to change as a result of surveys (such as are done during accreditation, which both schools went through during my fieldwork), and they felt like "guinea pigs" being observed. "Are you studying us?" was an uncomfortable question for me to address. At the same time, most enjoyed talking one-on-one about their schooling experiences with an interested, comparatively nonjudgmental person who wielded no formal authority over them; only one student, an African-American boy selected at random, declined to be formally interviewed.

About a month into my fieldwork, I began to worry that I would not meet and establish a rapport with the most disengaged students, particularly at Beacon. At La Fuente, I got to know new students through orientation class, including the most disengaged who sometimes did not even enter regular classes. At Beacon, these were the students who actively avoided sitting near me and prompted me to write in my journal: "I feel like a spy." At this time, the principal asked if I would be willing to teach choir. Instead, I persuaded him to let me offer a music appreciation class, emphasizing the roots of music popular on campus, especially heavy metal and punk rock, rap, and reggae. In addition to recruiting and getting to know a few highly disengaged students, I was able to observe peer group conflict and put myself in a continuation teacher's shoes in a way not possible otherwise.

Teaching the class and participating in the collaborative project contributed significantly to my understanding of the research site and yet created some difficult moments as well. First, students complained to me about certain teachers and asked me to take their case to the administration, arguing that adults would take me more seriously. At the same time, teachers asked me to advise them on how to deal with particular students. In both cases, I could usually beg off politely. Second, and more of an ethical dilemma, I witnessed events and overheard comments pertinent to my research that did not always cast participants in a positive light. And although school staff members were aware of my research purpose (and perhaps reminded of my researcher role, as opposed to my teacher or helper role, by my frequent note taking), many came to take my presence too much for granted or did not realize how widely I had cast my research net. In my quest for information, I hesitated to remind them, as perhaps a news reporter would remind an interviewee, "This is on the record."

Third, the students' stereotyped image of me as a hippie convinced many that I must be experienced with drugs, as of course quite a few of them were. For example, Janis, a Beacon student, confided in an interview: "See, I could see you hanging around in a stoner group." I consciously never initiated conversations about drugs, yet students, particularly those in my music class, loved to question me about what drugs I had tried, how often, and so on. In addition, drugs were a favorite topic among themselves, and because I was aware that certain students were trying to kick cocaine and marijuana habits and others were fighting peer pressure to try these drugs, I finally felt that I had to at least express my discomfort. The following excerpt from my field notes documents the approach I used:

> Rich mentioned his electric bong [water pipe] again. I saw this as a chance to discuss my attitude on drugs with the group as a whole. "I get concerned when I hear so much discussion about drugs. I think it is possible for some people to use some drugs occasionally, socially, and that doesn't mean you're a drug addict. But I just don't want you guys to be looking back years from now with a drug problem and wonder, 'Why did Deirdre hear me talking about this and never show her concern?' " Dennis asked if I was a counselor. "No," I said, "but I just feel that by now you're all my friends, and I'd share my concern with any of my friends if I thought there was a lot of focus on drugs. That's why I'm a little upset with all the talk in class about them." (Beacon, field notes, 1/23/89)

Apart from these methodological and ethical difficulties, gender affected the way others responded to me and vice versa. I set out to compare the experiences of boys and girls and spent equal time interviewing and observing the two sexes. Hanging out informally with groups of boys, however, was much less comfortable for me and them than it would have been were I male. Plus, the opportunities for doing so, primarily student activities, attracted more girls (as well as women teachers in supervising roles) than boys.

Partly because of this methodological deficiency, girls were more likely to discuss their feelings with me. However, I became convinced that, in general, the boys found it more difficult to discuss, for example, personal and family crises that affected their attachment to school. Sandra, a Beacon student, made a similar point: "I don't know if the opinions themselves are different, it's just the way guys go about expressing them. It's easier for a girl to say that education is an important thing than for a guy to say it." I got to know some boys who had interests and senses of humor similar to mine, but this did not always lead them to be able or willing to discuss their feelings. Some stated candidly that, in their opinion, women talk too much about relationships and emotions:

> Sometimes I just have the attitude that women are here for one thing and one thing only [sex]. I mean, some of them don't even do that right. Just like how they try to make sense out of everything, how they have to talk it out. I mean, sometimes it works, but sometimes they just talk in circles. It stresses me out.

. . . All women kind of degrade themselves, just so they can get compliments. I mean, everybody does; I don't mind that. But when they start getting out of hand: sighing and moping and crying. That pisses me off when I see girls walking around school crying, "Oh, me and Johnny just broke up." (Rich, Beacon)

Other boys and girls echoed this view of gender difference, although most felt it was due to socialization rather than some innate biological or psychological difference between males and females. If the boys did open up, students told me, it was usually to their girlfriends or other close female friends and relatives. The unwillingness to appear vulnerable was a definite liability in the classroom because boys seemed more reluctant than girls to ask for help. "Some teachers don't know how to look at somebody and say, 'He doesn't know how to do it.' I guess they expect you to know something [already], and it's like they're just saying it for routine" (Mike, La Fuente). In sum, the boys' relative reticence is reflected in the quality of the interview data and affects their style of disengagement from school, too, as subsequent chapters will show.

As a participant observer at Beacon and La Fuente, including its on-site SAM program, I attended all screenings of new students as well as orientation and other classes and activities throughout an entire school year and into the next. In phase one of the study, I attempted to see the continuation school through the eyes of a student: sitting with them, doing some of the classwork, talking with them informally.

On a typical day at Beacon, I would have a conversation with Bob, a seventeen-year-old of Mexican and Irish descent sporting dreadlocks, about his dream of going to Jamaica to help the victims of Hurricane Hugo. In my music class, Daniel would teach us about the different types of rap, incorporating video and record selections from such favorite groups as Public Enemy and N.W.A.; my role, apart from urging the heavy metal devotees to be tolerant and pay attention, was to ask questions and provide historical context. At the end of three periods of English, I would secretly agree with Serena as she pushed away her grammar workbook and exclaimed to nobody in particular: "This is boring!"

The next day I would be at La Fuente. Taking my seat in Ms. Wilson's orientation class, I would join in a rap session on self-esteem, followed by one on career plans. While helping out in the student-run store during lunchtime, April and Marsha would tell me about *Teen Angel*, a magazine for *cholos* and *cholas* (a subgroup of Mexicans often perceived as street tough and gang-oriented) that featured a titillating personals section; Anthony, the only boy in their cosmetology class; teachers' quirks; and the types of guys they preferred to date. My daily field notes from this observation phase provided a check on data gleaned from formal interviews with students and teachers conducted in phase two.

I also made systematic classroom observations. The student-focused observations aimed at assessing whether girls tend to disengage in different ways than boys. The teacher-focused observations aimed at assessing the range of teaching and discipline methods and policies toward tardiness and truancy, and whether these differ according to sex. In addition, I gathered available quantitative data by sex and ethnicity on course offerings, attendance, disciplinary actions, academic achievement, dropout and graduation rates.

In phase two I formally interviewed eighty-two students (forty-seven girls, thirty-five boys), selected to reflect each school's ethnic composition; pregnant and mothering girls were oversampled at La Fuente. I asked students to describe the transfer process, including perception of choice; to compare and contrast their experiences in the continuation program with those in the traditional school; to report on their behavior when bored in class or cutting school; to evaluate the various components of the alternative program, including the perceived value of its diploma; and to respond to hypothetical questions such as whether their experience in school would have been different if they had been born a member of the other sex.[4]

From this sample, I selected a subset of students and recorded their educational life histories with the aim of illuminating such issues as the relationship between early pregnancy, childbearing, and marriage and

---

4. Most of the hypothetical questions allowed me to explore with students the types of factors they considered in pursuing particular courses of action and the circumstances under which certain alternatives made sense. The question about whether their experiences in school would have differed if they had been born a member of the other sex asked students to put themselves in a position that, of course, was not actually open to them. But asking students to step into the shoes of "the other" frequently prompted a richer discussion of whether and how gender affected their school experiences than when they only considered the experience of their own gender. Commonly, students drew on what they knew of relatives and friends of the other gender. The question also allowed me to gauge the extent to which students perceived their subjectivity to be fundamentally shaped by gender—whether defined in biological, cultural, or political terms. A few insisted that, in school at least, gender did not matter, because underneath they would be "the same person" and thus have the same experiences, whether male or female; more commonly, students identified "socialization" as a powerful force differentiating boys' experiences from girls'. While it would be unwise to use the responses to such a hypothetical question to assess gender imbalances in structural rewards, the responses did help me understand students' ideological constructions of gender.

disengagement from school. I also conducted several focus-group interviews (on what turns kids off to school, on work and family plans) and schoolwide surveys (on why high school students fight with each other, on domestic and wage work responsibilities). After an initial analysis of interviews showed that a number of students described high school as a soap opera or prison, I returned to Beacon where more than eighty students agreed to write an essay (for English credit) on the metaphor that best captured their high school experience.

I interviewed almost all teachers (more than twenty), counselors, and administrators to discover how and why they came to the continuation school and to learn about their career goals, educational philosophies, and feelings about the continuation program's effectiveness and place within the secondary educational system. I asked people to share their observations on who drops out and why and what the early warning signs of disengagement are. I probed for differences by gender, ethnicity, and socioeconomic status. In addition, I interviewed thirteen teachers, one counselor, and two administrators at two comprehensive high schools, one a feeder into La Fuente, the other into Beacon. I also sat through a day of classes at the comprehensive high school that fed into Beacon. These interviews and observations provided some context for the views of continuation staff and students.

To summarize, data sources included: student surveys (pilot study interviews, fighting and peer mediation, domestic and work duties); student interviews, group discussions, life histories and journals; music class essays and observations; teacher, counselor, and administrator interviews; field notes (observation of schools, inside and outside of classrooms); school and district records; and historical data (state and other surveys of continuation programs, pertinent laws and regulations, newspaper articles, handbooks, and enrollment statistics).

Interviews and observations sometimes yielded different, even inconsistent, information. In general, students were less likely to be critical of, say, the continuation program during a formal interview than in an unprompted aside during class. Several factors may explain this. First, the audiotape recorder may inhibit harsh assessments. Although all students and staff who consented to formal interviews also agreed to let me tape our conversations (save one Latina), a few were more guarded than I knew them to be otherwise. Second, people tended to downplay certain complaints (recorded in field notes) as minor details in a formal interview. Third, program disadvantages do not occur to people as readily in a formal setting that is abstracted from actual circumstances. In contrast, the advantages of the continuation program are frequently spelled out to students in an abstract way: at intake, during orientation, in counseling. For these reasons, I make an effort in the analysis to indicate whether I am drawing on field notes, interviews, or both.

Informants' comments appear in quotation marks only if tape recorded or written down by me during or immediately after a verbal exchange. I consider these quotations data and use them liberally throughout the book, in part to give readers a sense of the different perspectives and voices informing the study. Nevertheless, I have extracted these quotations from long interviews (the shortest lasted forty-five minutes, the longest six hours), framed them with my words and concepts, and fit them into my analysis. This written account, in the end, reflects my unavoidably partial perspective; knowledge is always influenced by the values, biases, interests, and personal limitations of researchers.

In analyzing the data, I entered field notes into a database and coded key concepts, recurrent themes, and significant interactions with particular students and teachers. Using similar concepts and themes, I coded the eighty-two formal student interviews and entered the information into a statistical package and ran chi-square tests by sex, ethnicity (white versus other), and school where appropriate to determine whether observed differences were "significant" or not.[5] My sample was not strictly random; indeed, with new students enrolling weekly, this would have been impossible. What I know about the student population as a whole matches the characteristics of my two school samples well;[6] this fact is an important indicator that the student sample was random enough to warrant the use of inferential statistical methods.

SOME DEFINITIONS

Three key concepts—disengagement, gender, and subcultural style (itself informed by theory on class and ethnicity)—formed the framework for my research. I spent over a year comparing these theory-inspired concepts to what occurred in the daily lives of students at Beacon and

5. The chi-square tests were based on a sample of eighty-two students, analyzed by sex (thirty-five boys, forty-seven girls), ethnicity (twenty-four white, fifty-eight other including those of mixed ethnicity), and school (forty-three at La Fuente, thirty-nine at Beacon).

6. Examples of these characteristics include the sex and ethnic composition of the student body and students' curricular status (special education, SAM program). Because I selected students at random from classes I would be interviewing that day or week, there is probably a bias against students who were absent a lot. I kept students' names I had selected to interview and did not get to that day on my list, however, and succeeded in rescheduling most of these interviews.

La Fuente. My field experience reminded me that individual students do not think in terms social theorists use; the meanings they attach to such concepts as gender, class, and ethnicity depend on concrete situations, often shaped by peer group interaction. Further, what they disengage from at school extends beyond academics and teachers to other realms. In this section, I define and discuss these concepts, attempting to integrate social theory and student understandings when possible.

Subcultural Style: Nested and Multiple Identities

Subculture refers to a group of people who may or may not know each other or count each other as friends but who tend to share certain beliefs and values, give similar meaning to shared experiences, and emulate, as well as innovate within, the same style. Swidler (1986: 273) has emphasized that culture is a "repertoire or 'tool kit' of habits, skills, and styles from which people construct 'strategies of action.' " Subcultures form part of the wider, dominant culture and are not always as separate and distinct from each other and from the major culture as the sociological literature on deviancy sometimes implies. Furthermore, although I have emphasized shared beliefs and experiences, subcultures are also marked by power relations between men and women, for example, and are by no means homogeneous.

The subcultural styles that predominated at Beacon and La Fuente were stoners, rappers, punks, and Mexicans. Multiple, nested identities were associated with a particular style; Cohen (1978) notes the same situational quality and multiple identities associated with ethnicity. Stoners, for example, evinced an oppositional stance to school disciplinarians, school-sponsored activities, and students privileged by the school such as jocks and preps and included a wide variety of people, even students who got good grades. Most commonly, students who identified as stoners were white, dressed casually in jeans and t-shirts, listened to some form of hard rock music, smoked marijuana, and otherwise did not conform to the good student role. More specific expressions of the stoner style overlapped this relatively exclusive cluster of identifiers. Headbangers, for example, defined themselves as stoners who did not use drugs, excepting tobacco and alcohol.

Class and ethnic relations marked each subcultural style. Gender relations, too, influenced subcultural style; girls' experiences within youth subcultures differed from those of boys (see chapter 6). What follows is a summary of how students generally defined class and ethnicity situationally as well as some concrete measures of these concepts among the students interviewed.

Class versus Socioeconomic Status Most students did not spontaneously discuss issues related to class or socioeconomic status. When I was writing interview questions, the students advising me warned against asking about family income: "Financial would be too private." In contrast, students more often saw ethnicity and gender as readily observable traits, hence less private issues. They and others inferred socioeconomic status, sometimes mistakenly, mainly from the way a person dressed and talked.

These indicators are, of course, used by stratification theorists concerned with questions of inequality who categorize people based on income, education, occupation, and the like. Class theorists, concerned with the structural sources of change in society, categorize people based on their role in relations of control over production, investment, and labor as well as their opposition to other classes (Stolzman and Gamberg, 1974). Students did not use class in a Marxist sense, but some evinced a certain class consciousness and opposition to "rich people," their children—overrepresented among the jocks, preps, "prissy girls," and "snobby soshes" (short for socialites)—and their life-styles and attitudes. White students expressed these feelings most often, possibly because they could not articulate the differences between themselves and other whites through the language of ethnicity.

To continue with the stoner example within the context of class: the thrash metal music devotees, almost exclusively white male, considered themselves the most rebellious of the stoners. A common theme was their hatred of so-called young urban professionals. "Yuppyism is sick, disgusting," Ed told me. When I asked him what he meant by yuppie, he explained: "It's like a cross between a hippie and a rich stuck-up person, part naturalist, part professional," distinguished by a propensity to drink "designer" water and wine (never beer), buy "whatever is cool" and expensive, shun television watching, eat "exotic" food (quiche, Indian food), practice natural childbirth and permissive child rearing, and work on computers and "think up stuff" (as opposed to manual labor). These views were reflected in the music these stoners enjoyed. The leader of Megadeth, a favorite band of theirs, knew his audience well:

> These are kids in their mid-teens. They have something to be angry about. They're blue-collar kids. They're from low-income families, from the wrong side of the tracks. I identify with them. Thrash metal ain't yuppie music. (Hunt, 1988)

A disproportionate number of students in this study, compared with the comprehensive high school population, did come from low-income families, though not all. If children's class or socioeconomic status is derived from that of their parents or guardians, then most of the students at Beacon and La Fuente belonged to the working class. Only a third of the students were living with two parents or guardians; the most common living arrangement was with a single parent, usually the mother. In the United States in 1990, 44.5 percent of families with children under eighteen headed by single mothers were living below the poverty level; the poverty rate for such families was higher among African-Americans and Latinos than among whites (56.1 and 58.2 versus 37.9 percent; U.S. Bureau of the Census, 1991: 116). Two-thirds of the students interviewed had mothers with a high school diploma, GED, or less education. Most were employed in pink-collar (clerical, child and health care, maid, beautician) and blue-collar (electronics production and cannery) jobs. These and other socioeconomic realities generated major differences in experience and consciousness among students.

Ethnicity Interwoven with class, ethnicity[7] more obviously shaped subcultural styles: stoners and punks were largely, though not exclusively, white, rappers were mainly African-American, and Mexicans mainly of Mexican origin.[8] Perhaps the most striking aspect of the ethnic self-identification process is its fluidity and, for the purpose of this study, how academic ability, achievement, and scholastic orientation become bound

─────

7. I use the term *ethnicity* more often than race for several reasons. First, ethnicity designates cultural differences, whereas race in common parlance refers to differences in skin color. Few biological or genetic differences exist between groups of people that do not also exist within groups of people. Yet supposed biological differences among the so-called races have been used to justify the oppression of minority groups. Second, the current discourse on race tends to focus on black-white relations, whereas most of the non-white students in this study were Latino, Asian-American, Native American, or of mixed ethnicity. Third, many people of Mexican origin—the largest ethnic minority group represented in my study—identify themselves as white when asked to place themselves in a racial category. (This makes sense because there are Mexicans, for example, of African ancestry who consider themselves black.)

Of course, the term *race* does retain social and political significance. It is important to bear in mind that non-European ethnic groups are oppressed on the basis of visible differences and area of ancestry, and I will use the term *ethnic* (and occasionally *racial*) minority to signify the lack of power afforded to such groups as Mexican-Americans in relation to dominant culture whites.

8. One reason that identity and conflict tend to be focused through the lens of ethnicity rather than class in the United States has to do with the historic separation between work and neighborhood, the latter often segregated by ethnicity as well as class (Katznelson and Weir, 1985: 22). Also, ethnic minorities face discrimination inside and outside the workplace and have developed affiliations based mainly on ethnicity and territory.

up in the process. Some students felt they did not possess academic ability, others felt they were able but refused to put forth the effort to achieve,
and still others achieved at a reasonable level with minimal effort but
rejected the student role. Each of these distinct possibilities, in combination with other defining characteristics, influenced ethnic identity.
Dennis, for example, considered himself Mexican, and—at least within
the school setting—he excluded "the smarter students" of Mexican descent from his definition. In addition, students defined their ethnicity
situationally based on (1) skin and hair color, (2) a common national and
linguistic heritage, (3) neighborhood, and (4) life-style (drug and alcohol
habits, dress, slang, social activities, interests).

Ethnicity, like subcultural style in general, consisted of nested, multiple identities. A number of students of Italian and Portuguese descent
were considered "down with the homeboys and girls" (part of the Mexican subculture), although they listed themselves as white on official school
forms. Some light-complexioned Latinos passed for white at the comprehensive school and had hung out with the jocks and preps. The
daughter of Central American refugees preferred to identify herself as
Mexican at school. Students described an African-American male who
adopted the stoner life-style and loved heavy metal music as "that white
black guy." And Chicanos (usually second- or third-generation immigrants from Mexico) regularly put down Mexican immigrants as "moja-
dos" or "wetbacks" who overdressed and were too polite and quiet
("teachers' pets"), while Mexicanos saw Chicanos as disrespectful, shab-
bily dressed drug users who had lost their culture and Spanish language
(see also Rios, 1989; Matute-Bianchi, 1986; Haro, 1979).

Evidence from interviews and field observations lent support to the
argument that certain ethnic minority children may face peer opposition
for doing well in school if academic success is equated with "acting white"
(Fordham and Ogbu, 1986). Yet the same students who most distanced
themselves from what they scorned as the "school boy" or "school girl"
image had white friends and acquaintances who shared their antischool
values.

In sum, student subcultures often took on an implicit or explicit
ethnic identity. Yet they sometimes included other ethnic groups even
while excluding those of the same ethnic ancestry because they did not
meet other criteria of group identity such as life-style. This fluidity necessitated language of inclusion as well as exclusion. While certain white
and Latino students said they disliked "niggers" and "mayates," their
"black" friends were exceptions. When their nonwhite friends would
complain of ethnic prejudice by other whites, some Anglos would dis-

tance themselves from blame by distinguishing between themselves and "rich whites" or "white supremacists."

While students' definitions of ethnic identity were fluid and changed depending on context, the following is a breakdown of "nationality" a computer could process for those formally interviewed:

32 percent Latino (26 Mexican, 4 mixed Mexican and other Latino, 1 Puerto Rican, 1 Central American ancestry)
31 percent white (European ancestry)
12 percent black (African ancestry)
7 percent Filipino
1 percent Korean
1 percent Samoan
16 percent mixed ethnicity (9 white/Latino, 2 Mexican/Native American, 1 white/Pacific Islander, 1 white/Native American)

This sample reflected the ethnic composition of Beacon and La Fuente well (see table 1), particularly in light of the fact that most students categorized as mixed Latino/white or Latino/Native American ancestry tended to identify themselves as Latino (Hispanic) on school documents.

Students of partial or full Mexican descent—two-fifths of my sample—had the most within-group diversity.[9] But even this group had many experiences in common with the other students in the study. For example, most had been born and raised in the county where the cities of Beacon and La Fuente were located, and most spoke only English.

Gender

Like class and ethnicity, gender is a marker of collective identity, exploitation, and difference. I use the concept to refer to the social organization of the asymmetrical relationship between the sexes (Scott, 1986).

---

9. Two-thirds of the students of full or partial Mexican ancestry had been born within the county, usually in or near the cities of Beacon and La Fuente; one-fifth were born elsewhere in California and the United States, and the remainder in foreign countries (two in Mexico, one in Spain, one in Portugal). With the exception of an undocumented Mexican immigrant who arrived in La Fuente as an early adolescent, the Mexican-origin students had spent most of their lives in the county. A third of this subsample had one or both parents born in Mexico; the rest were born and raised primarily in the Southwest (California, Arizona, New Mexico, Texas). All but one student spoke fluent English, and 18 percent reported fluency in Spanish as well. Most (58 percent), however, said that although they heard relatives speaking Spanish at home, their own grasp of the language was limited. An additional 21 percent reported that only English was spoken in their homes, and they neither spoke nor understood Spanish.

It needs to be understood on three interlocking and reinforcing levels. At the individual and peer group level, girls and boys have different cultural identities and experiences. In seeking to redefine success, certain boys, for example, come to equate academic striving with imagery of homosexuality: they put down studious boys as "gay." At a second, organizational level, that is the high school, gender is a key factor in sorting out peer status, role models, the power hierarchy, and who is routed into what slots (Kessler et al., 1985)—all of this is critical to describing the disengagement process. Finally, at the macro level the societywide sexual division of labor and cultural definitions of masculine and feminine come to bear on high school students. Differences in class, ethnicity, sexual orientation, and age cut across gender, and each of these also influences the individual responses of boys and girls to schooling in important ways.

Disengagement: A New Way of Thinking about Dropouts and Pushouts

The term *dropout* puts inordinate blame on the individual; the term *pushout* puts inordinate blame on the institution. Dropout implies that the student makes an independent, final decision, whereas pushout implies that the institution acts inexorably to purge unwilling victims. Some recent work on early school leaving has emphasized that it is a mutual process of rejection (for example, Fine 1991; Wehlage et al., 1989), or what can be called disengagement. The metaphor underlying engagement is that of two toothed wheels of a gear, student and school, meshed together so that the motion in one is passed on to the other.

The concept of disengagement connotes a long-running, interactive process which may be reversible. It therefore encourages us to connect events in students' lives over time and look for cumulative effects. It also acknowledges the spectrum of ways that students are engaged: one who recognizes the need for a diploma can be very different from one who likes school. The terms *dropout* and *pushout* retain some usefulness in characterizing an exit from school—often the final outcome—as more student- or school-initiated. For a significant number of others, the decisive moment of dropping out or being pushed out never occurs; these students attend infrequently, leaving and returning several times, and thus may be more aptly described as fade-outs.

Because it occurs over time, disengagement can be difficult to document. Also, the process is not always observable (for example, passive resistance to learning), and it may be open to different interpretations. The literature on dropouts and pushouts suggests signs and styles of disengagement displayed primarily within school settings. I have grouped these into four categories: academics (including teacher-student relations), peer relations, extracurricular activities, and the credential (diploma) itself.

Indicators of disengagement from academics include: poor academic progress, classroom withdrawal (few instructional interactions, for example), participation in nonacademic or remedial classes and programs, grade repetition, and suspension and expulsion.

Ethnographic research has shown that youth subcultures mediate student outcomes like dropout and pushout. These outcomes are not simply a function of within-school factors as economic models often imply. Indicators of disengagement related to peers include: fighting, inability to make friends, alienation from and opposition to peer groups accorded status by the school, and bonding with peers marginalized by institutional practices. Indicators of disengagement from extracurricular activities include: lack of participation in and dislike of school-sponsored clubs, teams, and events. An example of disengagement from the credential is the belief that a diploma is either not necessary to realize future plans or will not bring promised rewards.

Students, of course, do not disengage from school or school from students in a vacuum. In order to examine and interpret constraints on student action, I drew from a number of theoretical perspectives. Each of these has informed my conception of disengagement, particularly as the process occurs within the continuation school, an organization that can neither select its students nor make policies independent of the mainstream schooling system's goals.

WAYS OF SEEING THE CONTINUATION SCHOOL

At the macro level, as Carnoy and Levin (1985) have argued, educational reform can be seen as a response to conflicts among constituencies with different priorities for schools, some interested in greater equality (democratization), others in greater efficiency (reproduction). According to Offe (1976: 5), educational change is limited because the advanced capitalist state must "reconcile dynamically the requirement of capitalist accumulation on the one hand and legitimation on the other." From this perspective, continuation schools may be seen as a response to public concern over dropouts and pushouts that helps legitimize the state insofar as they meet the needs of youth who are ill-served by the mainstream educational system. Such reform may forestall more far-reaching change to the extent that rebellious and failing youths are successfully segregated and labeled deviant and resistance is accommodated. At the same time, the more effective the continuation school is in reengaging students, the more parents and students will accept it, but the more financially burdensome it becomes to the state, and the more the regular schools may feel threatened.

More specifically, Clark (1960) argued that educational institutions create a "situation of structured failure" that operates to "cool out" particular students' aspirations. Seen from this perspective, the continuation school may serve to cool out downwardly mobile, low-achieving middle-class students and upwardly mobile, yet underprepared working-class and ethnic minority students. Whereas Clark saw the situation of structured failure emerging out of a conflict between high academic standards and nonselective recruitment of students, Karabel (1972) argued that the standards themselves performed a social function: to distribute students within the economic hierarchy (see also Bowles and Gintis, 1976).

Thus, at the organizational level, continuation schools may provide a safety valve—whether in response to demands for equal opportunity or class conflict—keeping the comprehensive schools pure while providing a second, yet devalued, chance to those who have been pushed out. Stated differently, institutional convenience may dictate that rebels and failures be put into a separate institution that, as a salve to conscience, aims to reconnect these students to the educational enterprise (compare Rothman, 1980; Tyack and Hansot, 1982).

These macro and organizational perspectives have been criticized as functionalist and overdeterministic. Alone, they imply, for example, that continuation students are unwilling dupes expelled from mainstream schools. As a corrective, therefore, I give equal weight to an individual and small peer group perspective. Viewed from this angle, those who end up in continuation schools may be engaging in incipient class (Willis, 1977), ethnic (Fordham and Ogbu, 1986), and gender struggle. For example, working-class, low-achieving girls who reject the official ideology for females in school (neatness, passivity, and so forth) and replace it with "a more feminine one, even sexual one" (McRobbie, 1978: 104; see also Anyon, 1983) or masculine one may be seen as resisting the middle-class standards of the mainstream school. Thus, some continuation students may revel in the feeling that they have tricked "the system" by getting themselves into a school that seems to expect less of them educationally, socially, and behaviorally while still awarding them a credential.

At the same time, students—many of them preconditioned to exclusion by virtue of their ethnic and class background, their previous schooling experiences, or both—may discover they are more comfortable in their new environment interacting with peers more like themselves. Mandy, a white student at La Fuente, described feeling out of place at the comprehensive school where "they're not rich but they're well off, whether they're black, Mexican, or white. And here . . . we all don't have that much money and stuff. And I guess it's weird because it's so true, that if you don't have as much money, you're more laid back." The following chapter takes up this theme, documenting historically how a disproportionate number of students excluded from the mainstream schools for violating white, middle-class norms have ended up in continuation schools.

2

HOW A CHAMELEON SURVIVES:
A HISTORY OF
CONTINUATION SCHOOLS

Plastic toy cowboys and Indians lay face down, strewn across a sheet of butcher paper that Mr. Ullmann had placed in the middle of the faculty room lunch table. The Beacon continuation high school teacher had arrived early to set this scene, indicating with a few marking pen squiggles that the battlefield represented the financially starved educational system. As Mr. Ullmann's colleagues gathered for an impromptu meeting, some joined in; Ms. Foster, a retiring teacher, portrayed herself parachuting out of Beacon and off the paper entirely. Others glanced at a front-page article Ms. Moore had clipped from the local newspaper, which announced that a nearby continuation school was threatened with closure. The headline: "Willows: Where Misfits Fit; Special School Faces Budgetary Ax."

Beacon teachers had felt embattled all school year. First came the news from the district office that they would have to give up their separate campus location and merge with the adult education center by the fall of 1992. The latest surprise was an edict from the central office telling them to decide which portable classroom building they would relinquish by summer. Ms. Moore explained her worst fear: "If enough districts get rid of their continuation schools, what's to stop our district from deciding it can do without one, too, and shutting us down altogether? A few of our students might make it at adult ed, but most of them would be lost—out on the streets."

By the end of the workday, some teachers had drafted one letter to school board members informing them of district office actions and another letter to parents and former Beacon students, urging them to

contact the superintendent and board members. Others pledged to telephone the local Rotary Club and probation officers for support. All
agreed: this was a fight for Beacon's survival as a last chance, alternative
school.

Theirs is not a new fight. Beacon may be only several portable
buildings stuck in a back lot, but it is the current incarnation of a sev-
enty-year-old history. Often during economic hard times, continuation
programs have been the first item on the budget cutters' checklist. Yet
they have managed to survive this long because of a chameleon quality:
an ability over the years to change colors and present themselves as an
innovative solution to the community's latest, most pressing fears and
concerns about teenagers. Continuation school teachers and administrators have been adept at forming constituencies and tying them into the
current way of thinking about students on the margins of schooling's
mainstream.

Anyone concerned with restructuring schools—with an eye toward
engaging all students—should be interested in why this has been so difficult to do. Examining the history of an institution that has served the
misfits from mainstream public high schools provides some clues. How
has the hidden world of continuation school survived as long as it has?
What militates against doing away with the institution altogether?

The logical place to search for answers to such questions is California, home to Beacon and La Fuente and the state where continuation
education has enjoyed an unbroken and robust existence for the longest
period of time. Just four years before the emergency teachers' meeting
at Beacon, state administrators characterized continuation education in
California as "one of the oldest and largest dropout prevention programs in the nation" (Calif. State Dept. of Education, hereafter cited as
CSDE, 1987: 4). The latest handbook terms "continuation education a
more important alternative educational program today than in the past"
(CSDE, 1987: iv). But to describe its history as simply a dropout prevention program glosses over its origins, purpose, and student body at point
of creation; to say that it is more important today than in the past dis-
regards how continuation education has changed over time.

In this chapter, where possible, I draw links between California and
the wider national scene in order to analyze how the evolving institution
of continuation education has fit into school systems and a capitalist
economy and social order. This history is essential to understanding the
world of Beacon and La Fuente as experienced by individual students
in their peer groups. I argue that in California and nationally reformers—led largely by professionals within urban school systems, state departments of education, and major university schools of education—have

repackaged the program twice since its inception, partly in response to social concerns over potentially disruptive youth. The first repackaging took place after World War II, when continuation education changed from part-time schooling for employed boys and girls to sites of "adjustment education" where students' psychological problems were addressed. The second—more rhetorical than real—occurred in the 1960s: although continuation schools were still said to serve employed youth and the "maladjusted," they were also touted as offering an "alternative" learning environment, a place for innovative curriculum and other institutional experimentation designed to reach students in all their diversity.

Throughout this evolution from part-time schooling for working youth to dropout prevention and recovery program, certain organizational characteristics of continuation education have remained largely constant (Stinchcombe, 1965: 153). These include: a flexible and reduced school schedule, individualized instruction, guidance counseling, small class size, open-entry/open-exit, and a curricular emphasis on "life skills" (for example consumer problems, health and personal care, understanding and getting along with people), basic academic skills, and prevocational training. In the meanwhile, though, broader social structures changed in pertinent and significant ways. The link forged between education and work grew even stronger, and today the belief that school should prepare young people for work is widely held. Over the same period, as school became the primary route to employment, high school enrollment and graduation steadily increased (Kantor and Tyack, 1982). Among the nation's seventeen year olds, 6 percent graduated from high school in 1900, 16 percent in 1920, 49 percent in 1940, and 76 percent in 1970 (U.S. Bureau of the Census, 1978).

Whether continuation schools have continued to serve similar types of students is open to question. In the language of continuation professionals through the years, new types of students came into the school and added to, but did not displace, old constituencies: first employed youth, then the "maladjusted," and finally those in search of an alternative. Other groups came and went, such as adults (students over eighteen years of age), while others seem to have been there all along only to be "discovered" recently: pregnant and/or married girls. Finally, the ratio of males to females has shifted direction twice (see figures 1 and 2), but it is the same today as it was the first year continuation schools opened: about 55 to 45 in favor of males.

Despite these changes, I will show that there has been a significant continuity in the student body. All students had been defined as misfits within the conventional schooling system and had either dropped out or been pushed out. These misfits included disproportionate numbers of certain ethnic minorities, working-class or low-income students, and those who had violated middle-class norms of sexual behavior. The latter were usually female—pregnant girls, mothering or married teens, runaways often assumed to have become prostitutes—and, although this is particularly hidden from history, overtly gay males.[1] Whether out of fear of

Number of Students

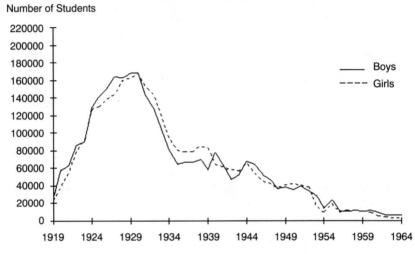

FIGURE I

Enrollment in Federally Funded Continuation Classes by Sex, 1920–1964

Source: U.S. Dept. of Health, Education and Welfare, Federal Board for Vocational Education, *Digest of Annual Reports of State Boards for Vocational Education to the Office of Education,* 1917–1965.

------

1. Although I did not find any references to gay and lesbian students in written historical documents on continuation schools, I did discuss the issue with some original and long-time staff members at Beacon. They recalled a few openly gay continuation students. Two of the students I interviewed mentioned gay siblings who had dropped out of school, one after having attended Beacon. The other explained how homophobia at school contributed not only to her brother's disengagement from comprehensive high school, but to that of other family members, as well.

> My oldest brother is gay, and he had a hard time. He didn't graduate because of pressure from school. Even his teachers, they were prejudiced. Then my second [oldest] brother had to hear, "Oh, yeah. I heard your brother is a fag, this and that." That's what put pressure on my other two brothers, and that's why my second brother didn't graduate, but my third brother did. When people find out about your family problems, that puts pressure on. I remember my [oldest] brother came home and he was crying cuz he was so mad. His teacher was teasing him about being gay, and he didn't like him. . . . So I heard all this, and you get that little thing in your

juvenile delinquency or other threats to social order or as a salve to conscience, continuation school advocates have pressed the need for an institution to deal with this diverse group of outsiders.

EARLY YEARS: A PART-TIME BRIDGE
BETWEEN SCHOOLING AND WORK

In its original form, continuation education took place largely in compulsory part-time schools designed to provide young workers, aged fourteen to eighteen years, with four to eight hours per week of schooling aimed at increasing their "civic or vocational intelligence." The 1917 legislation that supplied federal money to this part-time bridge between

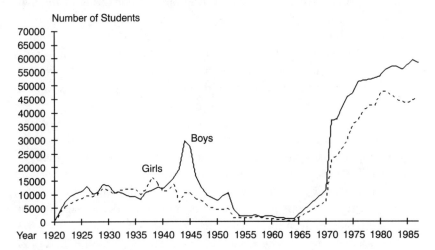

FIGURE 2

Enrollment in California Continuation Programs by Sex, 1920–1987

Sources: CSBE, *Biennial Reports,* 1921, 1923a,1924, 1926; CSDE, *Biennial Reports,* 1932a, 1934, 1985, 1988; CSDE, *Enrollment in California Public Schools,* 1955, 1970–1979; CSDE, *Report for the Governor's Council,* 1948, 1951, 1952; Shaffer, 1955; U.S. Dept. of Health, Education and Welfare, Federal Board for Vocational Education, *Digest of Annual Reports of State Boards for Vocational Education to the Office of Education,* 1917–1965; White, 1962. Data for 1965–1970 were not available. Data for 1971–1979 were estimated from fall enrollment rather than from cumulative enrollment.

---

head that's telling you, "I hate that teacher. I guess all teachers are like that." And the students! See, if you stick up for gay people, then they [other students] look at you like you must be gay. It gets you upset. Cuz there was this girl who was gay, and she dressed like a guy. And she was my friend because she was also being outcast, and the rumor around our class was that we were together. (Renee, Beacon)

schooling and work came about through the intense lobbying efforts of vocational education advocates.

At the turn of this century, a coalition of professional educators allied with businesspeople, labor leaders, politicians, and social reformers grew increasingly concerned about the number of students dropping out after elementary school as well as the new entrants to the high schools and began to push for vocational education.[2] School people were especially alarmed over what became known as the "boy problem." Educational researchers amassed evidence that boys did less well academically, were forced to repeat grades more often, and quit school in larger numbers than girls (Tyack and Hansot, 1990). Many of these boys were of working-class and immigrant backgrounds. Tyack and Hansot argue that "much of progressive education, especially the vocationalizing of the high school, can be understood as a campaign to fit schooling better to boys, particularly those who seemed non-academic in inclination or ability." Rury (1988), using 1900 census data, found that socioeconomic status may have been a more important variable for male retention, while ethnicity was the more critical factor in determining which females went to school.

Fueling this concern over dropouts were the changing forces of production. New technologies—high speed machinery, telephones, cash registers, pneumatic tubes and other devices—were eliminating many of the unskilled jobs held by young people (Tyack, 1978). Child labor and compulsory school attendance laws and protective legislation for women, backed by trade unions and social reformers, limited the participation of women and children in the labor market (Hartmann, 1976: 159–67).

Vocational reformers believed that "hand-minded" children and those who had to leave full-time schooling out of economic necessity needed occupational and moral guidance. They disagreed about what form this guidance should take, however. Alternatives ranged from differentiated tracks within the comprehensive high school to separate vocational schools divided by sex to continuation schools for young workers outside of the public schooling system. The national champion of the part-time continuation school model was Charles Prosser, executive secretary of the National Society for the Promotion of Industrial Education. Prosser, joined by the National Association of Manufacturers, favored opening continuation schools inside factories, where young workers would alternate

2. Karl Marx also liked the part-time education concept. Writing in the mid-1800s, he noted that "the combination of paid productive labour, mental education, bodily exercise and polytechnic training, will raise the working class far above the level of the higher and middle class" (quoted in Silver, 1983: 49).

learning the general principles behind specific occupations with attending school (Kett, 1982).

Opposing this model, John Dewey and other humanitarian progressives argued that vocational education should focus on general industrial knowledge and should not be administered separately from general public education (Cremin, 1964: 53). A dual school system would deny young people, particularly those from working-class backgrounds, an equal opportunity by forcing them to specialize in a trade too early. Trade unionists, too, argued against separate continuation schools, interpreting them as an attempt to sanction child labor, whose cheaper rates undercut the unions (Katznelson and Weir, 1985: 155).

Some professional educators tended to gloss over the class interests inherent in the debate over continuation schooling. Argued the principal of a Boston continuation school: "The continuation school is an institution typifying the real democracy of education. She has no aristocratic standards for admission" (McDonough, 1921: 255). This claim of non-elite admission standards was seriously misleading because continuation schools were originally designed for young workers, not children from more privileged backgrounds who would hardly choose to attend them.

Allied to this attempt to construct a discourse of schooling that appeared classless were progressive educators' plans for citizenship training, which found their way into federal and state legislation on continuation schools (compare Hendrick, 1980). Citizenship training would "assimilate" foreigners and introduce them to "our customs and to the ideals peculiar to America"; it would make illiterates "self-supporting citizens" and more "responsible"; and it would help select leaders from the lower classes "whose ideals are in harmony with the ideals of democracy," according to a U.S. Bureau of Education bulletin (Jones, 1907: 140–41). This assimilationist vision ignored existing ethnic and racial divisions deeply embedded in U.S. society and implied that an uncontested set of customs and ideals existed. The stress on harmony, duty, and sense of community appealed to those in power who feared social disruption and divisiveness.

Industrial employers were also preoccupied with foreign economic competition. The National Association of Manufacturers hoped to emulate the German system of continuation schools, which the association saw as closely linked to Germany's preeminence in international markets (Kantor, 1982: 26–27). Once business leaders began to press hard for vocational education, labor leaders eventually changed their position and supported it, but within a unitary public school system (Katznelson and Weir, 1985; Kantor, 1982). The Smith-Hughes Vocational Education Act, signed into law by President Wilson in 1917, stipulated "that at least one-third of the sum appropriated to any State . . . shall, if expended, be applied to part-time schools or classes for workers over fourteen years of age [and less than eighteen] . . . ." (*United States Statutes at Large*, 1918: 934–35). This legislation represented a substantial victory for the "administrative progressives"—members of business and professional elites, including school administrators, who, as characterized by Tyack (1974: 126), "urged that schooling be adapted to social stratification"—and they busily set about implementing its provisions.

State legislatures rapidly enacted the provisions of the Vocational Education Act necessary to receive federal matching grants, although the available evidence suggests that enrollments in general continuation classes did not swell except in cities that enforced accompanying compulsory attendance laws (Trout, 1937; New York State Teachers' Assoc., 1929: 304–6). In 1911, only Wisconsin had a statewide compulsory continuation school law. By 1920, twenty states had passed similar laws, and by 1930, three-fifths of the states had done so. During 1930—the peak of the part-time school nationally—nearly 340,000 boys and girls in thirty-four states attended general continuation classes, about half of the total enrollment in all federally aided schools providing trade and industrial classes (U.S. Dept. of Health, Education, and Welfare, Federal Board for Vocational Education, *Annual Report*, 1931: 84–85).

While most states received federal aid for part-time general continuation classes during the 1920s and 1930s, much of the enrollment was concentrated in large industrial centers in a handful of states: New York, Pennsylvania, Massachusetts, California, Illinois, Wisconsin, and New Jersey. This fact is not surprising, considering that part-time schooling had been designed primarily for city school personnel and their perceived problems: poverty, large influxes of non-English-speaking immigrants, and juvenile delinquency.

State departments of education, working with local universities to train teachers in continuation education, advised school districts to provide students affected by the part-time law with an opportunity to study trade, industrial, or commercial subjects. In the absence of a vocational focus, the professionals warned, these pupils "will constitute a problem which will be very difficult to handle" (CSDE, 1919: 4). Reformers believed that part-timers, especially boys, were vulnerable to recruitment into crime (Calif. State Board of Education, hereafter cited as CSBE, 1923a: 100). The continuation school was well placed to prevent delinquency, explained a New York principal, "for the continuation school alone deals with the young person in a man-to-man fashion at the most critical period of his life" (Mayman, 1933: 198).

Several student surveys from this period show that children of foreign-born parents were significantly overrepresented in continuation schools: in Pittsburgh, Pennsylvania (Goldberger, 1931: 40–1); Oakland, California (Kantor, 1982: 132–36, citing Palmer, 1930); and New York, where a statewide survey of pupils found that two-thirds of the boys had parents born abroad, mainly in Italy, Russia, and Poland (New York State Teachers' Assoc. 1929: 302). The principal of Boston Continuation School observed that "children of foreigners from non-English speaking homes" made up a large proportion of his students. For this group, he warned, citizenship and vocational training were particularly vital because: "In their homes conversations are constantly held in their native tongue and foreign newspapers are read, reeking as they are with radical theories. These children ... at the age of fourteen years are automatically forced out of school and compelled to go to work to help support their parents" (McDonough, 1921: 204).

Critics of the day charged the continuation advocates with promising too much, given that students were required to attend for so little time. Proponents countered that compelling more than four to eight hours of attendance "would disrupt every employer's business, cut the child's wages in half and impose a crushing burden of expense upon the state" (Douglas, 1921: 266). In theory, reformers exhorted part-time schools to develop the mental, physical, moral, civic, and craft capacities of their students (CSBE, 1924: 126; New York State Teachers' Assoc., 1929: 294). In practice, continuation personnel were advised to focus on "the organization and direction of the pupils' interests outside of school" (CSBE, 1924: 36). Much of that direction, carried out by trained coordinators, was apparently aimed at placing students in jobs (Tibbitts, 1935).

Yet girls' labor market experiences seem to have been much different than boys'. A survey of more than 125,000 continuation students in New York state found that girls earned about half what boys earned and were subject to frequent and lengthy bouts of unemployment, in contrast to the boys. About one-fifth of the girls worked at home for no pay. Those girls who did wage work had found their jobs on their own or through relatives and friends; only 5.5 percent received help from a continuation placement officer or teacher (New York State Teachers' Assoc., 1929: 301–3).

Liberal supporters of continuation education such as Paul Douglas believed that part-time schools should prepare boys and girls for divergent vocations. Despite the increasing labor force participation of females and the fact that many working-class women did not leave the work force once they got married and had children, most reformers insisted with Douglas that "training for home-making and for life, as well as for industry, should then be an integral part in any system of vocational education for women" (Douglas, 1921: 175). A partial exception to this was Willystine Goodsell, who rejected the popular notion that "the wage-earning life of women is only from five to seven years in length." She suggested public coeducational day schools of household arts be set up, but that these should be administered separately from trade or industrial schools so that "girls would not suffer, in their education for wage-earning, by being compelled to divide their energies and time between two vocations" (Goodsell, 1923: 211). Federal and state legislation did not reflect this view, however, and homemaking courses for girls were strongly promoted.

In fact, the principal of Brooklyn Girls' Continuation School acknowledged that in her ten years of experience, most girls had to be persuaded to apply for homemaking upon first enrolling in continuation school. "The average girl from the public elementary or high school believes that she has received an ample amount of instruction in homemaking, so we must be prepared to interest her in new possibilities." Creating such "interest" was done by limiting entrance to popular commercial (clerical) courses to elementary school graduates—thus placing "homemaking courses within a narrower range of subjects than would otherwise be the case"—and by making the "homemaking annex particularly attractive" (New York State Teachers' Assoc., 1929: 314–15).

While the variety of course offerings differed depending on the size and resources of the school district, all continuation education programs included home economics classes and these seemed to be the main fare for girls in the smallest programs. While enrollment data by sex are scanty, several large eastern cities formally segregated their classes by sex and, when enrollments were high, taught boys and girls in separate schools, buildings, or departments (McDonough, 1921: 205; New York State Teachers' Assoc., 1929: 298, 302–5). In California, the state advised continuation administrators: "Except in hygiene, physical education and home economics, sex should not be considered a governing factor in class groupings" (CSBE, 1923b: 40). Richmond, and perhaps other school districts, did not follow this advice, however (Olson, 1945: 93). And, in practice, enrollment in strictly vocational courses tended to reflect the degree of sex-segregation of particular occupations.

Immigrant girls seem to have been overrepresented in home economics classes, where they studied cooking, dressmaking, and millinery, and short-unit courses ranging from "story telling for children" to "household mechanics." California's Commissioner of Industrial and Vocational Education reported that "enrollment in some of the [home economics] classes is almost entirely composed of foreign-born children," which, in his view, presented an opportunity "for vital instruction in citizenship" (CSBE, 1921: 101).

The state Department of Education showcased a "citizen-homemakers" course offered mainly to Mexican immigrant girls in Bakersfield. The main purpose of instruction was the transmission of middle-class norms of self-presentation, morality, and housekeeping (CSDE, 1920: 21). Half the girls were working as maids in local homes, and their middle-class women employers telephoned the teachers to report on their work daily. During the sewing hours at school, according to their teacher, "all kinds of weighty problems are discussed, salaries, good taste, husbands, preference of country, U.S. or Mexico, homelife, whether it is right to break an engagement of marriage, and the right age for marriage" (CSDE, 1920: 19).

In the large cities, girls had more courses from which to choose. The *San Francisco News* reported: "Although classes for girls include dressmaking, millinery, cooking, nutrition, diet, care of the home, home decorations and maid work, the most popular courses are bookkeeping, typing and shorthand." Vocational classes for boys included automobile mechanics, printing, woodworking, and commercial art. Both boys and girls enjoyed a course in journalism (*San Francisco News*, 9/30/30; see also New York State Teachers' Assoc., 1929: 302–3).

YEARS OF UNCERTAINTY DURING HARD TIMES

The part-time continuation school as originally conceived peaked in 1930 throughout the United States. The immediate and most obvious explanation for its decline was the onset of the Great Depression and lack of work opportunities. As school districts across the United States began to feel the fiscal crunch, many of the programs introduced earlier in the century were cut back (Tyack, Lowe, and Hansot, 1984: 40; Katznelson and Weir, 1985: 129).

In addition, more and more students were remaining in the full-time school, for a variety of complex and interrelated reasons. Manufacturing and commercial employers were requiring a high school diploma for the better jobs, a trend not lost on parents and adolescents. Cities stepped up enforcement of compulsory attendance laws. The discourse about those on the front lines of enforcing these laws was changing: "hookey cops" gave way to "truant officers" (Tyack and Berkowitz, 1977). The "main duty" of attendance officers and teachers, according to reformers, was "that of selling education to the children and to their parents" (CSBE, 1923b: 50). School people did not describe nonattending pupils as lacking in moral character so much as "maladjusted," either overwhelmed by environmental problems or deficient psychologically.

When hard times hit, compulsory attendance laws were strengthened, and some states maintained a role for continuation education. California, for example, passed an "anti-loafing" law in 1929—the year the stock market crashed—to prevent "idle minors" from competing with unemployed adults for work. The law required proof of employment from part-time students; those unemployed were required to attend continuation classes for at least three hours per day. In some cities, notably Los Angeles, students were not allowed to leave the full-time high school for the continuation school unless they had first secured employment (CSDE, 1932a: I-74).

Furthermore, the administrative progressives had succeeded in expanding the range of what was taught as well as developing systems of tracking and ability grouping in the regular junior and senior high schools (Tyack, 1974: 194). These developments led the chief of New York State's Bureau of Industrial Education to observe that continuation schools had probably "attained their maximum size," partly because mainstream schools now offered "programs of education and training suited to the needs and interests of nearly all boys and girls, whether they plan to go on to college or university, or not" (New York State Teachers' Assoc., 1929: 295–96). Or, to put the matter more sharply, "comprehensive high schools . . . were now in a position to accommodate continuation school pupils with less danger of contaminating the others" (Imber, 1978: 12).

As enrollments declined in continuation classes, girls began to outnumber boys for the first time. This trend, evident across the country, continued throughout the 1930s in both smaller and larger communities (CSDE, 1934: 3–4), with the biggest gap occurring in 1938–39: out of a total enrollment of 141,265 students, females outnumbered males almost three to two (see figure 1).

At the same time, adults made up an increasing proportion of total enrollments. In California, for example, between 1922 and 1926, about 80 percent of students enrolled in part-time general continuation classes were sixteen or seventeen years old. Of the remaining students, boys were more likely to be younger (fourteen or fifteen) while girls were more likely to be eighteen or over. Enrollment data for 1932–34 show that as total numbers declined and females began to outnumber males in continuation classes, one-third of those enrolled were eighteen years or older, while less than 4 percent were younger than sixteen (CSBE, 1924: 196–98; CSBE, 1926: 161–65; CSDE, 1934: 5).

Although evidence is scanty, these demographic shifts in continuation enrollments can be accounted for in several ways. First, females who had married and had children early may have remained in the continuation school, not having been allowed to attend the regular high school. The principal of San Francisco Continuation School reported that although he excused married women under eighteen from attending, many chose to attend the school voluntarily (*San Francisco News*, 9/30/30).

Second, girls may have left the comprehensive high school in increased numbers during the Great Depression to engage in domestic labor while adults sought work outside the home. Girls in this situation (and others) also could not afford to attend a regular junior or senior high school (Lightfoot, 1933; Ching, 1935: 188). Edwards (1976), in a related analysis, found that post–World War II "teenage girls accelerate their school-leaving in times of depression, while teenage boys either do not respond (all races combined) or are more likely to remain in school (nonwhites) during such times." She argues that the main reason for this gender difference

> is that opportunity costs of teenage boys are determined primarily by labor market conditions, while those of teenage girls are determined both by home productivity and labor market conditions. Since home productivity sets a floor to declining opportunity costs in the downward phase of the [business] cycle, opportunity costs vary less over the cycle for girls than for boys. (Edwards, 1976: 201)

A third reason girls outnumbered boys in continuation classes during the 1930s may be that a disproportionate number of boys went into New Deal programs such as the National Youth Administration (NYA) and the Civilian Conservation Corps (CCC).[3]

Fourth, continuation education leaders began to de-emphasize job training and placement for those under eighteen while encouraging continuation program heads to enroll adults (Mayman, 1933: 201). This change in priorities may have reduced the program's attractiveness to

---

3. Although the CCC ostensibly accepted single men between the ages of eighteen and twenty-four, a survey of participants revealed the average age of the youth in the camps was nineteen years, and two-thirds of them were younger when they entered. Moreover, their background characteristics closely matched those of continuation students, and it seems likely that at least some boys under eighteen slipped into the CCC (CSDE, 1939: 179–80). Even more likely, they secured employment on a NYA project, because NYA participants could be as young as sixteen years. Girls also participated in the NYA: they comprised 45 percent of the participants nationwide (Tyack, Lowe, and Hansot, 1984: 126; compare CSDE, 1936: 92).

younger males seeking employment. Job placement of continuation school pupils in California, for example, decreased by 60 percent between 1929 and 1932 (CSDE, 1932a: I-73–74).

Rather than job placement, the state departments of education advised continuation school administrators to focus on vocational guidance, which was broadened to include recreational, social, civic, and health guidance. Guidance for girls involved preventing or modifying sexual behavior that seemed to challenge the middle-class family form (heterosexuality, female virginity, marriage). A Chicago high school principal wrote of the "maladjusted" girl: "The seeming casualness of her acceptance of promiscuity and her declaration of the right to smoke, drink and 'go the limit' with her 'boyfriend' make the need for guidance more necessary" (Smithies, 1933: 261). At the same time, continuation school personnel were urged to educate students "through life experiences." Thus, teachers were advised to use "such home problems as occur to increase the understanding of home making and of happy home relationships" (CSDE, 1932a: I-74–75).

The curriculum also began to shift away from traditional vocational education courses toward academic subjects during this period (CSDE, 1932b: 12; CSDE, 1934: 27–28). Presumably, an increasing number of students, especially girls interested in clerical work and their families, felt basic English and math courses were a safer investment than training for occupations with an uncertain future. The shift away from job preparation and placement called into doubt the purpose of continuation schools. The advocates (largely urban school people and "child savers") and opponents (largely small district and rural school people and some parents of truants and employers) put forth arguments that echoed the debate of the previous decade and were still being invoked as the economy began to turn around in the late 1930s.

Advocates of the part-time continuation school law held that everyone should be given all the education possible and that compelling sixteen to eighteen year olds to attend helped prevent juvenile delinquency. Critics countered that the law was unenforceable and largely ignored by students, parents, and employers and that "part-time education should be given evenings when it does not interrupt the day's work and when many part-time students now roam the streets or frequent pool or dance halls" (Calif. Commission, 1931: 53; see also Trout, 1937; New York State Teachers' Assoc., 1929: 304–5). Advocates further contended that part-time school made young employees better workers and encouraged them to pursue their education as adults in evening school (Bogan, 1932). Opponents, on the other hand, argued that young workers would learn more on the job itself while earning more and upsetting their routine, and that of their employers, less. Finally, while continuation education proponents pointed to the success of the law in the large city school districts, critics noted that the plan was not adapted to small towns and rural areas (Calif. Commission, 1931).

Two additional points of contention came to the fore in the 1930s. First, critics charged that continuation education was too costly. The original advocates had argued that this type of school would cost less per pupil, but this seems to have been true only during periods of " 'indecent' overcrowding of pupils" in the largest city schools. In New York, for example, costs rose because of "mandatory increases in teachers' salaries and persistent efforts to reduce the size of instruction groups" (Mayman, 1933: 201, 203). In California, teacher salary costs per unit of average daily attendance in continuation schools were about 25 percent more than for high schools (CSDE, 1934: 23). Class size in 1931–32 averaged fourteen students overall and sixteen pupils per class hour in the largest cities, the highest being twenty-three in San Francisco (CSDE, 1932b: 11). Continuation proponents argued that the higher cost per pupil was "proper" because "smaller classes, individual programs, teachers specially qualified to deal with problem cases, and a constantly shifting personnel [student body] necessarily increase the costs of educational services" (CSDE, 1934: 23–24).

Second, even those sympathetic to the continuation education cause argued that continuation students formed a diverse group whose needs could not be addressed by one teacher. The director of adult and continuation education in Burbank wrote:

> Whoever had the idea that one person could take twenty or thirty or even ten continuation students and instruct them in the things they should know and make them like it must have been the champion day-dreamer of the ages. I say it's a joke to place a group of these people under one person, because, if ever any class needed real practical help, these students do. They represent the moron and the genius, the social misfit and the socially unfit, the rich man's misunderstood daughter and the poor man's understood son, together with the bewildered and groping foreign born. (Trout, 1937: 183)

Burbank's situation was not uncommon. At Snyder Continuation School in San Diego, a survey of the student body revealed that pupils ranged in age from fifteen to fifty-three (although most were between the ages of sixteen and eighteen) and had come from twenty-nine states and eight foreign countries. A third of the students were employed, primarily in low-level service occupations such as clerk, janitor, or wait-ress. Most worked to help with family finances. While other pupils were seeking jobs, they had been assigned to the continuation school for a wide variety of other reasons:

Reason for Continuation School Attendance	Boys	Girls
Employment	152	88
Over age	131	116
Substandard academic performance	67	36
Truancy	43	82
Placement council (school maladjustment)	32	6
Special arrangement	24	13
New to city	22	15
Probation office (delinquency)	20	7
Rehabilitation bureau (physical handicap)	8	4
Health	3	9
Total (877)	501	376

In what would become the new watchword in the continuation educa-tion movement, a teacher described how the San Diego School District had expanded the continuation concept to include "adjustment":

> ... the Snyder Continuation School's function as a psychologi-cal adjustment agency has long since supplanted its importance as a structure where the underage employed must be enter-tained for four hours a week to comply with the law. There is a place for anyone and everyone in this unique institution. (Mar-key, 1940: 160)

While the shift from a vocational to an adjustment model might seem to support the continuation believers' psychological perspective that deviance was evidence of individual or family pathology, the fact that the clientele remained fundamentally unchanged lends credence to a more structural perspective.

ADJUSTMENT EDUCATION: 1945–1965

Continuation school advocates had, from the beginning, discussed the role that part-time schools could play in "adjustment," although they were never entirely clear about what it was (how did it differ from ed-ucation?) or who was adjusting to what, or vice versa. Typically, reform-ers assumed that a certain proportion of school-age children were mal-, ill-, or unadjusted to the full-time school, the workplace, the home, so-ciety, or life in general.

California was well situated to keep the system of continuation education alive, while in other states continuation programs were already in steep decline, most never to recover. School people nationwide perceived a need for "adjustment" education, but California appears to have been one of the few states to weld this to the existing institutional structure of continuation programs. When, decades later, the nation's economy and educational opportunities expanded and school dropouts became a concern again, state officials and youth advocates could build on an organizational and legislative framework already in place.

Compared with other states, California was in a fiscal position to maintain continuation programs during the Depression and managed to do so, despite a conservative governor's attempt to cut them from the state budget (Hendrick, 1972). Early on a coalition of continuation administrators and teachers, probation and truant officers, youth advocates, and university leaders formed the California Continuation Education Association (CCEA). The CCEA was directly linked to the Department of Education through a state-employed consultant, who was an ex officio member of the CCEA and acted as a lobby on behalf of the association's interests (for a summary of early CCEA legislative proposals, see Bash, 1945). When the "life adjustment" education movement began sweeping the country in the years following World War II, continuation advocates labored to show that "adjustment" had been part of their program since its inception and should be made the cornerstone of a revised program.

Early in the implementation of California's continuation program, Emily Palmer began to distinguish between the adolescent worker who drops out of the full-time school and the maladjusted. As the person in charge of the Research and Service Center, State Board of Education, and the Division of Vocational Education at the University of California, Berkeley, Palmer wrote most of the early reports and handbooks on continuation education and also became the special agent for training part-time teachers. Based on teachers' reports, she noted that the problem of maladjustment was concentrated among students, especially in small towns, who "seem to have no interest in preparing for future employment" and "often become school rebels." By default, Palmer argued, it fell on continuation teachers to try to adjust these students' attitudes toward school, work, and authority early in order to prevent delinquency (CSBE, 1924: 150–51).

Thus, even in its heyday, the continuation school served not only immigrants and others working out of economic necessity or assuming domestic responsibilities so that others in their family might earn a wage, but also truants who did poorly in school, discipline cases, and bright students bored with regular school fare (CSBE, 1926: 109–10).

During the Depression, as ever more pupils remained in the high school, a greater proportion of the continuation student body seemed to be made up of those "maladjusted" to the full-time school—or labeled as such. By 1932, Palmer argued:

> If it is the policy of the school district to place such [maladjusted] pupils in the continuation school, then the school becomes an opportunity school and must make its curricula flexible enough to include pupils whose problems are not primarily vocational. (CSDE, 1932c: 28)

As the number of unemployed minors subject to fifteen hours per week compulsory attendance in continuation education classes increased, teachers and school administrators claimed to focus more on adjustment education (Markey, 1940; Trout, 1937).

By 1950 continuation advocates were on the defensive against charges that the program was increasingly irrelevant, ineffective, costly,[4] and stigmatized as "the stepchild" of secondary education (Hicks, 1945). As discussed in the previous section, the need for a part-time school for employed minors had diminished because of the decline in youth employment and the increased holding power of the regular full-time high school. School-age youths who wanted or needed to work could now participate in cooperative education, work experience, or apprenticeship training programs through the regular school. In light of these changes, most continuation leaders favored recasting the program as an adjustment school (Warner, 1954: 302).

Continuation people no doubt rallied to the leadership of the same Charles Prosser who championed vocational continuation schools and now was spearheading a curricular movement known as "life adjustment education." Prosser saw the need for a curriculum aimed at the middle 60 percent of high school students, who did not plan to attend college or study a skilled trade. Rather than academics, this curriculum would emphasize work experience and practical arts, home and family life, health

---

4. After World War II, the state Department of Education calculated the average cost of a continuation program at 40 percent higher than the cost of a regular high school program (CSDE, 1946a: 13). In 1947, after much lobbying on the part of the Continuation Education Association and the state Department of Education, the legislature allowed that three hours rather than four should constitute a day of attendance for apportionment purposes. It also authorized the holding of continuation education classes on Saturdays, which allowed smaller districts to use regular school buildings and teachers while segregating continuation pupils (Smith, 1945). Both of these changes helped districts meet the higher costs of continuation education, though most continued to ignore the law.

and physical fitness, and civic competence (Cremin, 1964: 334–37). These ideas had already been put into practice in many continuation classes. Not surprisingly, the Commission on Life Adjustment Education for Youth's reports were sharply criticized by a number of educators who recognized the concept of adjustment as a rehash (some might say bastardization) of some of the tenets of progressive education of the 1920s. Critics also charged that this sort of curriculum encouraged conformity to the status quo and failed to prepare the nation's future work force to meet the challenges of a rapidly changing economy (Cremin, 1964: 344–47).

These concerns did not deter continuation advocates. After all, the reason many students were said to end up in continuation classes was that they did not conform enough or their academic performance was below average or both. The national life adjustment movement lent legitimacy to their enterprise, and for most school administrators in the 1950s, the name adjustment education did not carry the stigma that continuation education did. Continuation administrators, through the CCEA, stepped up the statewide effort to repackage the program (Warner, 1954).

Although the organization, administration, and curriculum (with its emphasis on guidance counseling) of the adjustment school would resemble that of the continuation school, its primary purpose would change. Rather than serving mainly as a bridge from school to work, the school would provide a "treatment" program for "the problem cases of the regular full time school." The adjustment school was intended "to redirect the student, who has dropped from a regular school program, back into the regular full time school program with a much better understanding of the requirements of society" (Warner, 1954: 307). The "unadjusted" were already familiar to continuation school personnel. According to the *Handbook of Continuation Education,* they included:

> students who are retarded in school, students with little interest in the school program, students needing remedial work in certain fields, students with limited physical capacity, students returning to school after long periods of absence, transfers, late enrollees, students needing special guidance such as habitual truants, juvenile court problems, behavior cases, health problems, and students requiring rehabilitation. (CSDE, 1950: 3)

Personal, family, and environmental "handicaps," it was assumed, "cause general maladjustment" (CSDE, 1950: 4). The solution was psychology-based: counseling to overcome "disturbance from within" (Morena, 1953: 107).

Continuation educators had a solution in search of a problem. Workers in other agencies serving youth had a problem in search of a solution. The "problem" was juvenile delinquency, which, so it was argued, was caused by maladjustment in school. Concern about "teen-age problems" prompted at least two large-scale studies of continuation education as a means of preventing youth crime. In Illinois a juvenile court judge authorized a committee to survey continuation schools in fifty U.S. and four Canadian cities (Voss, 1958: 151–52).

California, more than any other state, thoroughly embraced continuation education as a solution and in so doing recolored the program as "adjustment education." The process was boosted when the Governor's Advisory Committee on Children and Youth appointed the Committee on Continuation Education in 1953, with a mandate to study the program and make recommendations for its improvement. The study was co-sponsored by the California Youth Authority, the state's prison system for young people.

Two decisions helped ensure that the study's findings and recommendations would draw attention to the need for a shift in direction toward adjustment education. First, Charlotte Elmott, a Santa Barbara school administrator, became chair of the committee, and her interest was clearly in maladjusted students—her Ed.D. thesis concerned how to develop a "mental hygiene" program. Elmott argued that the "emotionally disturbed should get financial help as do the physically handicapped and mentally retarded" (Rosenberg Foundation, interview with Charlotte Elmott, 3/16/56).

Second, the committee appointed E. Evan Shaffer, assistant director of research, San Diego Public Schools, to design, direct, and write up the study funded by the Rosenberg Foundation.[5] San Diego's Snyder Continuation School (named after California's first commissioner of industrial and vocational education) had pioneered the idea of an adjustment school in California during the 1930s (Markey, 1940; Landon and Cox, 1945; Jacobs, 1951: 433).

While many continuation students at this time had jobs, Shaffer ar-

---

5. Max Rosenberg, a San Francisco businessperson, established the foundation in 1935. In 1953, the Rosenberg Foundation requested the study's sponsors (notably, progressive Governor Earl Warren's Advisory Committee on Children and Youth and the California Youth Authority) "to broaden the membership to include businessmen and representatives of school administrators." Later, in evaluating the completed study, a foundation staff member wrote that the sponsors had "failed to involve probation officers effectively" and "community membership [was] too heavily weighted in [the] direction of professional education" (Rosenberg Foundation, administrative reports, 1953–59).

gued that employment was a symptom rather than a root cause of why many students left school, even during the Great Depression:[6]

> Many who left full-time school for a job on the *pretext of economic need* were in no greater financial difficulties than others who relied upon after-school employment. *Lack of adjustment* to the program or the environment of the regular full-time high school led these youth to drop out ... (Shaffer, 1955: 1; emphasis added)

His analysis of the study's data convinced him that only a quarter left because of economic need.[7] While this group could continue to benefit from continuation education, he argued, it did not pose nearly the problems that maladjusted youth did to California's system of public education (Shaffer, 1955: 2–3, 53).

Redirecting the emphasis of continuation education from working youth to the maladjusted, however, created a new dilemma for continuation advocates. In claiming to serve more than employed students, continuation education people reinforced the growing public perception that the program was a dumping ground for "mentally retarded and disciplinary cases" (Voss, 1958: 154). The stigma attached to continuation schools made students and their families reluctant to have them attend (Boldenweck, 1978; CSDE, 1950: 20–23).

Indeed, the Shaffer study was prompted in part by "the active and passive attacks upon continuation education" and the need to address the fact that "in many localities a stigma became attached to continuation education in the minds of students and teachers in the regular high

---

6. From the beginning, some educators had maintained that most part-time students were not really compelled to leave the full-time school by economic necessity; rather, they desired "to earn, have, and spend money" and took a "greater interest in adult life and occupations than in school work" (CSBE, 1923b: 33). A number of historians have argued that school people tended to underestimate the degree to which urban working-class families needed their children's wages or help at home while one or both parents worked for wages (Hogan, 1985: 113; Tyack and Hansot, 1988: 254).

7. In the 1954 California survey of 1,073 students, about half (529) affirmed the statement "I quit regular school and got a job because of need of the money," while 544 denied it. Students were classified as having left full-time school due to economic need if they affirmed the statements "I have to work because I pay all my own bills" or "I have to help my family pay bills." About one-sixth of the sample mentioned leaving school due to academic failure; 13 percent said they could not get along with a teacher or teachers (Shaffer, 1955: 51–53; compare the results of a survey sponsored by the Bureau of Adult Education of 700 continuation students in CSDE, 1951: 6–7).

schools and in the minds of the general public" (Shaffer, 1955: 6, 25). Shaffer found that one-fourth of the continuation students sampled had been on probation, usually for minor offenses like public drunkenness; the statistic was not analyzed by gender. But in a later study, Elder (1966: 333) reported that most girls were on probation for running away from home or for sex offenses. At the same time, continuation students studied by Shaffer averaged only slightly lower on IQ tests than the general population, a considerable number were capable of college work, and 88 percent had sufficient ability for regular high school classroom instruction.

This finding contrasted sharply with the views of regular high school principals, half of whom had been surveyed by the state a few years before. Almost half of those polled checked "inability of [continuation] pupils to do high school work" as a problem. Three-fifths of the principals felt that a combination of citizenship, social living, and vocational training would best meet the needs of continuation pupils, while only 14 percent listed opportunity for high school graduation as a need (CSDE, 1946b: 12–13).

In contrast, continuation administrators had recommended at a 1944 meeting that credits toward a high school diploma should be provided as an attendance incentive (Warner, 1954: 274–75), and a number of districts were already doing so. Student and parent demand seemed to prompt this shift. Shaffer's survey of more than a thousand continuation students showed a four-to-one majority believing that the main goal of the continuation school should be to help them graduate from high school (Shaffer, 1955: 54). Earning high school credits also gave students the option of returning to the regular school, though apparently few did.

Shaffer's finding that continuation students were academically capable was consistent with a study by Evraiff, who compared boys in both the continuation and regular schools in Fresno and Stockton, matching his sample on age, grade, scholastic aptitude, and father's occupation. Despite the similarity in father's jobs, though, he noted statistically significant differences between the two groups in terms of socioeconomic status. The continuation students' parents had less education. These students were also more likely to come from single parent families and to live in homes where a foreign language was spoken; fewer continuation boys had telephones or television sets in their homes or received an allowance. The continuation boys also made earlier and more frequent claims to adult status: they had held more jobs and were more likely to smoke, drink, and go steady (Evraiff, 1954).

Evraiff concluded that continuation schools were more "realistic" and tolerant in dealing with students than regular secondary schools, which were biased toward "middle-class standards." The existence of continuation schools called into question the regular schools' effectiveness and commitment to equality of opportunity: "the regular secondary schools are failing to meet the needs of many students and are turning their 'problem children' over to a kind of segregated educational program" (Evraiff, 1954: 90). He felt that lessons learned from continuation schools regarding curriculum, guidance, and less demand for student conformity could be incorporated into the regular school program.

Shaffer, in his report, met these charges head on. "Reduction of the student-teacher ratio to fifteen to one is financially possible only in special classes or special schools." Likewise, establishing "a permissive situation" was probably only possible in a separate school because the "regular school staff may not tolerate the differences between two types of classes in a single school" (Shaffer, 1955: 70, 73). An earlier qualitative study lent some support to this argument. Continuation staff told Jacobs (1951: 434) that their program would be more effective if held in a separate building because the pupils, teachers, and their problems were not understood. One coordinator described being placed in a basement room with no telephone; continuation pupils were not allowed in the main halls, on the playground of the high school, or at school dances and could go to the auditorium and library only under full supervision (compare Hicks, 1945: 76).

Not surprisingly, the California Committee on Continuation Education—based on the Shaffer study—recommended "that the responsibility of continuation education be redefined in terms of a program serving all those students who have limitations, unusual problems, or responsibilities which make it inadvisable for them to attend the regular secondary school program." This modified program was referred to as "adjustment" and "continuation" interchangeably (Shaffer, 1955: 105).

Continuation leaders touted the Shaffer study "as the most significant contribution since the original part-time education law was enacted in 1919" (Voss, 1955: 465). It failed, however, to create much immediate interest among county, city, and high school superintendents, all of whom were sent three copies each. In a passage that could have been written by the equity conscious critics during the academic excellence, back-to-basics climate of the 1980s, the committee sponsoring the Shaffer study lamented that society was devoting a disproportionate amount of money and attention to gifted students (Rosenberg Foundation, evaluative report, 3/10/58: 2).

Continuation advocates began lobbying on behalf of "socially maladjusted children." A San Francisco continuation teacher wrote: "If our aim is salvage, not punishment; if we keep one lifer out of San Quentin or Napa; if we keep one girl off the streets; or if we keep one youngster away from heroin, we have certainly accomplished something worth while" (Born, 1957: 286). A former continuation school principal warned, "this group of kids could be the spot that would endanger democracy" (Rosenberg Foundation, notes from interview with Carl Bash, 4/10/56; compare Shaffer, 1955: 5).

These ideas did not resonate with school districts, however. A number of individuals, including some educators, and newspaper editorials argued that everyone would be better off if so-called maladjusted sixteen- and seventeen-year-olds were allowed to leave school. One paper urged the schools to "Kick Them Out" (*San Francisco Examiner,* 11/14/58).[8] Most school districts refused to take action to create continuation/adjustment programs without further financial subsidy (Rosenberg Foundation, evaluative report, 3/10/58: 3). In retrospect, the most significant outcome of the Shaffer study was the establishment of a special committee on continuation education within the Department of Education charged with developing legislation aimed at providing an "excess cost" formula for continuation education and putting teeth in the compulsory attendance laws (Voss, 1958: 152–53).

The committee helped persuade the state superintendent of public instruction to shift responsibility for continuation education from the Bureau of Adult Education to the Bureau of Secondary Education in 1961. Continuation advocates felt that the latter Bureau would be more sympathetic to their idea of an adjustment school.

Various state education associations called for state funding to study the characteristics and needs of "divergent youth," and in 1962 the state

------

8. This editorial was published after a group of merchants operating near the continuation school complained to the police of "noontime hoodlumism." As a result of the ensuing controversy, the district was forced to change its policy of sending chronic truants and disruptive pupils to the continuation school.

Educators who felt that disruptive students should be allowed—even asked—to leave school and forced to go to work argued that: (1) it was unfair to the majority of students to keep "problem" students in class, (2) they wasted tax dollars spent on their education, and (3) they undermined the authority of teachers and the school by flaunting the rules with impunity (Silverman, 1958). Of the 80 percent responding to the sample survey of regular secondary school principals in California in the spring of 1954, only a slim majority agreed that there was a "need for supervision of instruction on a part-time basis for 16 and 17 year old youth who work full time" (Shaffer, 1955: 76). An administrator for the Los Angeles City Schools made the case for why his district "let them go" in a *California Journal of Secondary Education* symposium that echoed the sentiment of many state legislators reluctant to toughen compulsory attendance laws (Jacobs, 1958: 119–22).

senate held hearings on this topic. "Divergent" was clearly just a new tag for the "maladjusted": "those students who don't work up to their mental ability in school, who resist academic learning, and who make up the larger portion of social problems, academic failures and school dropouts" (Calif. Legislature, 1963: 53).

ALTERNATIVE EDUCATION FOR "DIVERGENT YOUTH"

Despite increasing state and national concern over dropouts and divergent youth in the early 1960s—especially "the subcultures of minority and estranged" males without jobs (Calif. Legislature, 1963: 53–56)— school administrators across the country were largely ignoring or evading the continuation program ostensibly designed to help these young people.[9] At the federal level, policymakers reasoned that school-work cooperation, work experience, and apprenticeship training programs had superseded the original function of continuation education, and its funding was no longer mandated in the Vocational Education Act passed by Congress in 1963 (U.S. Dept. of Health, Educ. and Welfare, 1968: 2).

Fully aware of this trend, the Rosenberg Foundation nevertheless decided to grant $32,800 to the Institute of Human Development at the University of California at Berkeley to study the eleven continuation schools operating in California during 1964–65. The rationale behind this funding decision indicated an understanding that some dropouts were more properly described as pushouts. One staff member wrote that the study might "have real possibilities in suggesting approaches to perhaps our most baffling school problem: devising ways of fitting the outcast child into the educational system" (Rosenberg Foundation, administrative report, 1965).

The pushout issue—as well as community fears about juvenile delinquency and the threatened lack of an adequately large, productive labor force—had also captured the attention of California school people and legislators. Continuation leaders identified as a major problem the need to help youth exempted or expelled from school (White, 1962: 405); through the CCEA and a half-time consultant within the Department of Education, they lobbied for recognition and increased funding of their program as the solution.

---

9. A California Department of Education survey done in 1961 revealed that less than 10 percent of the state's 330 school districts were operating the required continuation program. The department estimated that between 65,000 and 200,000 youths were eligible, but only 5,449 boys and 2,824 girls were enrolled during 1961–62 (White, 1962: 399–400).

Meanwhile, an Assembly Legislative Reference Service study of long-term suspensions (authorized by the Legislature beginning in the 1961–62 school year) showed that "the long-term suspension mechanism has, at least in part, been substituted for the traditional and more formal [expulsion] process." [10] Validating the claims of the CCEA and other youth advocates that continuation education was a solution to the pushout problem, researchers found that four-fifths of long-term suspensions occurred in districts that did not operate continuation classes or schools (Calif. Legislature, 1965: 8–10). This study persuaded the legislature to pass a law requiring all school systems to provide continuation education (or transfer to a "parental school" designed for hard-core truants and delinquents) for youths suspended ten days or more.

School districts that did not comply with the 1965 law faced having 10 percent of all state apportionments withheld annually (Calif. *Education Code,* 1965, Sec. 7757). These were the teeth that continuation leaders had been fighting to put into the compulsory attendance laws; the effect was immediate. Further, in another victory for the CCEA, state funding favored the establishment of separate continuation schools under the Necessary Small High School foundation program over continuation classes within the regular school. [11] In four years, the number of continuation high schools in the state increased from 13 to 183 (Weber, 1972: 571). In 1967, the legislature extended the length of time a student could be suspended from ten to twenty days and declared its intent that continuation education classes be maintained to provide:

> (1) an opportunity for the completion of the required academic courses of instruction to graduate from high school, (2) a program of individualized instruction that may emphasize occupa-

10. During the three years that long-term suspensions had been allowed, they increased seven times faster than expected given increased average daily attendance in secondary schools. "In the main, [the suspended student] is a boy who is sixteen years old, doing very poorly in school, with low reading ability but a fairly normal I.Q.

"He probably has three or four brothers and sisters living with him in a one-parent home, and the family income is substantially below average, although not in the poverty category. He is most likely to be a member of a minority group, although not Oriental" (Calif. Legislature, 1965: 1).

11. Separate continuation classes received regular high school apportionment for only those pupils who were present each day. Excused absences were not counted toward accumulation of average daily attendance (CSDE, 1966: 12, 21). Without this financial incentive, the Assembly Legislative Reference Service concluded, districts would continue to evade existing compulsory attendance laws already mandating continuation programs (Calif. Legislature, 1965: 17).

tional orientation or a work-study schedule . . . , (3) a specially
designed program of individualized instruction and intensive
guidance services to meet the special needs of *pupils with behavior
or severe attendance problems,* or (4) a flexible program combining
features in (1), (2), and (3). (Calif. *Education Code,* 1967, Sec.
5950; emphasis added)

The years of lobbying for an adjustment program, begun by the CCEA
as early as 1945 and supported by youth advocates inside and outside of
state and local government, had paid off.

The Rosenberg Foundation–funded, U.C. Berkeley study of the
state's continuation schools confirmed the findings of previous surveys
and first-person accounts: that the effectiveness of, and community support for, the program varied widely. A number of schools were lacking
in resources, meaningful vocational education or work experience opportunities, and remedial instruction. In the one school profiled, Elder
(1966) found that, proportionate to their residence in the community,
African-Americans were about twice as likely to be enrolled in the school,
yet only 23 percent of the non-white male students were employed compared to 53 percent of the white males. This school, noted Elder, was
open to the charge of being a "dumping ground" for African-American
students (1966: 327, 331, 340).

On the positive side, Elder pointed to the tutorial method, the tendency to treat students more like adults, flexible scheduling, and the
chance to get a high school diploma (identical to the regular one) as
promising. Other researchers, some with funding from reform-oriented
foundations, also saw continuation schools as fertile ground for experimentation (Rosenberg Foundation, administrative report, 1966).

Within the wider context of a developing counterculture ideology—
the protest against the war in Vietnam and racial injustice in the United
States as well as a shifting economy—attitudes toward education were
changing. In Berkeley, the city that has come to symbolize the reform
wave of the 1960s, the first of the school experiments was the transformation of McKinley Continuation High School "from a dumping ground
for school rebels and failures into an innovative educational environment."

Students were given careful personal attention in an atmosphere of respect and support, and the curriculum was trans-
formed to emphasize racial and ethnic identity alongside basic
skills. This freer, more intimate, more egalitarian school then
began to attract alienated white students who purposely sought

expulsion from Berkeley High so that they could attend Mc-Kinley. (Swidler, 1979: 36)

Under a new principal in 1965, the school was eventually relocated to the Berkeley High campus; it seemed to be a case of experimentation leading to racial integration (Kirp, 1982: 172). A former teacher recalled that when the riots broke out, "the only kids who would come to school went to the continuation school. It embarrassed the regular staff" (Hill, 1988). Now a school within a school, McKinley was renamed East Campus in 1967 in an attempt to remove any lingering stigma.

By the late 1960s, a curricular reform movement was underway throughout the country, and many of those working in or writing about continuation education touted its potential as an alternative. Curiously forgotten or ignored were the ideas and practices of progressive continuation and other school people writing in the 1920s and 1930s. While these reforms were not always put into practice (Hendrick, 1974), earlier advocates had identified many of the same failures in the schooling system that critics in the 1960s now sought to correct.

These early reforms ranged from the physical layout of the school to philosophy. An early observer of continuation education reported that "most schools try to avoid the appearance of the formal classroom." This was accomplished by providing conference tables and chairs, open book shelves and an inviting assortment of magazines (CSBE, 1924: 150). From the beginning in 1919, continuation schools served a diverse student body, and this prompted a recognition of different student interests and abilities and an experimentation with methods of instruction. Indeed, the Part-time Law had banned a "minimum uniform standard."

California's manual for teachers (CSBE, 1923b: esp. 40–41) clearly foreshadowed "a school without failure," a revaluation of instruction on an artistic or vocational theme, a recognition of diverse learning styles and aptitudes, and a de-emphasis on competition—themes prominent in later decades (Elder, 1969a; Galas and Winans, 1969: 323). One key difference, however, between the reform movements of the 1920s and the 1960s was the more widespread assumption in the latter period that institutions rather than individuals had failed (for example, Reed, 1969).

There is some evidence that the public was receptive to alternative ideas in education. The Gallup poll of attitudes toward education in 1972 showed that nationally, 71 percent of those surveyed favored a non-graded school where students worked at their own pace, according to ability; support was higher among public school parents (74 percent) and professional educators (87 percent). A general question was also posed about alternative schools:

> For students who are not interested in, or are bored with, the usual kind of education, it has been proposed that new kinds of local schools be established. They usually place more responsibility upon the student for what he learns and how he learns it. Some use the community as their laboratory and do not use the usual kind of classrooms. Do you think this is a good idea or a poor idea?

While professional educators gave the idea high approval (80 percent thought it was a good idea, 15 percent a poor one), 62 percent of public school parents thought it was a good idea, 28 percent a poor one, and 10 percent had no opinion (Elam, 1973: 146, 163–64).

When the *Handbook on Continuation Education* was revised in 1973, the program was referred to as "alternative" and a third major constituency singled out: while continuation schools continued to serve employed youth and dropouts and potential delinquents (that is the "maladjusted"), those bright but bored students could also benefit (CSDE, 1973: iii, 2).

Owing in part to the statewide law mandating and supporting continuation schools, California, followed by New York and Washington state, has had the largest number of public alternative schools in the nation since the movement flowered in the early 1970s (Barr, 1975: 4; Raywid, 1982: 6). Nationally, California has been credited with having "pioneered" continuation education (Bill, 1972: 27). And although a number of different types of alternative schools exist, continuation programs remain the most prevalent. In the first extensive survey of K-12 alternative programs, continuation schools comprised the single largest category (20 percent of the total); they provided "for students whose education in the conventional schools has been (or might be) interrupted." This definition included dropout centers, reentry programs, pregnancy-maternity centers, evening and adult high schools, and street academies (Barr, 1975: 8). The most recent national survey, focused at the secondary level, found that about two-thirds of public alternative schools are intended for potential and actual dropouts (Raywid, 1982: 1; see also Young, 1990).

THE "DISCOVERY" OF AN OUTCAST GROUP: PREGNANT AND MOTHERING GIRLS

One outcast group "discovered" early in continuation education's alternative phase were pregnant and mothering girls. Until the late 1960s, it was common educational policy to exclude pregnant and mothering girls from public schools in the United States. Nevertheless, some young mothers, particularly those who were married, seem to have been quietly accommodated in continuation and adult schools (Born, 1957). In 1928 the following item ran in *Vocational Education News Notes:* "San Francisco Part Time School is proud to have enrolled a pupil who is believed to be the youngest part-timer in the State. . . . Thomas and his mother are both enrolled in the part time school. The mother has only 16 years to her credit and Thomas has only 6 months" (quoted in Warner, 1954: 15).

Married girls in high school were an issue of concern during World War II, and the continuation school, an isolated facility where these young women could be segregated from other adolescents, seemed an appropriate solution. The girls' vice principal at Metropolitan, Los Angeles's continuation high school, reported that hundreds of girls between the ages of fourteen and eighteen had married boys who were leaving for training or combat and were therefore no longer welcome in the regular junior and senior high schools. In response, Metropolitan created the "Brides' Class," which consisted of such topics as home management, child care and development, the art of entertaining, and home care of the sick (Bullock and Weiss, 1945: 91).

In a rare mention of the "unwed mother" issue, the executive secretary of the California Association of Secondary School Administrators excerpted the written policy of several schools across the state regarding married and pregnant girls. These policies, put forth as possible models for other districts, revealed the strong fear that girls who had deviated from the norm in terms of their sexual behavior might contaminate other students. Example: one high school would allow married girls to continue school only if they agreed to "exert no unwholesome influence. Discussions which might be considered undesirable for unmarried girls to hear may be sufficient cause for cancellation of enrollment. Physical evidence of pregnancy will be sufficient cause to request a girl to check out of school" (McGowan, 1959: 487). Some districts allowed unmarried girls to return once they had given birth, but usually transferred them on a "social adjustment" permit to the continuation school, "especially if the circumstances have been given publicity in the girl's own school" (McGowan, 1959: 488).

Sedlak argues that by the 1960s, teenage pregnancy "had become less of a problem, or at least one that no longer required intensive rehabilitative treatment out of the public's view. Adolescent emotional maladjustment became identified as a more serious social and health problem." Changing attitudes as well as federal policies and financial assistance encouraged states and local districts to establish nonresidential, community-based, comprehensive care centers in public schools, but apart from regular classes (Sedlak, 1983: 22–23). For example, the Children's Bureau of the Department of Health, Education and Welfare funded a demonstration project that led to the establishment of continuation schools for pregnant and mothering girls throughout Iowa (Zober, 1967).

What is not clear is the extent to which pregnant and mothering girls were being served in continuation schools prior to the 1960s, without being singled out as a group worthy of special attention and funding. In a profile of one continuation school, Elder (1966: 324) noted that half of the young women students surveyed were married, pregnant, or mothering. At this time, pregnant girls were considered "physically handicapped" and therefore classified under the Special Education program, which meant they had to attend school full-time, unlike other continuation students.

Prior to 1965 a number of continuation schools had child care classes for pregnant girls. At McKinley Continuation, for example, the home economics teacher instructed girls about pre- and postnatal care, then they attended academic classes across the street at Berkeley High (Hill, 1988). Some had full-fledged nursery facilities (Knoeppel, 1969: 299). These programs were eventually singled out for special state funding in 1979. Others, such as Beacon's, were transferred to more suitable sites and expanded once financial incentives became available. In 1985–86, 13 percent of these programs were located in continuation schools; such schools served 26 percent of all students enrolled in the pregnant minors and teenage mothers programs in California (Cagampang, Gerritz, and Hayward 1987: 26).

While pregnant girls could be found in continuation school classrooms from the beginning, the original program was tailored and sold to meet the bigger concern of its day, the working-class and immigrant boy problem. Boys enrolled in the 1920s when the continuation schools helped place them in jobs. Their participation declined in the 1930s when continuation personnel by law could not help youth find paid work, given high adult unemployment. Boys flocked to the continuation schools again during World War II when the nation faced a labor shortage. In the 1950s and early 1960s, when juvenile delinquency (with its implied threat to private property and social order) and school pushouts (who threaten physical confrontation with authorities) emerged as largely boy problems on the public agenda, males outnumbered females in continuation programs.

Girls seem to have experienced the continuation school differently, yet none of the theories put forward to explain its origins and transformation draws attention to the gender dimension. Girls' reasons for disengaging stemmed from some of the same root causes as boys (for example, a dislike of school), but they sought to restore their dignity through traditional means not tolerated within the conventional high school: marriage and motherhood. Others rebelled in ways similar to boys but were seen as less threatening to social peace. Still others responded to their family's need for domestic or paid labor. In reading these girls' reasons for leaving the regular high school, however, the continuation school did little to challenge the traditional ideology bolstering the subordination of women within the home and workplace. This occurred in spite of the fact that many of these working-class and low-income girls would spend years in the paid labor force, earning much less than their male counterparts.

In continuation education's more vocational phase, immigrant girls were concentrated in home economics classes and the paid extension of these, maid work. Other girls sought out clerical training and jobs and non-sex-segregated courses like journalism. Although the conventional high school had failed to challenge the unequal sexual division of labor, too, the situation in the continuation school was arguably worse. The curriculum was less rigorous and academic (although seemingly in response to the majority of girls during the Depression, it returned to the basics), and this put girls at a greater disadvantage in the labor market because they had fewer opportunities than boys for on-the-job training in skilled trades (Carter and Prus, 1982).

Further, girls' deviance was defined almost exclusively in sexual terms. For girls to have sex outside of marriage was evidence of their maladjustment. Those not under direct family and school supervision (for example, runaways) were assumed to have been sexually corrupted. Thus, one of continuation education's explicit goals until recently was "to help the student develop principles for home and family living, including preparation for marriage" (CSDE, 1973: 1). Although framed in gender-neutral terms, this goal was clearly aimed at girls who were far more likely to be in family living and home economics classes and stood to lose the most if labeled sexually deviant, given the still prevailing double standard that affords boys more sexual and social freedom.

In sum, continuation programs historically have failed to challenge the idea that the family sphere is the primary domain of women. Home economics and family preparation courses may have seemed useful and even interesting to girls but did not allow them to continue their academic education or provide them with job skills. Vocational training prepared them for sex- and class-segregated jobs that did not usually provide a living wage. Overall, then, continuation programs reinforced the idea that the girls' financial security depended on association with a man rather than direct participation in the economy.

On the day that the Beacon staff gathered around the faculty lunch table to plan its counteroffensive against the central office's proposed changes, veteran teacher and counselor Ms. Foster turned to me for advice. She knew that I had been doing consulting work for a task force charged with developing an action plan for restructuring high schools throughout the state. I told her that I had sensed few advocates for alternative education in general on that task force. In fact, a number of members had argued that if we restructure schools and make them better for all students, then we do away with the need for continuation schools and the like—and around the state continuation school advocates were organizing a defense and sending representatives to our meetings. Most of these education professionals were advocates for alternative education and saw themselves as representing students and families poorly served by the state traditionally. It was a loose network ideologically: some wanted continuation schools to be one of a broad range of schooling options, the better to accommodate flexibly choice and diversity throughout the system. Others were more traditional in seeing continuation schools as places for "treating" misfits.

The notice sent by Beacon faculty to parents and students brought many phone calls of support. In the end, however, it was a faculty-written letter to all school board members that raised the superintendent's ire—and seemed to be the biggest reason for Beacon's eventual partial victory in its battle for survival. Citing the latest "literature on safe schools," Beacon's teachers argued that it would be a bad move to undermine their school's "controlled environment . . . conducive to dealing with students at risk." Beacon kept its portable building and its distinct identity for another year at least. Nearby Willows, a day after the newspaper gave front page, color photo treatment to its threatened closure, was saved. "The board has listened to you," said the superintendent. "We will maintain Willows High School. We need to make someone happy in all of this [other budget cutting]."

The ongoing survival of the continuation education program in California is the story of many such episodes in which its workers and advocates rally others around the mission of the continuation school even as its self-described purpose changes to fit the times.

Institutional convenience, framed by a larger conflict between advocates of democracy versus efficiency, best explains the origins and transformation of the continuation program. In response to a changing, hierarchically structured economy and an influx of immigrants, professional educators were experimenting with ways to deal with students, particularly boys, who could not or would not conform to the dominant culture and class standards. Social reformers argued that juvenile courts, detention homes, reformatories, jails, penitentiaries, sanitariums, and asylums already strained community coffers. They hailed continuation education as a humane, preventive response to these individuals' neglected needs. Yet by segregating rebels and failures from the mainstream high school, educators stigmatized them and the continuation program while easing their disciplinary load and scaring other students into relative conformity.

When policymakers and school administrators later looked for solutions to the problems of juvenile delinquency, pushouts, and teen pregnancy, the chameleon-like continuation program changed its colors. Its expansion was boosted by the climate of the late 1960s, for example, when civil rights and other protest movements were demanding greater social justice in education, and continuation schools—recolored as alternative programs—were a ready solution. Victories for greater equality in schooling were being won, such as the recognition of the right to an education for girls regardless of pregnancy and the funding of small schools for them and other continuation students. As Carnoy and Levin (1985: 232–33) argue, high levels of employment and economic growth in the 1960s helped create a climate in which such victories became possible. At the same time, comprehensive high schools did not have to accommodate students in all their diversity; rather, those who did not fit the mainstream mold could transfer to separate, almost always devalued institutions.

3

SAFETY VALVE VERSUS SAFETY NET: THE PROCESS OF STIGMATIZATION

"My dad used to lecture me: 'Do good or you'll end up in the school with no windows. First it's juvenile hall, then La Fuente,' " Matt told me. La Fuente's safety valve reputation—as a place where the comprehensive schools sent "bad kids"—troubled Matt, and yet he needed a safety net. In eighth grade, he "got into drugs and started to notice girls. It was downhill from there." By Matt's sophomore year, he had "wised up about drugs" but found himself severely behind on school credits. One summer he signed up for an entrepreneurship class held on La Fuente's campus, and he saw for himself that the school was not the prison he had imagined. As a result, Matt resolved to ask for a transfer so that he could make up lost credits and perhaps even graduate with his class.

To Matt's surprise, the vice principal at his home school did not want him to transfer because "I only had a problem with my grades, and he offered me extra help, tutoring. I guess, [like my dad] he thought La Fuente was a bad guy school, too." Matt's counselor and teachers at the comprehensive high school also opposed the move. "They thought it would be hard to return [from La Fuente]." A classmate of Matt's recalled a similar experience. When she asked to transfer to La Fuente after a "horrible sophomore year," the principal responded: "This is weird—someone *wanting* to go to La Fuente."

Once enrolled at La Fuente, Matt liked the smaller campus and thought he was learning more. But he missed his old school's dances, sports, and yearbook. La Fuente's reputation as a "school for druggies" bothered him, and he was not earning credits as fast as he had hoped. At the time of our formal interview, he seemed to have resigned himself to not graduating on schedule, joking: "My parents are always saying that high school is the best four years of your life, so I figure why not

67

the best five years?" Would he graduate at all? He told me, "I'd rather be at home" but "no way would I have dropped out" even if La Fuente had not existed: "My dad, he says the family name is not for quitters." Then again, Matt told me he was "unsure" of the value of a La Fuente diploma—would it carry the weight of a conventional diploma?

Like many of the students I came to know, Matt was caught in the contradictions of attending a stigmatized organization. Continuation schools did meet some of the needs of students like Matt, although such needs existed in part because mainstream schools were relatively inflexible. Young people learned to fear continuation schools because administrators, parents, and others portrayed them as places for losers. Once enrolled in the continuation program, embarrassment replaced fear as the main anxiety that stigma produced in those in the hidden world. Students were usually left to cope with the stigma on their own, and they drew on different resources and developed different strategies to maintain a sense of self-respect.

Is it possible to create an alternative environment for pushouts, dropouts, and potential dropouts without stigma? This was a goal of many of the people who worked at and attended La Fuente and Beacon. Yet it was also true that the schools were not constantly trying to shed stigma. Some regarded stigma as a useful tool for maintaining the safety valve function of the continuation program. A safety valve provides a mechanism to rid mainstream schools of failures and misfits without holding school administrators fully accountable for the consequences, a mechanism that reinforces students' disengagement from school. By devaluing the program, administrators districtwide could use the continuation school as a threat in order to marshal students into conformity. By contrast, a safety net provides a program geared to meet the intellectual and social needs of those that the mainstream schools cannot or will not help, a program that meets with some measure of success in reengaging students. In trying to create a safety net, however, continuation teachers and administrators sometimes found themselves stigmatizing the most disengaged students as well as the few options left open to them.

In the last chapter, I examined the historical context in which the continuation school was created and institutionalized. This history has shaped its reputation as the "stepchild" or "wastebasket of compulsory education" (Markey, 1940). Generally, its academic standards and resources have increased over time. But the process has been a perpetual game of catch-up because the continuation school remains subordinate to the comprehensive high schools, dependent for its clientele on the mainstream's evolving definition of failure.

Thus, the continuation school is stigmatized partly because of the types of students it commonly serves, but these categories are created by the conventional schools' standards of deportment and academic and social success and do not inhere in individual students. As Becker argued, *social groups create deviance by making the rules whose infraction constitutes deviance,* and by applying these rules to particular people and labeling them as outsiders" (1963: 9, emphasis in original). Ultimately, who gets defined as deviant and for what purpose is "a question of political and economic power," and in the struggle to publicly define deviance, some groups have the advantage by virtue of age, gender, ethnicity, class, and so on (Becker, 1963: 17). As the last chapter showed, young people who violate white, middle-class, heterosexual norms have always been overrepresented in continuation schools.

This chapter discusses the relationship of the continuation to the comprehensive school and the factors that have contributed to the continuation school's stigma, analyzing these factors at three levels: the community, the organization, and the individual participants. The persistence of the negative label lies partly in its grounding in the routines of daily life, and this, in turn, makes it more difficult for students to reengage within the continuation setting.

As the chapter will show, girls tended to feel less stigmatized by the continuation school than boys, or they experienced the stigma in different ways. In general, the girls exercised and perceived more choice in transferring to the continuation school. In contrast to the large number of boys who felt they had been pushed out of the comprehensive school, girls were more likely to say they wanted an alternative learning environment or, if pregnant or mothering, to appreciate the special services provided them within the continuation setting.

COMMUNITY AND FAMILY INFLUENCES

The continuation school has few means of generating positive publicity because it maintains no athletic teams or college preparatory classes and activities, two traditional sources of prestige for comprehensive schools. The few community members who do interact with the continuation school often reflect and maintain its stigma: the police, social welfare workers, judges, substance abuse counselors, probation officers.

The mass media, through a selective depiction of events, can reinforce negative stereotypes. Journalists tend to cite a youth's attendance at a continuation school as evidence of criminality. Example: In a feature exploring the murder of a teenager by a group of other boys, the author wrote: "Most [of the alleged attackers] went to continuation school.

Two were gang members. At least one of the boys, age 14, had a knife in his pocket and a troubled past, police said" (*San Francisco Examiner, 2/4/90: B-1*). Left out of this story was the fact that the victim also attended a continuation school. Curiously, this fact did surface in a related article, which identified the victim as a "Churchill Continuation High School" student, yet the school's official name did not contain the word "continuation." Indeed, a review of the 422 schools listed in the *1987–88 State Directory* of the California Continuation Education Association reveals that only 23, or 5 percent, have "continuation" in their name (Calif. Continuation Educ. Assoc., n.d.). Yet rarely do the media mention a continuation school without inserting the word. Thus, continuation personnel's efforts to avoid the label are often futile.

Beacon did, however, succeed in lessening the perception of the school's stigma among local employers. Clubs like Rotary sponsored academic debates and awarded promising students vocational and academic scholarships. The school had an active Employers Council, made up of businesspeople who hired Beacon students enrolled in an award-winning work experience program. According to a statewide evaluation of continuation schools, the single most powerful factor associated with the retention and graduation of students was the proportion of students a continuation school had enrolled in a work experience program (McCormick, 1990: 14).

Nevertheless, Beacon and especially La Fuente still had stigmatized reputations in the community, and parents and guardians frequently reacted with alarm at the prospect of their child attending a continuation school. (District-level statistics suggest that disengaging Asian-Americans and middle-class whites were underrepresented at La Fuente and Beacon, probably avoiding continuation school in favor of private schools, independent studies, community college, or even dropping out altogether.[1]) Administrators described their first task as reassuring fam-

---

1. Potential and actual dropouts and pushouts among the Asian-American and middle-class white populations were more likely to avoid Beacon and La Fuente. Take La Fuente as an example. Only 3 percent of La Fuente students were Asian-American, yet Asian-Americans comprised one-fifth of districtwide high school enrollment. This underrepresentation would hardly be surprising except that the Indochinese (Cambodians, Laotians, and Vietnamese)—who made up the vast majority of Asian-American students—dropped out at a rate equal to the district's average. Asian-Americans were also underrepresented in the district's independent studies and GED programs.

Whites made up nearly 30 percent of all students in the district but only one-fifth of La Fuente's students. Yet white students left the district's comprehensive schools at a rate not substantially lower than for nonwhites. From this I inferred that disengaging whites might pursue other alternatives at a higher rate. Although no data regard-

ilies. In their former roles as comprehensive vice principals, the continuation principals had seen initial parental reactions: "Parents would panic. They assumed this was the end of the line for their child."

The student interviews revealed three equally likely patterns of family response to the continuation transfer: upset and continued unhappiness (33 percent), happiness (31.5 percent), and pragmatism (31.5 percent). A few parents, all first generation, non-English-speaking immigrants, were apparently unaware of the transfer or of its significance (4 percent). Beacon was more successful in converting a significant portion of skeptical parents' distress into pragmatism, that is concern combined with acceptance that the transfer might be for the best. Beacon's orientation session—in which the entire staff greeted assembled newcomers and then teacher-counselors met one-on-one with the parents of each child—made the difference, according to student accounts.

Virtually all families were aware of the continuation school's stigma, but how they adjusted to the transfer depended largely on how disengaged their child was from the educational system and why. The least disengaged, and males in particular, tended to report the most upset parents, while those who had already left school or were on the verge of dropout/pushout, and females in particular, reported the least upset parents. For those out of the schooling system, the continuation school offered a route back, albeit devalued.

Overall, 40 percent of the girls said their parents were happy versus 27 percent unhappy, while for the boys, 23 percent said their parents were happy versus 39 percent unhappy. One explanation for this gender difference was that some parents had different expectations for boys and girls, and these were reinforced by the proximate reason for a child's disengagement from school. For example, parents appeared to interpret their daughters' pregnancy and decision to bear a child as a personal

---

ing transfer to private schools were available, whites comprised 40 percent of the students enrolled in the district's independent studies and GED programs—a significant overrepresentation.

Based on conversations with out-of-school adolescents and continuation students, I speculate that Asian-Americans and middle-class youths, particularly whites, associated continuation schools with "lower class" and ethnic minority cultures, which in their minds were discredited and to be avoided. Lisa, half white and perceived to be Anglo, tried La Fuente briefly, then left because she "felt totally outnumbered"; she subsequently returned when her boyfriend, who "looks Mexican," entered La Fuente. Many of the Latino and African-American students at La Fuente also saw the continuation school as a place for ethnic minorities and were surprised, during a regional spelling bee, to see that whites made up the majority at nearby suburban continuation schools (field notes, 5/21/89).

choice, having little to do with school and indicating a weak attachment to the labor force. Thus they looked favorably on La Fuente offering pregnant and mothering girls a chance to complete their education, an opportunity denied to many of the parents' generation:

> My mom thought it was great! Every time she had friends over she'd say, "My daughter goes to La Fuente." . . . for a person like me to still go to school is remarkable to them cuz they figure at their age, kids that got pregnant, they didn't go to school. (Anna, La Fuente)

In contrast, the parents of boys, particularly of those boys who wanted to remain at the comprehensive high school and felt they had no choice about the transfer to the continuation school, seemed to believe their sons' potential to be a good breadwinner had been reduced by the school: "The only reason my parents are mad is that I was in honors English and was working on a scholarship, and that's burned. They were planning on me getting a [wrestling] scholarship" (Max, La Fuente). Maria, who "messed up" partly to join her boyfriend at Beacon, perceived that her father would not allow her younger brother to do what she had done. "I kind of got away with going here, but my brother, he won't get away with anything. My dad will push him [to stay at the comprehensive high school]."

Family members appear to hold three interrelated fears. First and foremost, they perceive the transfer to continuation school as concrete evidence that their child is losing in the status competition in which schooling and the type of credential one receives play a key role in determining access to future rewards (Collins, 1977). Second, even if parents believe that their child will return to the comprehensive school or that a continuation diploma is an equivalent credential, they may fear that their child will be contaminated by "typical" continuation students.[2] Third, although some parents may believe that their child will resist negative peer influences thought to be concentrated in the continuation school, they nevertheless fear that their son or daughter will be labeled a "bad kid" by the wider community.

These concerns can overshadow any success that a student may experience in the continuation school, thus adding to the stress that many

---

2. This fear of "contamination from their poorer school-fellows" is nothing new. In mid-nineteenth-century England, parents of full-time students reportedly removed their children from school once half-timers began attending. They saw half-time students as coming from "the neglected class," perceived as lower than the working-class (Silver, 1983: 51).

students reported feeling. This exchange from a student interview illustrates the tension a parent feels between wanting to reinforce the reengagement process but not within a devalued organization:

DK: How did your mom feel about you coming to Beacon?

Joan: Um, she was glad. See, but she thinks [my boyfriend] made me come here, so she was kinda resentful. . . .

DK: I'm not sure if I understand that. She's mad at [trails off].

Joan: I don't know. I don't know. . . . like lots of times I got [honors] letters home in the mail from my school [Beacon], and she sent a copy to my dad and she'd be really happy. And other times, she's talked about moving, and she turns to me and she's like, "So where are you going to stay, cuz you know you're not going to be able to graduate from anywhere except that Mickey Mouse school. And now that you've gone there, no one will take you back at a regular school. You've blown all your chances. You're too intelligent to be there, but once you've enrolled in a school like that." I was like, I just let it go.

Students themselves experienced the same tensions, and field notes, more so than formal interviews, reveal numerous instances of students alternately talking about, for example, how easy the continuation school was, then defending the program as good and in some ways more difficult than the comprehensive school. No doubt these ambivalent feelings inadvertently fueled their parents' concerns.

ORGANIZATIONAL INFLUENCES

Recruitment of Administrators, Teachers, and Students

The recruitment of administrators, teachers, and students tended to reflect and maintain the continuation school's stigma. Each of the principals had served as vice principal in charge of discipline at one or more of their district's comprehensive high schools just prior to their current position. Two of the men aspired to a "regular" principalship; indeed, one of them was promoted halfway into this study. The third (at the pilot study site) said he wanted to create a "true alternative" program, but the district's use of the school as a punishment for tardy and truant students made this impossible; he has since left the position. In short, the districts under study tended to use the continuation school as a proving ground or way station for administrators. According to teachers in one school, central office administrators have also transferred at least one past comprehensive school principal into the continuation position as punishment for poor performance. Whether proving ground or punishment, these recruitment patterns usually ensure a turnover of principals about every two years. This compares to a 20 to 35 percent statewide turnover in continuation principals over a recent two-year period (CSDE, 1985: 25).[3]

This instability in leadership positions can hinder the program's overall effectiveness, as the literature on effective schools has suggested. An extreme example of this occurred at La Fuente where the organization was without a principal from halfway through the school year under study until well into the next year. Teacher morale went from bad to worse when district leaders decided not to replace the principal and instead assigned a central office administrator to oversee the school part-time. He lost support when he told teachers, who had expressed their desire that he spend more time on campus, that he could "run this school with a beeper" (field notes, 10/11/89). In the absence of leadership, disagreements over the school's goals, teaching strategies, and student discipline seriously divided the staff.

Teacher recruitment patterns are more complex. Two factors help shape the overall stigmatization process. First, as an alternative organization, the continuation school seems to attract a fair number of teachers who are critical of mainstream schooling, and their beliefs are reinforced by continuation students' generally negative experiences in, and perceptions of, the comprehensive high school. For example, one teacher, who had been a comprehensive school counselor, told of coming under attack from fellow counselors and teachers for being too much of a student advocate; they perceived her as undermining their authority. These differences seemed to contribute to the poor lines of communication that existed between the continuation and its feeder schools in both districts.

Second, there is some evidence to suggest that continuation schools sometimes attract disengaged teachers, and in some districts continuation assignments are "a form of teacher punishment" (Weber, 1972: 572). I did not set out to evaluate teacher performance or interest in teaching, and interviews revealed that continuation teachers equal comprehensive teachers in educational background and teaching experience. Nonetheless, the perception on the part of administrators that, in the words of one principal, "some of the worst teachers end up at the continuation

---

3. The turnover rate of continuation principals appears to be significantly higher than that of traditional school principals; the latter has been estimated as high as 7 to 10 percent per year (Weindling and Earley, 1987, cited in Hart, 1991: 451).

TABLE 2

Student Perceptions of Choice regarding Continuation Transfer by Sex
(In Percentages)

Degree of Perceived Choice	Female	Male	Total
Perceived more options			
Asked to come (alternative)	34.0	20.0	28.0
Simple yes	23.4	14.3	19.5
Or another comprehensive school	10.6	5.7	8.5
Subtotals	68.0	40.0	56.0
Perceived fewer options			
Chose to "mess up" to get in	2.1	2.9	2.4
Or another continuation school	2.1	2.9	2.4
Or GED/adult education/ISP	12.8	5.7	9.8
Or drop out altogether	8.5	5.7	7.3
No, but now yes	2.1	5.7	3.7
Simple no	4.3	37.1	18.3
Subtotals	31.9	60.0	43.9
Totals	99.9	100.0	99.9

Note: Chi-square $(1, N = 82)$ for "Perceived Options" by Sex 2 x 2 contingency table $= 6.43$, $p < .02$; phi coefficient $= .280$.

school" is a factor maintaining the schools' stigma. Informal comments by a few teachers that they came to the continuation school mainly in search of shorter hours, fewer nonclassroom duties, and less pressure— not unlike many continuation students—fueled these perceptions.

Most important to the maintenance of continuation education's stigma is the nonselective recruitment of students and dependency on the comprehensive schools for its base. Although the majority of Beacon and La Fuente students were not technically involuntary, their choice to attend was often constrained. (Indeed, all high school students can be considered involuntary in the sense that state laws generally require children to attend school until at least age sixteen and as long as age eighteen in the case of California.)

Students were asked to describe the transfer process and whether they considered it their choice. Table 2 presents a summary of their views, arranged by degree of perceived choice as measured by the number of options they said were available to them and the value of the credential attached to each option. Student responses were grouped under "perceived more options" if they indicated that obtaining a traditional diploma was still open to them. Significantly more girls than boys felt that they chose the continuation school, reflecting in large measure the fact that boys more often were disciplinary referrals whereas girls came as counseling and pregnancy referrals.

Insofar as the continuation school acts as a dumping ground for students who pose a problem to the mainstream schools, it reinforces the idea that the problem rests with a minority who can and should be segregated. Principals at Beacon, La Fuente, and Willows (the third pilot site) were all clear that their districts used the continuation school as "the ultimate scare tactic," as one put it, to maintain discipline at the comprehensive schools. They were equally forthright in saying, particularly in the districts allowing involuntary transfers, that the continuation school serves to keep the mainstream high schools "pure":

> [In this district], the philosophy is send everybody here, just get rid of them, dump 'em; *it cleans out those kind of kids from the regular school* and makes the regular school a better school. And it does that. It makes the regular school less impacted by resistant kids, truant kids, tardy kids, behavior problem kids. (principal, Willows; emphasis added)

As La Fuente's principal argued, however, there then emerges a trade-off between offering a safety net and serving as district safety valve:

> I always felt that the biggest loophole in dropouts was in La Fuente. . . . But as soon as we plug that hole [by trying to reduce the high turnover rate in the continuation school], it creates other problems for the district's comprehensive high schools because it becomes a bottle neck [of at risk students]. (principal, La Fuente)

Given these arguments of institutional convenience, continuation teachers had little or no say over which students ended up at their school. Indeed, they joked freely about the "dumping" cycle. The first dumping occurred at the beginning of November. The comprehensive schools routinely hold on to disengaging students until enrollment levels have been established for staffing purposes, and these are reported to the state at the end of October. The second dumping occurs late in the spring as comprehensive school principals rid themselves of disciplinary cases they do not want to deal with the following year.

Beacon, unlike La Fuente or Willows, held a "screening" every other week where all teachers and the principal would meet with comprehensive school vice principals, counselors, and a district psychologist to be briefed on incoming students. Theoretically, if Beacon's principal and teachers felt that a particular student recommended for transfer to their school by one of the comprehensive high schools would not benefit from the continuation program, they could veto the transfer. I attended every screening save one during 1988–89, however, and not a single student was screened out, despite several instances in which Beacon's teachers and principal expressed strong concern or doubt about the wisdom of a particular transfer.[4] Further, I recorded four separate instances in which comprehensive high school vice principals explicitly stated that a particular student would not be allowed to return to their schools, thus suggesting that the transfer to Beacon was coerced by comprehensive school staff, despite an official policy to the contrary.

Two examples, drawn from field notes taken during two screenings, illustrate this process:

> The counselor from [one comprehensive high school] presented the cases of two behavior problem, "special day" students (that is, students who attend one self-contained special education class all day). After their involvement in a gang fight, they had been "decertified" from the special education program so they could attend Beacon. Beacon's principal pointed out that these boys "aren't well suited to Beacon since they're mainstreamed into all our classes." This prompted the following exchange:
>
> Beacon teacher 1: We're setting ourselves up for failure.
>
> Beacon teacher 2: We do do that sometimes. . . .
>
> Beacon teacher 3: That's the law. (field notes, 10/25/88)

> The vice principal from one comprehensive high school told us that an Asian immigrant boy had been suspended for pulling a knife on a kid during a fight at school. He has since been charged with assault with a deadly weapon. The comprehensive school counselor noted: "His parents didn't want him to come to Beacon. They think it's a bad school." A Beacon teacher-counselor replied, "We're too good for him!" This prompted the vice principal to announce: "He won't be accepted back at our school." Several Beacon teachers exchanged uneasy glances. (field notes, 10/11/88)

---

4. As vice principal of discipline, Beacon's principal told me, Beacon only denied him one transfer request, and that was because the student was under sixteen years of age. Although vice principals sometimes ask students to demonstrate good faith by improving their attendance for six weeks prior to transfer, there is no hard and fast rule. Plus, a few students explained that they had subverted this rule by dropping out altogether for a quarter and then entering Beacon from outside the schooling system.

To an outside observer, it appeared that the comprehensive school administrators exercised the most control over which students would come to Beacon, and this was accomplished ahead of time. The screening was a ritual rubber-stamping that made the Beacon staff feel as though they were participating in the process. The comprehensive school staff's presentation of what was known about each case tended to put a human face on individual students. This regular exchange mitigated the feeling that Beacon was merely a dumping ground, and the ensuing discussion of how Beacon might benefit particular students assured teachers that their role was appreciated. The process of student transfer was only publicly called into question in extreme cases, with teachers usually following the principal's lead. So infrequent were these breaks in the ritual that at least one teacher believed that Beacon could not refuse a student ("That's the law").[5]

In summary, both districts (and Willows as well) used their continuation schools, even Beacon which billed itself as a "school of choice," as safety valves, and this fact often overshadowed their role as safety net and contributed significantly to their stigma. But, as later chapters will show, students reacted differently to the program depending on their particular circumstances and the degree to which the program met their individual needs.

Staff Development and Diffuse Goals

Continuation school staff members in this study, with the exception of a few founding teacher-counselors at Beacon, were not expressly selected for an alternative teaching philosophy or trained in alternative methods. In the early days of continuation education, such training occurred informally. Shaffer surveyed principals, who agreed that it took two years "to make a regular teacher into an effective continuation teacher . . . to break down his dedication to a particular subject field, to the idea that high school is college preparatory, and to the value of conformity of all students to the regular classroom standards of 'normalcy' " (1955: 24). After more than twenty years, the believers in continuation philosophy and methods, diffuse even in the beginning, seem to have dwindled in numbers. The true believers' message seems muffled, partly by

---

5. Individual school district policies and the range of local secondary education options influence whether or not continuation schools can refuse particular students. For example, a district must decide whether it will allow for involuntary transfers to the continuation school bearing in mind the state law prohibiting the long-term suspension of students without first sending them to a continuation or other comprehensive school.

their fellow teachers and administrators who, in an effort to reduce the continuation stigma, have pushed for a more academic curriculum and student adherence to hierarchical authority.

Both groups believe that if the other would join forces with them, then they could do a better job at reengaging students. One could argue that both sides fail to see that the problem of student disengagement, and hence the pressures for something like continuation schools, persists because jobs, wealth, education, and power are distributed unequally, and thus a fundamental solution must include restructuring the economic, political, and social context as well as the schools. Granting the truth in this argument, nobody expects teachers to stop trying to engage students, and schools can make a difference. But in the absence of a clear, systematic philosophy to guide and unite them—and sufficient resources to carry it forward—teachers sometimes lower their expectations for success and begin to blame themselves or others (fellow teachers and administrators as well as students and their families) for failure.

Neither Beacon nor La Fuente had systematic philosophies, and consequently the schools' goals seemed diffuse at best. In continuation education historically, an inherent tension has existed between the desire to become an alternative center—with the goal of accommodating differences in learning styles, schedules, and the like—or a treatment center—with the goal of returning students to the comprehensive high schools. Teachers and administrators with a more traditional teaching philosophy have tended to favor the latter while those with a more developmentalist approach have favored the former.

Despite initial plans to the contrary, few students returned to their home schools (less than 5 percent at both schools; see part B of flow charts 1–3 in the appendix). Reflecting La Fuente's treatment orientation (as opposed to Beacon's relative emphasis on being an alternative model), it allowed "turnaround" students to go back to their home schools in the last few weeks of school to graduate; they comprised a quarter of the fifty-two La Fuente students who received a diploma during 1988–89. This fact hurt certain teachers' morale because these were among their "success stories." This occurred despite the fact that most teachers were happy for individual returning students, who in turn usually appreciated the help that teachers had given them.

Teachers talked up the continuation graduation ceremony and otherwise tried to motivate students to stay. Yet traditionalist teachers at La Fuente successfully argued against recognizing a valedictorian because, they argued, "a 2.5 GPA [grade point average] is a joke" (field notes, 5/31/89). They looked to academic standards set by the district's other high schools rather than to an alternative standard such as one based on academic improvement, as developmentalists did. This reflected a general strategy whereby underperforming or misbehaving students had to be stigmatized as losers, through failure and exclusion, in order to motivate the rest to work harder and remove the stigma attached to the school as a whole. Developmentalists wanted to maintain La Fuente and Beacon as last chance mechanisms, a strategy that risked all students being tainted with a higher degree of stigma.

When students returned to their home schools, developmentalist teachers sometimes felt disheartened. "Our students definitely feel the stigma. They'll say, 'I need to get back to [the home school] to get the diploma,' " said one Beacon teacher, who confided: "That presses some of my buttons, obviously, because I think this is the neatest place in the whole world to go. I would love to go here; I see all its value." In addition, the return of students to their home schools undercut teachers' efforts to lessen the stigma for those who liked the continuation school and planned to remain.

Those who could have returned but chose not to, whether for continued child care, bad memories of the home school, or loyalty, tended to be most critical of their peers who returned.

> There's people here with so much potential, and they just came here because there's not as much homework and it's easier. . . . Like Bill, . . . he's going back to his other school after doing all these extra credit things here to get to his 230 [credits]. It's like using La Fuente to get what he wants from another school. (Mandy)

> Everybody says, "I'd rather have [a diploma] from a high school." But if you're gonna learn and get the credit from here, I don't mind getting the diploma from here at all. *They're the ones that helped me graduate, not the other school.* I don't see [my home school] over there trying to get me to go and do this and making things easy. (Carla, La Fuente; emphasis added)

Limited Resources

Historically, many districts have housed continuation students in poor facilities (Shaffer, 1955). The schools in this study were attractive and adequate, but both La Fuente and Beacon were made up of portable buildings. In the case of Beacon, this "temporary" solution came in response to real estate developers and neighborhood groups' outrage at the prospect of a stigmatized institution being permanently constructed.

California exempts continuation and other small schools from maintaining a library, and Beacon did not have one. (The two English class-rooms were stocked with books, however.) La Fuente used its library, in part, to distribute textbooks to students who wanted to take them home overnight. The rationale, endorsed by teachers, was that student turn-over was so high that the school could not risk losing the books. At the time of the study, the state was considering exempting continuation schools from providing physical education as well. Thus, districts con-cerned with cost-cutting could eliminate two elements—libraries and athletics—that go to the heart of what a school is, further devaluing the continuation program.

Another issue, more symbolic, related to resources and stigma in-volved chairs. Especially at La Fuente, the number of chairs in each classroom was based on the low percentage of students administrators had calculated would actually attend on any given day. Occasionally, most students would show up and then there would not be enough chairs for everyone to sit down. This subtly conveyed low expectations.

One could argue that more resources in continuation schools go into funding staff positions because, theoretically, they maintain lower stu-dent to teacher ratios. (In fact, however, a state study found that in many districts, student-teacher ratios were actually higher at continua-tion high schools than they were at conventional high schools [CSDE, 1988: 9]). Districts can undercut the promise of more individual atten-tion for students, however, when central office administrators load con-tinuation principals with extra duties under the rubric of "alternative education." At a regional meeting of continuation administrators, prin-cipals complained that they were expected to oversee independent stud-ies, GED preparation, pregnant minors, opportunity classes for students under age sixteen, and other programs; serve as their district's atten-dance officer, compiling dropout and other statistics; and assume other duties associated with "at risk" students. Districts argue that because con-tinuation schools are generally small, have low student-teacher ratios, and teach some students only part-time, the practice is justifiable. The fact that continuation funding is not set aside particularly for that use but instead goes into a school district's general fund encourages this add-on approach, too. Administrators thus found it difficult to concen-trate on, and achieve success in, one area.

Intensive counseling is thought to be one of the continuation school's high cost features. Yet if one assumes a comprehensive school counsel-ing load of 400 students to 1 counselor, then neither La Fuente nor Willows offered significantly more services. Beacon, in contrast, did pro-vide intensive counseling via its teacher-counselor model, and, surpris-ingly, this arrangement was even more cost effective than the traditional approach, given the student enrollment ceiling of 140. According to the principal, each of six teacher-counselors received a counseling stipend ranging from $1,900 to $2,500 in addition to their teaching salaries. Thus, the school budgeted between $11,400 and $15,000 extra for counseling versus $20,000 it would have had to pay to a half-time counselor with no teaching duties. Although the district aimed to equalize per pupil costs for resources, Beacon received more in teacher salaries because it maintained a ratio of twenty students to one teacher versus twenty-seven to one in the comprehensive schools. Elsewhere, however, "in spite of small class sizes, reported average expenditures per pupil are no higher in continuation schools than in other public schools" (Stern et al., 1985: 47).

Academic Standards and Devalued Curricula

During the 1980s, continuation schools sought to bring themselves into closer alignment with the competitive, high status academic curriculum. Most notably, they increased graduation requirements. In California each district governing board has the authority to establish local graduation requirements, including the number of credits required for graduation. The number of districts requiring the same graduation credits for continuation as for comprehensive high schools increased from 25 to 75 percent between 1979 and 1987 (CSDE, 1988: 25). This was true for both districts under study, but the statistic is misleading.

First, both schools offered a way for students significantly short on credits to get around the credit floor. Beacon and its comprehensive counterparts all required 220 credits for graduation. If, however, students could pass GED tests in Science, English, and Math at an average of 50 percent or better (a more rigorous standard than for the actual GED), they earned 50 credits, usable only toward a Beacon diploma. La Fuente and its district counterparts required 230 credits for graduation. But students who did not plan to return to their home school and did not arrive with senior credits could graduate with 200 credits; the rationale for this difference was that La Fuente offered fewer elective courses.

Second, both schools used their flexible hours to squeeze out more credit-earning opportunities, in ways that reflected their different styles. Beacon, more an alternative-traditional hybrid, compressed class and break times and let students out for the day at 1:00 P.M. Students earned credits for attending and working in increments as little as one-quarter of one class. Nobody could fail a class. At La Fuente, more traditional in style, students could fail (although this was usually tied to attendance and productivity) and earn zero credit for a particular three-week grading period; thus, in contrast to Beacon, La Fuente did not award credit in direct proportion to attendance and productivity. In the amount of time saved by shortening class time, La Fuente added a seventh period. There were six grading periods per semester, and each class passed in a grading period was worth one credit. So a highly motivated student could earn 42 credits in a semester compared with 30 at the comprehensive high schools.[6]

Both schools offered early dismissal, allowing students more time to earn credit through work experience and vocational training programs as well as adult education or community college classes. In addition, Beacon permitted students in good standing to match credits through homework. Many La Fuente teachers did the same informally, although some expected a certain amount of homework as part of the course grade, so homework did not automatically yield extra credit.

These are all ways continuation schools offer students behind on credits a chance to graduate in a reasonable amount of time (say before age nineteen). This is, of course, the second chance they were designed to offer. But these routes to "easy" credit, at the same time, leave them vulnerable to charges of offering a second-rate credential. In addition, the struggle to help continuation students garner credits did nothing to challenge the mainstream schools' academic standards, defined as the achievement of a rather arbitrary number of credits as opposed to some defined learning objectives.

Beacon and La Fuente, like many dropout prevention programs, offered mainly remedial and vocational courses, which provided students with weaker linkages to higher education. The curriculum was not that different apparently from what many, but not all, continuation students had been exposed to in the comprehensive high schools. Both schools offered the state-required courses, and students had to pass district proficiency exams in reading, computation, and writing like all other high school students. Neither school, however, offered college preparatory classes, such as a foreign language or advanced math and English,

---

6. Beacon students could also earn as many as 42 credits per semester (without doing homework), even though only six periods were offered. Six extra credits could be earned through the bonus system: for five straight days of attendance in each class, a student received a bonus of one productive "hour." Fifteen bonus hours in a class garnered over the course of the semester yielded one credit.

Teachers sometimes argued that continuation credit was harder to earn for many students who had been able to do the minimum at the comprehensive high school and study hard enough at the end of the term to pass with a D and collect all five credits. Comprehensive schools in both districts had begun to allow teachers to deduct partial credit after a student amassed so many absences (excused and unexcused) to discourage this behavior.

required for entrance into four-year colleges and universities. Further, a number of teachers felt they had relaxed their standards in terms of grading, not so much regarding the quality of the student's work, though this was a factor, as the amount of time allowed to finish it.

For most students, the number of credits and how difficult they were to earn determined the value of a credential. At both Beacon and La Fuente, they saw the GED as "the easy way out" and worth no credits per se. Next in the hierarchy of alternative credentials was the adult education diploma, worth 20 to 40 credits less than the comprehensive diploma. The continuation diploma was rated lower than the traditional diploma by 46 percent, largely because although it was worth the same number of credits, these were easy credits. This also accounts for the sizable group of students unsure of the continuation diploma's value (14 percent), despite assurances from staff members that it did not have the word *continuation* on it.

For those who felt the diploma was the same (32 percent), this reasoning was common: "I don't see any problem with it because it just says Beacon High School, not Beacon Continuation. No one's gonna know the difference in the world. Unless they know what Beacon is, but you go to find a job, they won't know" (Simone). The perspective still assumed stigma; indeed, it was not uncommon for continuation students at both schools to try to pass as "regular" students in the world outside the hidden world.[7] Finally, those who rated the continuation diploma higher (8 percent) interpreted value to mean better for them personally for various reasons rather than better compared to a comprehensive diploma in any absolute sense.

Responses to the question "Do you think a continuation high school diploma is an advantage or disadvantage?" revealed few differences by ethnicity or school. But significantly more girls than boys said that it was the same or provided them an advantage.[8] The observed gender difference can be explained in much the same way as the differential family reactions to the transfer: fewer girls had been sent involuntarily to the continuation school in the first place, and more were focused on being

---

7. Carmen, for example, told me she let new acquaintances think she attended La Fuente Community College rather than a continuation school (for a discussion of "passing" and other strategies for managing a "spoiled identity," see Goffman, 1963).

8. The difference in the degree to which boys and girls attached stigma to the continuation diploma was statistically significant. One-half the girls versus three-quarters of the boys said the continuation diploma was devalued or of unknown value, whereas one-half the girls versus one-quarter of the boys believed that continuation and conventional diplomas were equivalent. The chi-square $(1, n = 77)$ was 4.50, $p < .05$; the phi coefficient was .242.

wives and mothers than future breadwinners. Five of six girls who felt the continuation diploma was an advantage were in the SAM program. These girls felt that the continuation school was less stigmatizing than the alternative: remaining at their home school and being one of the few to be pregnant or a mother.

Among those who said the continuation diploma was a definite disadvantage, girls tended to give different rationales than boys. Six girls versus one boy said it marked them, usually unfairly, as a "bad person." Boys and girls were equally likely to say simply that the diploma was considered "second class." But a subset of six boys and only two girls said they wanted to return to their home school to graduate with friends and enjoy senior activities, and only the boys claimed this had nothing to do with feeling stigmatized. These boys were eager to assert that they did not "care what other people say." Only a small group of students expressed concern that employers (two girls, one boy) and colleges (one boy) might devalue a continuation diploma, though this probably influenced the others' thinking, too.

There seems to be little research to indicate whether these concerns are well founded. A few related studies suggest that GED holders do not fare as well as traditional high school graduates in the labor market or higher education, an indicator that the two are not equivalent credentials (Quinn and Haberman, 1986, cited in Kolstad and Kaufman, 1989: 21). But one researcher found that a GED was better than no diploma at all (Passmore, 1987, cited in Fine, 1991: 86). Anecdotal evidence suggests that employers may not distinguish between continuation and traditional diplomas, but military recruiters do, arguing that alternative-program graduates are twice as likely to leave the service because of drugs and disciplinary problems (Leedom, 1988). In sum, despite increased standards, doubt remains concerning the equivalence of continuation and traditional diplomas.

Programs that diverge from the high status academic curriculum become devalued when they are not as directly linked to the society's wider system of rewards. As Connell observes, the competitive academic curriculum is "hegemonic":

> To say it is hegemonic is not to say it is the only curriculum in those schools. It is to say that this pattern has pride of place in the schools, it dominates most people's ideas of what real learning is about; its logic has the most powerful influence on the organisation of the school, and of the education system generally; and it is able to marginalise or subordinate the other curricula that are present. (Connell, 1985: 87)

The comprehensive high schools' competitive academic curriculum definitely subordinated the remedial, vocational, and occasionally experimental curricula at La Fuente and Beacon.

Poor Communication between Continuation and Sending Schools

Few channels existed for continuation and comprehensive school staffs to communicate. I interviewed four teachers and a counselor at a Beacon feeder school and nine teachers and two administrators at a La Fuente feeder school. All were either involved with dropout reduction programs or concerned about the dropout problem in their schools. Only one teacher had more than a vague idea of what the continuation school was and how it operated, and she gained this knowledge informally (through former colleagues, now at the continuation school). Said one teacher: "It has the connotation that if you're bad, you go there. The feeling I get from the district is that La Fuente is less than the other high schools, which I feel is unfortunate."

Continuation teachers complained that some comprehensive teachers at districtwide union meetings were completely unaware of the continuation school's existence. La Fuente was sometimes left out of official statistics or lists of the district's high schools, thus prompting a group of teachers to circulate a facetious petition to secede from the district (field notes, 12/12/88).

One channel of communication was the Beacon screening, but comprehensive school participants did not display much knowledge of the specifics of the program. In explaining why a particular student would benefit from Beacon, comprehensive staff members would use vague and sometimes contradictory concepts. For example, a counselor described a male student as "a discipline problem in the classroom; he's lethargic, then explosive." Conclusion: he would benefit from Beacon's "more structured" program (field notes, 11/8/88). Another counselor from the same feeder school described another boy as "not a discipline problem, but he confuses teacher standards for harassment. He sees himself as the victim of circumstance." Conclusion: he would benefit from Beacon's "less structured" program (field notes, 1/4/89). "Structure" seemed to be a code word signaling adherence to a particular teaching philosophy and set of values.

INDIVIDUAL AND SMALL GROUP INFLUENCES

The stigma that continuation schools bear stems from their place within the larger society and educational system and is shaped by and manifested through their organizational characteristics. But individuals, alone or in groups, react differently to the stigma, sometimes in ways that challenge it or at least turn it on its head, sometimes in ways that reinforce it. This section analyzes these patterns.

Competing Philosophies of Teachers and Administrators

Many comprehensive school teachers and administrators feel that students must adhere to certain standards of academic achievement and behavior. A subset of these teachers hold to traditional teaching methods and authoritarian discipline styles; they emphasize conformity, and deviants are little tolerated. This creates an obvious problem for nonconforming students and the teachers and administrators subsequently charged with teaching them. As long ago as 1906, proponents of the ungraded classroom, a precursor to continuation education, complained that certain standardized grade teachers

> refuse, at least fail, to co-operate with the efforts of the ungraded rooms to give a fair chance to these very pupils who have been forced on to disadvantageous ground by this same overmuch standardized teaching and management. With these teachers, school work is a question of survival of such as can come up to standard. *With these the ungraded rooms are to be judged, not by what they do for certain types of pupils whom the grades cannot reach, but rather by the power or lack of power to make these pupils over into a new type that will conform to standard.* It is the old idea of the Procrustean Bed, with the ungraded room to do the cutting and stretching. (Los Angeles Public Schools, 1907: 65–66; emphasis added)

The highlighted passage recalls the conflicting goals of providing an alternative ("what they do for certain types of pupils whom the grades cannot reach") or a treatment program ("to make these pupils over into a new type that will conform to standard").

Why should there be antagonism between continuation and comprehensive school teachers? Little tension exists between the traditionalists in both organizations because they agree that the continuation school should aim to reform "bad kids" and academic failures. This view obviously reinforces the continuation school's stigma. Developmentalists in the comprehensive schools tend to favor many of the organizational features of the continuation program but are either unaware of them or devalue them because of the overall stigma. The sharpest conflict, however, emerges between the traditionalists at the comprehensive school and the developmentalists at the continuation school. To simplify: Comprehensive teachers devalue the continuation school's successes by pointing to the "easy" curriculum and "lax" student discipline. In contrast, continuation teachers consider the dropout/pushout rate to be an indictment of the comprehensive school generally rather than of certain students. Further, they feel they have helped pioneer some methods and curricula that could benefit many students at the comprehensive school, but these go unappreciated.

This same dynamic is played out to a lesser extent within the continuation school. A traditionalist La Fuente teacher spoke of most continuation schools being "loosely structured" and having poor reputations. He saw himself as part of a group brought in to increase academic standards and tighten student discipline, with the comprehensive school as the model:

> When I got here, this one [continuation school] wasn't that bad, but boy it's a lot different now. Most of the teachers that were teaching here had never taught at another school, at a comprehensive school, number one. Number two, they were doing almost completely all individual instruction, which I think doesn't lend itself to enhancing learning. . . . And it made it tougher on discipline. . . . I wanted to get into teaching more the way you would in a comprehensive school, in terms of lecturing.

Developmentalist teachers agreed that La Fuente had changed, and, in their view, for the worse. They disagreed among themselves over the impact of increased academic standards, but all decried the return to traditional methods by many of their fellow teachers:

> We have to offer all the academic course requirements, but one of the reasons these kids have failed in other schools is because their talents lie outside the academic areas. . . . Some of these teachers would die if they ever walked into my class. What I do in my classroom and how I relate to my kids is not traditional and not accepted by a lot of people who are pushing for the basics. But I think that if I lectured to my kids and made them do those kinds of assignments, I would have lost a lot of them already.

Maintaining the Credential Hierarchy

In trying to persuade students to reengage, teachers and administrators throughout the schooling system often use negative motivations as a last resort. Unwittingly, they reinforce a hierarchy of stigmatized organizations in the students' minds. Many comprehensive staff members cast the continuation school in a negative light in the hopes of scaring misbehaving or truant students into changing their behavior. Students who ended up in the continuation school anyway sometimes repeated the horrors they had been told, to the dismay of the staff. Ironically, when continuation staff members' bag of tricks to motivate disengaged students grew empty, they reached for the same "dirty" trick: they disparaged the educational alternatives that remained open, usually adult education, the GED, or independent studies—even the continuation school's own afternoon shift in the case of Willows.

A teacher-counselor, who had taught in one such alternative program before coming to Beacon, fretted over this contradiction:

> We say [to students], "You're blowing your APP [Attendance, Punctuality, and Productivity] period; we're going to send you to adult ed." And they're saying, "Well, is adult ed OK?" Here I'm in a position of saying, "I want to keep you here," and how do you keep someone here other than by saying, "This is the best place to be." Any time you say, "This is the best place to be," it's leaving another message for the other place. . . . In a way it's a threat, and when we kick you out, we kick you out over there. Well, it's a lower place on the ladder. There's no way you can't assume that. If they're good there, they can come back up the ladder, and if they're really good, they can climb back up the ladder to [the comprehensive school] or whatever.

Student Peer Influences: Recoiling at and Reveling in Stigma

Students' peers, both inside and outside the continuation school, played a major role in their perception of the stigma attached to the program. A number of students reported that their noncontinuation friends—many of whom, by all indications, were somewhat disengaged from school themselves—put down the continuation school as a place for losers. In a few cases, they even broke off the friendship. "Some of the friends I had, it was like, 'Oh, you're going to Beacon? Screw you, then,' " explained Ed. "Others are like, 'I'll see you there,' cuz they knew they were going." Once at the continuation school, friends continued to exert pressure on students to return to their home school, if possible. Said Paul: "The reactions I get from my friends is like, 'You should just transfer back to [comprehensive high] and graduate and get your diploma there.' I don't really care all that much. They're all, 'You go to Beacon, huh?' "

A comprehensive high school teacher said in an interview that every year she showed a video about a continuation program and asked her students to write about whether they would be willing to pay taxes to support such an organization. She said most students supported the idea as "one more option," including her college prep classes. Apparently, students feel differently when their own friends attend a stigmatized place, perhaps because it accords them automatic stigma by association, or what Goffman (1963) called a "courtesy stigma."

Friends also mediated student perceptions of stigma within the continuation school, particularly when someone was deciding whether or not to return to the comprehensive school. The students who did not want to or could not return then sometimes tried to influence their friend's decision. For example, David exhorted his friend, " 'You're going to still be short on credits. That means you can't be absent twice. This is a regular high school with a regular diploma.' I tried to explain that to Bob, but he had this continuation thing in his head" (Beacon).

In interviews with a few students who returned to their home schools, they stressed a dislike for the negative peer influences and—because they themselves had changed or never were that "bad"—being lumped in with the stigmatized group. Not all continuation students were "druggies" or "slackish" with respect to school work, they conceded, but outside observers do not make distinctions. At the same time, the return group acknowledged what it felt were the strengths of the continuation program, none having to do with former peers: extra counseling, closer relationships with teachers, flexible scheduling, opportunities to make up credit, and the emphasis on taking responsibility for one's own actions.

Whereas some continuation students recoiled at the outsider image, another group turned the continuation school's stigma on its head and reveled in it. At a student activities meeting scheduled to discuss the design of a school t-shirt, a group of boys amused each other with the following suggestions: "the La Fuente roaches" (as in marijuana cigarettes), "make it black and white with stripes and a number," "the La Fuente babies or peewees," "Support your drug users: Buy a t-shirt," and "Alcatraz" (field notes, 11/23/88). Others exaggerated the time they had been at the continuation school to their newly arrived peers and hinted at pasts much worse than reality. Carmen explained that former La Fuente students told her that only "really big troublemakers" attended the school. "I heard that you were caged in, you can't leave campus, you couldn't do a lot of things. . . . A lot of them told me, 'Well, you might want to watch your back: you might get shot.' "

Boys were much more likely to play up the outsider image once at the continuation school. In a sardonic and revealing orientation class essay, Gerardo, a senior close to graduation, reflected back on why he decided to attend La Fuente and how he saw himself fitting in:

Maybe on any other day I would have said "why bother," but then I pictured myself up on stage wearing my blue cap & gown and shaking some guys hand, which I have probably never seen before. Picking up my diploma, and putting behind 4 years of cutting classes, setting off fire alarms, and basically just "screwing around." Those 4 years will probably be the last time I'll be able to do the stuff I did and get away with it. Yeah, growing up really does suck.

So with all this in mind, I got up & took a long hot shower. Then I put on my most comfortable pants (the ones with the holes in the knees) and a sweatshirt. *I basically looked like a Mexican with an attitude, but I had to fit into my new environment.* (5/10/89 essay; emphasis added)

In sum, Gerardo indicated two criteria for fitting in at La Fuente: committing acts of adolescent rebellion and conforming to the "Mexican" subcultural style defined by dress and self-presentation.

The outlaw folklore generated by continuation students was not lost on teachers and administrators. According to one comprehensive school teacher, "In some groups it's almost a status symbol to go to Beacon, and students will misbehave here in a traditional high school, hoping to get kicked out so they can go to the continuation school." In formal interviews, a boy and a girl said they purposely "messed up" to get into Beacon (see table 2); others boasted of it informally. Like the high school students that Page (1987) studied, who deliberately dropped down into the lower track to get an easier schedule, continuation students sometimes felt they had outwitted the credentialing system: they could attend a "kickback" school and still receive their diploma. Vice principals in charge of discipline said if they sensed a student wanted to go to the continuation school, they would not threaten them with it because it would not be an effective disciplinary strategy.

Students arrived at Beacon and La Fuente with more than one image of their new schools in mind. And the "stigma contest" (Schur, 1980) that was waged between traditionalists and developmentalists, both within the continuation schools and across districts, heightened the contradiction between serving as an "alternative" and "treatment" center, between providing a safety net and a safety valve. The resulting confusion—both institutional and personal—was well illustrated by the Student-to-Student (STS) project that had Beacon students addressing junior high classes.

On the first day at Hart Junior High, the thirteen students whom I had helped train as peer counselors sent out mixed messages about the continuation school. One by one, they described how difficult the transition from junior to senior high had been and how they had ended up at continuation. A number of junior high students strongly identified with these difficulties and began to ask questions about Beacon. Alarmed that some of the younger students thought Beacon sounded like an attractive alternative, the peer counselors emphasized how Beacon had stigmatized them:

Dennis: You guys don't want to be fuckups. People look down at you; they don't look up at you.

Alfredo: They always make fun of you. "You go to Beacon, you're not smart."

Dennis: Opportunity [the junior high equivalent of continuation], that's like what we're in, man. It's the lower class school. You're not going to like it at Beacon. (5/19/89 group discussion with seventh- and eighth-graders)

But at another session Maria told some sixth-graders: "Beacon's not really a low-class school or anything. I mean, they help us a lot, to tell you the truth. I'm speaking for myself. They put me back on track; they've helped me want to graduate." Her friend Leslie quickly cut in: "We're not saying, 'Go to Beacon.' " At this, the room erupted, and Beacon students and their junior high audience began openly debating the contradictions that had come to the fore.

The contradictions inherent in a stigmatized safety net were discussed again the following week when letters from junior high students arrived at Beacon. One sixth-grade boy wrote: "When I grow up I think I'll go to Beacon. It was fun sharing problems. I wish they would come again. They told us to be in school and not to drop out." This attitude clearly made the STS participants uncomfortable. Maria, whose brother was an eighth-grader at Hart, argued that junior high students needed to know that attending a continuation school made one an "outcast" (field notes, 5/22/89).

Ultimately, the mixed feelings that resulted when students were enlisted to present the hidden world to a wider public were too much for Dennis and Alfredo. They decided to quit STS, and the following year nobody, including the teacher who sponsored it, wanted to continue. To a place so clearly and consciously reserved for what Goffman called "undesired differentness" (1963: 5), community leaders, school administrators, and parents all ascribed a dishonor that weakened its official purpose as safety net. One-third of Beacon's students and more than one-half of La Fuente's students dropped out or were pushed out during the 1988–

89 school year—including Matt, the student who at the beginning of this chapter said he had elected to come to La Fuente despite the stigma conveyed by his father, teachers, and vice principal, and who declared himself no "quitter."

Over the last twenty years, La Fuente and Beacon have tried to reduce the stigma attached to the continuation program: they have raised academic standards, garnered more resources, and removed the word *continuation* from their name and diploma. Yet the schools' poor reputation persists and is reinforced by community perceptions, organizational arrangements, and the responses of their participants: teachers, administrators, and students. This chapter has presented evidence to suggest that each district maintained the continuation school's devalued status by using it as a disciplinary threat and then making it dependent on the comprehensive schools as a base for its nonselective student recruitment.

In dealing with students considered "at risk," school administrators face a tension between addressing "special" needs and separating—and seemingly inevitably, stigmatizing—targeted groups. When special programs operate within mainstream settings, traditionalists oppose them on the grounds that they undermine standards and the regular staff's authority. In trying to avoid stigma in alternative settings, special programs such as continuation often revert to traditional or hybrid models in a bid for legitimacy. But unless students have access to the same high status academic curriculum available in the mainstream schools, which in turn provides entry to higher education, the professions, and other material and social rewards, then second-chance continuation programs will continue to be seen as second rate.

Reengaging within, or bonding to, a stigmatized organization requires a mental juggling act. This is particularly true because the continuation school serves late adolescents, who perhaps have more fragile egos, less self-knowledge, and a greater tendency to identify with oppositional subcultures (or rebel against institutional authority) than adults do. In the chapters to follow, I explore the symptoms, styles, and causes of disengagement from school, as students perceived the process within both comprehensive and continuation settings and as I observed it within the latter arena. I then examine who reengaged within the continuation school and how, seeking to explain why girls were relatively more successful at it than boys.

4

SLIPPING IN AND OUT OF THE SYSTEM: SYMPTOMS AND STYLES OF DISENGAGEMENT BY GENDER

I don't want someone to hold my hand, but I don't want someone to totally overlook me. At Beacon, they're not going to just
let you slip out of the system like you can at a regular high
school.
—Sandra, Beacon

Girls tend, I think, to be the ones that fall through the cracks
in that there's not so much attention placed on them.
—Teacher, feeder high school into La Fuente

Though still a place for traditional education's "misfits," today's continuation school has become more of a clearinghouse as the array of alternative education choices and credentials for disengaging students has
expanded. Students who stop attending high school outright often by-
pass the continuation school. But those who keep some tenuous hold,
who still show up to class occasionally, are prime continuation candi-
dates. Those attempting to slip back into the educational system via the
continuation school include students who have stopped out for a semester or more, or are coming from juvenile penal, mental, or substance
abuse institutions. (See the appendix for flow charts that document by
sex and ethnicity how many entered, stayed, and left the schooling system via Beacon and La Fuente during 1988–89.)

Generally, girls tend to slip in and out of the schooling system, both
continuation and conventional high schools, more quietly than boys. If

simply truant without being defiant of institutional authority or sexually "improper," girls were not pushed out by administrators or teachers. Disengaged girls favored strategies of classroom withdrawal or manipulation (for example, "sweet talking"), whereas boys were more prone to clowning or fighting. Thus, girls tended to hedge their bets, while boys engaged in acts of major confrontation that jeopardized their survival in school.

When cutting, girls were more likely to stay home, do chores, or be with older, out-of-school boyfriends, whereas boys hung out in large groups that sometimes engaged in acts of public delinquency. As a consequence, boys were more likely to be in alternative settings (opportunity classes, community schools, juvenile hall) and closely monitored. Girls were relatively free to drop out altogether, with fewer warning signs, and more prone to cite moving as a reason (this left open a face-saving option for returning to school at a later date).

Once at the continuation school, boys continued to be more vulnerable to pushout, although a significant subset of "tough" girls were, too. Based largely on classroom observations, I argue that gender relations affect how teachers define and act out their work in classrooms as well as how students respond to these values and practices; gender and sexuality critically influence teacher-student relations, a key component in the engagement process. For example, traditionalist men teachers expected more of male students and acted to maintain hierarchical control in the classroom; at the same time, boys acted out differently for these teachers, up to and including physical confrontation.

WARNING SIGNALS: QUIET AND LOUD

Student stories of how they ended up at the continuation school, an examination of attendance patterns, and my own observations convinced me that girls slip in and out of the schooling system more quietly than boys. Girls, for example, were significantly more likely to cite pregnancy (La Fuente) and truancy (Beacon and La Fuente) as reasons for their transfer to the continuation school. In contrast, for two-thirds of the boys in my sample, a discipline problem other than truancy precipitated their transfer; usually, however, they had also been in trouble for cutting classes and many now wanted to make up credits (see table 3).

Girls were also slightly underrepresented at both schools, as has often been true of the entire continuation program. Several factors explain why fewer girls ended up at Beacon and La Fuente, as well as why those who did were more likely to be counseling and pregnancy rather than disciplinary referrals.

TABLE 3
Primary Reason for Continuation Transfer by Sex (In Percentages)

Primary Reason for Transfer	Female $n = 43$	Male $n = 39$	Total $N = 82$
Truancy/desire for credits	72.3	34.3	56.1
Discipline problem	6.4	65.7	31.7
Pregnancy only	19.2	0.0	11.0
Other	2.1	0.0	1.2
Totals	100.0	100.0	100.0

Note: Chi-square $(3, N = 82) = 34.898$, $p < .0001$; phi coefficient $= .652$.

First, girls' irregular attendance did not seem to alarm administrators as much, especially if they were "nice girls" (sexually proper). Ruth, unusual in having initiated the continuation transfer herself, described how difficult it was to persuade the principal in charge of discipline to let her change schools:

> [The vice principal] told me, "You have to get up and go to your first period class." So I did, and he was all happy. But I wanted to come to La Fuente, and he told me I'd have to mess up. So I didn't go to my classes the next day. Even then, he was going to send me to [names two comprehensive schools]. "You're a nice girl, Ruth. I could send you to these other schools." But I said, "What makes you think I'm going to get up any earlier to go to those other schools when I didn't do it [here]?" He said I had a good point. The way I see it, La Fuente starts later, and I heard it was easier, too.

In contrast, a number of boys said they were told to either "quit wasting time and attend school, or drop out and get a job." More than one-half of my male sample (57 percent) said they were referred to continuation by a principal, while only 11 percent said a counselor told them about Beacon or La Fuente. In contrast, girls were slightly more likely to have been referred by a counselor (26 percent) than a principal (23 percent).

Second, by their own accounts, the girls in my study were less likely to disengage in class in ways that would bring them to the attention of school authorities. Simone, a Beacon student, explained:

> When I was at [the comprehensive school], I had this class and ... I missed a lot of school. My teacher never really noticed until I didn't come for a week straight. . . . Some of the teachers don't really pay attention to girls, they don't think they would

be [out causing trouble]. Cuz my teacher liked me. She was always: "Are you OK? Were you sick last week?"

If students were relatively quiet in the classroom and seemingly studious when there, at least some teachers in the feeder schools—and later, according to what I saw, in the continuation schools—appeared to ignore their absences or excuse the truancy longer.

Third, perhaps because girls were more willing to discuss their problems with significant others, they were more likely to find their way to the continuation school through informal networks: family (15 percent of the females versus 3 percent of the males), friends (21 percent versus 11 percent), or—more rarely—a special teacher (6 percent of the females, none of the males). Girls and boys were equally likely to say that they referred themselves to the continuation school (9 percent each).

Fourth, boys were more likely to have been sent out of class, suspended, placed in opportunity classes, and transferred to other schools for disciplinary purposes (at the secondary school level, compare Alvord, 1979; Duke, 1976: 71).[1] Students seen as hard-core discipline problems are usually sent to the continuation school as soon as they turn sixteen years old. Of the 125 sophomores sent to La Fuente during 1988–89, only 35 percent were females (and more than half were pregnant); 65 percent were males. Boys were also more likely than girls to have been put on probation or parole or to have served time in juvenile hall: less than one-tenth of the girls in my sample mentioned being on probation, while one-third of the boys had been or were.[2] Nine percent of males and no females said a probation officer had referred them to the continuation school.

Not surprisingly, therefore, twice as many boys as girls transferred to Beacon from alternative programs. In contrast, 23 percent of the girls

---

1. Although I could not obtain disciplinary and alternative placement statistics for La Fuente's and Beacon's districts, the number of suspensions by sex and ethnicity for the third pilot site, Willows, were available: In 1985–86, girls accounted for one-fifth of all suspensions, boys for four-fifths. Within ethnic groups, these figures ranged from 18 percent for Asian-American girls (including Filipinas and Pacific Islanders) to 27 percent for Native American girls.

Further, I visited the opportunity classes at one of two feeder junior highs in Beacon's district and found that almost all of those enrolled were boys.

Of continuation students interviewed, significantly more boys than girls said they had attended more than one comprehensive high school (63 versus 34 percent), often because they were being punished.

2. "Youthful offenders" (those aged fifteen to nineteen who are either on parole or in penal institutions) are 95 percent male in California (California Youth Authority data for 1989).

versus 10 percent of the boys reentered the educational system having dropped out completely (see the appendix). Similar patterns existed at La Fuente and the third pilot site, Willows. Explained Lilia, "I've never been in trouble by the law, and nobody in my family is on welfare, so they [the authorities] didn't make a big issue that I wasn't in school" (Willows).

Once at the continuation school, girls' styles of disengagement continued to differ somewhat from that of most boys. I noticed, and a number of teachers and students confirmed, that boys in general seemed to have a more well-defined direction; for a subset, this necessitated a diploma, and they attended fairly regularly. Others, disengaged and often enrolled primarily under duress (pressed by a vigilant probation officer or social worker), hardly attended at all, refused to do much school work, and were usually pushed out as a result.

Girls attended and worked more sporadically and thus were more likely to give the impression of being uncertain or without set long-term goals that might inspire more consistency. Much of this uncertainty derived from girls' propensity to view their future in terms of family commitments, rather than to separate these from paid work as boys did:

Linda: I think guys nowadays know what they want, more so than girls. . . . They know if they want to be bums all their life, they're going to be bums, and if they want to have nice things, they're going to work.

DK: What's the difference between them, do you think?

Linda: I think the difference is that some girls, especially young girls, are naive. And a lot of nice things are said and a lot of nice promises, and that's exactly what it is, *broken* promises. And they don't realize that until . . . it's too late. (La Fuente)

Various school statistics reflected the boys' more polarized response to La Fuente and Beacon as well as the girls' more ambiguous one. Not surprisingly, mothering girls' attendance was particularly sporadic; caring for sick infants kept many out of school. La Fuente's principal did a study of attendance and found that while the school's overall attendance rate was between 70 and 75 percent, the rate for girls enrolled in the SAM program (who made up one-fifth of all students) was 55 to 60 percent; he contrasted this with an 85 to 90 percent attendance rate at the district's comprehensive schools (field notes, 11/16/88).

To the extent that girls perceived childbearing or marriage as alternative routes to status, they seemed more susceptible to "cooling out" messages conveyed when educational institutions create a "situation of structured failure" (Clark, 1960), such as transfer to a continuation school.

Continuation schools have their own mechanisms for cooling out the aspirations of unsuccessful students. For example, Beacon's Attendance, Punctuality, and Productivity (APP) system allowed me to track attendance. Every three weeks, students' APP records were assessed. To stay "clear," students had to earn ten of fifteen hours in each class; those who, in addition to being clear, had a 90 percent attendance rate overall made "honors." Students who failed—whether due to absenteeism, tardiness, or lack of productivity in class—to achieve clear status were put on step I of probation. If they did not improve their APP record in the next three-week period, they were put on step II. In the next APP period, a student could either move back up to step I through improved attendance or, failing that, down to step III. I analyzed one-third of the twelve APP periods (spread over the school year) by gender and found that a higher proportion of boys than girls always made honors, sometimes at twice the rate, and boys almost always formed the bulk of those on the verge of being pushed out (step III). The largest proportion of girls, on the other hand, was usually on clear status; roughly similar proportions of both sexes were on the intermediate probation steps (I and II).

Students who attended minimally and ended up on step III of academic probation were usually given the choice of going through the furlough program or being transferred to adult education. The furlough program was a three-week, independent studies course that required students to engage in "reality therapy"; they had to write a resume, apply for a job, talk to a military recruiter, calculate their living expenses, and contact an obstetrician to find out the cost of prenatal care and childbirth. Students met with a teacher-counselor once a week for an hour to report on their progress.

Of those enrolled during 1988–89, girls were less likely to have *ever* been on furlough: 24 percent versus 30 percent of the boys. Perhaps because of their greater ambivalence, this group of ever-furloughed girls was sometimes able to increase attendance significantly: compared to boys, over twice as many furloughed girls eventually graduated by fall 1990 (45 versus 21 percent).

The relationship between teacher-counselors and students affected what happened to students when they reached step III. I observed that if teacher-counselors were aware of personal or family crises in students' lives, they sometimes intervened to keep them from going on step III and furlough, despite poor attendance records. For example, Mrs. Foster announced to me that she would "never" put Sandra—a girl who had been abused and suffered from depression—on furlough, adding, "I'm going to save that kid" (field notes, 12/5/88). The fact that girls seemed, on average, more willing to confide such information than boys and less likely to disengage in ways that disrupted class and school activities may have motivated some counselors to give girls, on average, more time to improve their attendance and "productivity" and possibly graduate.

More girls also seemed to interpret being on step III as an indicator that they were not succeeding and might as well quit, as a message of rejection by the school, or both: one-third of the girls on step III dropped out without first going on furlough or transferring to adult education versus only one-fifth of the boys. Further, more girls than boys dropped out without ever reaching step III: 58 percent versus 27 percent. Relative to their continuation classmates, these students' records of attendance and "productivity" did not warn of impending exit.

Most of the girls who slipped quietly out of Beacon cited "moving" as the official reason for leaving but did not subsequently request their transcripts (see the appendix). Some liked school well enough and had achieved success at Beacon but were having problems with their families or boyfriends (discussed in the next chapter) that prompted a move. Others did not actually move but found this a convenient excuse to tell teachers and friends at school; it had the advantage of leaving the door open if they decided to "move back" later—as at least two Latinas did— because they could portray the decision to change residence as beyond their control.

La Fuente did not track students' progress through the system nearly so systematically, but available statistics revealed a similar pattern. For example, La Fuente referred a sizable proportion of its most disengaged students to the on-site independent studies program. Reflecting a tendency to slip more quietly out of the system, girls (Latinas in particular) were more likely—compared to their representation in the overall school population—to be no-shows, while boys (Latinos and whites in particular) were more likely to enroll for awhile before dropping out altogether (see the appendix, flow chart 1).

ABSENTEEISM AND CUTTING CLASSES

For the most part, absenteeism and class cutting indicated passive resistance to schooling, specifically academic competition, overcontrol of student behavior, and social ranking. In the past, researchers have had difficulty interpreting the greater nonattendance of girls, particularly when they stay at home. Stinchcombe (1964: 190), for example, speculated that girls' higher rate of absenteeism in the high school he studied had "to do either with the physiology or with the social definition of menstruation." But the girls in this study made clear that they were quietly saying no to the sometimes conflicting demands of teachers, administrators, and peers. "If I was going to be late and get into trouble and have Saturday school, I'd just stay home and tell them, 'I'm not feeling good. I'm not going to do good in class.' And my mom would call in . . ." (Martha, Beacon).

Being absent from school (truant), cutting classes, and being tardy are often linked to low achievement because students spend less "time on task," which in turn is associated with less learning (Karweit, 1984). Also, students are punished for this behavior by low grades (possibly failure and, later, loss of credits) and suspensions, which may contribute to a student being held back a grade. School delay and being overage for one's grade are highly correlated with dropping out, particularly for low socioeconomic status youth, Mexican-Americans, and males (Hirano-Nakanishi, 1986; Nielsen and Fernandez, 1981). In one of the few studies to examine the causal relationship between grade repetition and dropout, Grissom and Shepard (1989) found that being retained a grade increased the probability of eventually dropping out of school—across three city school districts—by 20 to 30 percent, *after* achievement level, socioeconomic status, and sex were held constant.

Research in England using student self-reports of behavior found that girls were as likely as boys to be truant, but they more often stayed home or cut classes while remaining at school. Boys tended to be truant in groups outside the home, and their truancy was associated with delinquency (Davies, 1984: 8, 136–37). My student interviews largely confirmed these findings.

Almost every student interviewed had cut school, and cutting patterns were roughly similar across ethnic and school categories. About one-sixth of both boys and girls began by cutting some classes, got "a taste" for it, and then stayed out of school for whole days. (It was a truism among students that "cutting is addictive.")[3] More girls than boys said they usually just cut a class or two (28 versus 20 percent), while more boys than girls reported only cutting full days (29 versus 13 percent). Two-fifths of the girls and one-third of the boys said they did both (sometimes cutting a class, other times cutting all day).

Significantly more Beacon students reported staying home (62 versus 23 percent), but similar proportions at both schools cut to be with friends and "party," defined by them to include drinking alcohol and

---

3. Students who miss long periods of school for legitimate reasons may be at risk of truancy. A number of students' first cutting jags were touched off by illnesses, accidents, or parents' taking them on extended trips.

using drugs, usually marijuana, sometimes cocaine. A number of non-white La Fuente students believed that partying was ethnic minority behavior. Anita, a Latina who had earned all A's and B's while living in a suburban town before moving to La Fuente City, explained: "I don't mean to be racist, but there was a bunch of white people there, and . . . I don't really know them to party. So it was like nothing else to do, so I'd just come home and do my homework." Yet in individual interviews whites were equally likely to say they cut school to party (58 versus 52 percent). One-quarter of all students cited peer pressure to cut, and sometimes do drugs, as the main factor responsible for their disengagement.

> If most of your friends go, you're going to go. Because you don't want to be here when you know your friends are having fun and you're in school. Then you'll want to cut. . . . Your friends, they go, "Try this, try that [drug]." (Luis, La Fuente)

At both schools, girls were significantly more likely than boys to cut to stay home (53 versus 26 percent). About eight in ten students cut to be with friends, and significantly more boys than girls spontaneously mentioned drinking and taking drugs while doing so (69 versus 43 percent). This matched students' perceptions that more boys were "partiers." Still, a fair number of girls did use, or had used, drugs and alcohol. More than boys, they stressed that drugs can become a cause of school disengagement rather than just a symptom because they can inhibit or damage teacher-learner relationships and poison communication between students and their families. Two girls reported that their families eventually kicked them out of the house for using drugs that had made them argumentative and paranoid; this then forced them to leave school.

In addition, girls were significantly more likely to report cutting to be with boyfriends (68 versus 37 percent), who were usually older than they were and out of high school (55 percent of the boyfriends had dropped out, 23 percent had graduated, while the rest were still in school). The influence of boyfriends will be discussed in the next chapter.

Finally, girls, particularly young mothers, more often than boys mentioned cutting to attend to domestic responsibilities (17 versus 3 percent). Few mentioned this as a major problem; I explore the issue using data from a special survey in the next chapter.

CLASSROOM SURVIVAL STRATEGIES

Classroom Withdrawal

Most of the empirical research on gender and classroom interaction has been done at the elementary school level, where, it is frequently noted, girls achieve at or above the level of boys; further, they are less disruptive and speak out less than boys (for example, Lockheed and Klein, 1985). Thus girls' behavior and attitudes seem more in line with the norms that define the "good student." Even at this stage, however, a significant subset of girls may be at risk academically.

In a study of sixth-graders in a white working-class suburb, Lahaderne and Jackson (1970: 98) found that "the tendency to deny one's human failings is associated with a general strategy of withdrawal in the classroom among girls (fewer self-initiated interactions, fewer instructional interactions, more inattentiveness), but a similar pattern does not appear for boys." This strategy, used by the group of girls who were most concerned about what others thought of them, was associated with lower academic performance. And the relationship between withdrawal and the need for social desirability held true holding ability (as measured by IQ scores) constant, while the relationship between the need for social desirability and academic achievement disappeared. Given the competitive intellectual setting, the girls who emphasized withdrawal may have been seeking to avoid the disapproval of the teacher, their peers, or both (ibid.: 101). Interpreting these findings from a sociological perspective, one could argue that the withdrawal strategy is symptomatic of girls' low expectations for competence, which, in turn, results from the girls' low gender and academic status (Cohen, 1982).

Subsequent classroom studies of teacher-student interaction have found that females, particularly white girls, receive less communication—both positive and negative, academic and neutral—from teachers because they are more likely to be "on-task and manageable" (Irvine, 1985: 343; for a review see Sadker, Sadker, and Klein, 1991: 294–307). Through neglect, then, teachers may inadvertently reinforce the withdrawal strategy among certain girls. Peers, too, may play a part. In an ethnographic comparison of four kindergarten classrooms, Goodenough (1987: 440) found that boys' "sexist behaviors" adversely affected the classroom performance of girls, who, overtime, answered fewer questions and were more timid and less spontaneous.

In my music class, three students (two white girls and one white boy) pursued a withdrawal strategy. Much of my energy was spent encouraging group activities, which these students were content to let their classmates dominate, and maintaining discipline; none of these students ever posed a problem. To my dismay, very often at the end of the day as I wrote up my field notes, I could not even remember whether these students were present let alone what, if anything, they had said or done in class. They reluctantly made their two required presentations to the class, but their shyness was compounded by the reaction of their peers who expected to be bored, so were inattentive.

Classroom withdrawal may become less viable as students enter junior and senior high. More teachers use a lecture format and expect students to give formal presentations. This may further upset students prone to withdrawal because they are more on the spot individually than in the more fluid elementary classroom. In a study of science classrooms, Morse and Handley (1985, summarized in Sadker, Sadker, and Klein, 1991: 296–97) found male students interacted more with teachers, and this gender gap grew as students moved from seventh to eighth grade: "In the seventh grade, girls initiated 41% of the student-to-teacher interactions, a figure that dropped to 30% by the eighth grade. In contrast, male initiation of class comments rose from 57% to 70% over the same 2-year period, suggesting that girls were becoming less assertive over time."

My student interviews lent some support to the idea that girls become less assertive in the classroom. On the one hand, girls and whites at both schools were 1.8 times more likely to report reading something else or pretending to work when bored in class. More girls than boys reported daydreaming (19 versus 12 percent). (Although these are not exact indicators of withdrawal, I found that they best identified students I had observed to be withdrawn in the continuation setting.) On the other hand, more boys reported doodling (31 versus 17 percent), sleeping (33 versus 22 percent), and making jokes (17 versus 0 percent), while girls said they talked more (32 versus 12 percent)—activities that tended to attract the teacher's attention. One girl argued that even the most disengaged girls, herself included, will attempt to "survive" school while their male counterparts will simply drop out:

> [When I'm bored] I just sit there and stare at everybody and the walls. But I can't go to sleep cuz I won't get credit, so I make it look like I'm working. . . . It seems like more males are stubborn about things. If they don't want to go to school, they're not going to go to school. If it was a girl, she wouldn't want to go to school, [but] *she probably would find a way to go to school and survive.* (Frances, Beacon; emphasis added)

Surviving through a strategy of withdrawal became more and more difficult at the comprehensive high school, according to some students. A subset of girls reported being punished or severely criticized for refusing to read aloud or give oral reports and the like; above all, they feared they would embarrass themselves in front of classmates. "I'm not good at reading," Carmen told me, "and some of the students that are in a classroom, they might make comments about it. That's what I don't like. . . . I told the teacher, 'Kick me out, but I'm not going to do it' " (La Fuente).

Depending on the student's overall demeanor and personality, teachers interpret this refusal to participate as shyness, lack of ability, or insolence. Elena, who often appeared sullen, got into more trouble when she withdrew than other students did:

> [If I'm bored] I just sit there and don't answer. They get mad and kick me out of class. . . . Sometimes they treat the smarter people better, too. It's weird. Like a teacher, Mrs. H, *I'd sit there and always do my work,* but I'd never answer questions. I'd do good. *I'd just mind my own business,* and all of a sudden, she told me I was stupid. She called me a juvenile delinquent. I didn't tell. I just didn't care. Ever since that one day, [if] she tells me to do something, [I'd say]: "No, I'm not going to do it for you. Do it yourself. Tell one of your other students to do it." Before, I used to have respect for her, but when somebody acts like that, you can't act like the way you used to. Especially for no reason: *I was quiet in class.* (La Fuente; emphasis added)

Elena was puzzled and hurt that her survival strategy no longer worked as well as it had. In elementary and junior high school, she could get by if she was quiet and completed her written work. She respected her teachers and helped them; in return, she expected not to be pressed to participate in class discussions.

Renee said she tried to participate, but withdrew again when faced with sarcastic remarks from teachers. "Usually when I've said, 'I don't know,' the teachers have said, 'Most likely.' Then they'll pick somebody else, and you're sitting there with your mouth hanging open and you just don't want to say anything anymore" (Beacon). She observed that other students, following a teacher's lead, will tease shy students, thus contributing to their withdrawal. I saw this dynamic in play with a few teachers at La Fuente where classrooms were organized more traditionally. Beacon's individualized program allowed students to withdraw, but some teachers succeeded in coaxing shy students out of their shells socially.

Clowning versus Sweet-Talking Teachers

If the strategy of classroom withdrawal was more prevalent among a subset of girls as a means of masking low ability (real or perceived), low achievement, or lack of preparation, acting the clown was almost exclusively a male strategy, across ethnic groups. Like the girls who refused to participate verbally, class clowns seemed most concerned about what their peers thought of them.

About one-sixth of the boys interviewed described clowning as a way of dealing with boredom; eventually, they said, this behavior got them into trouble. I observed them and other boys not interviewed using this strategy within the continuation setting as well. Sometimes their antics were physical, but more often they would make jokes. Tim was tardy and the teacher commented, "Late again, huh?"; Tim responded with a grin, "Not really. I'm early for tomorrow" (La Fuente, field notes, 3/16/89). This usually elicited a laugh from the class and even a reluctant smile from the teacher. Even when a teacher felt that such students had gone too far in subverting their authority within the classroom and disciplined them, they tended to see their behavior as part of the "boys-will-be-boys" variety (compare Davies, 1984: 142).

Often, too, these boys seemed to be emulating fathers who had bragged of their high school exploits. Example: Kurt, whom I had observed climbing on top of a classroom table and pretending to sleep (Beacon, field notes, 2/6/89), noted: "I would always hear my dad talk about things he did when he was little, and I'm eighteen now. It went by so fast. I'm glad I got to do what I got to do and get away with what I did." I did not see girls playing the class clown, so I can only speculate that perhaps teachers, peers, or both subtly discouraged this behavior as unfeminine.

Although I did not observe girls clowning, some did report enjoying the feeling of "getting away with things," as Kurt put it. Manipulating "the system" allowed these girls and some boys to avoid the "goody-goody" label while not directly challenging school authorities. "I liked that I knew all the loopholes in the system," Estelle told me. "I was friends with all the teachers and then a couple of classes, I didn't have to do any work and I received A's. . . . There wasn't one class that I didn't get out of every day for at least fifteen minutes" (La Fuente). Some girls would do homework for their boyfriends or help them cheat. Other students, girls and boys, acting as assistants for teachers (almost always men), would alter their friends' grades or attendance records (Beacon, field notes, 4/28/88, 1/9/89). Carla described with pride how, for friends, she doctored "admits" (passes admitting tardy or absent students back to class) from unexcused to excused:

> Everybody'd come to me cuz I used to always carry around nail polish remover, hairspray, and Q-tips. All you do is hold the admit and get the Q-tip, rub it around in a circle and write, scribble with ink and then turn it around and circle it, like carbon. (La Fuente)

Students used their sexuality not only to break the classroom routine, but also to get out of work or bend the rules. "You could totally sweet-talk a male teacher" (Sandra, Beacon, 4/28/88 group discussion). Lupe, for example, wanted to avoid her science class so attended exactly enough hours within a grading period to maintain her honors status before cutting to hang out in Mr. LaBelle's class. Although she lost credit in her science class thereafter, she "sweet-talked" Mr. LaBelle into giving her extra credit in the class she had with him earlier in the day (Beacon, field notes, 6/5/89).

Boys did not seem to sweet-talk teachers in the same way, or if they did, they purposely overplayed it to comic effect; thus, I categorized the behavior as a clowning strategy. Rich described how he teased a woman teacher into giving him more latitude:

> If teachers don't get a response that they enjoy or they want, they get frustrated, send you to the office, and make you write sentences. I mean, one teacher I had, Miz K., whenever she'd start yelling at me, I'd just be all, "I guess that means no on our date?" And she'd just be all, "You're impossible," and walk away. I'd compliment her, "Gee Miz K., may I call you Mary? That dress is really attractive on you." She'd just be all, "Ahhh." She'd just leave me alone. (Beacon)

By thus embarrassing the teacher, Rich may have furthered his reputation among his peers, but jeopardized his survival in that class. Girls were more likely to hedge their bets, playing up to teachers in ways that allowed them to bend the rules to benefit themselves and possibly their friends without angering teachers (unless their cheating came to light).

BOYS' AND TOUGH GIRLS' GREATER VULNERABILITY TO PUSHOUT

Discipline, Gender, and How Schools Disengage from Students

Official disciplinary actions such as in-school detention and suspension are well-known correlates of disengagement. Data from the national High

School and Beyond study show that 31 percent of the sophomores who dropped out of school had been suspended or put on probation versus 10 percent of those who stayed in school. Of those who dropped out or were pushed out, 13 percent of the males and 5 percent of the females cited the reason "expelled or suspended" (Ekstrom et al., 1986: tables 1 and 6).

The pattern of fewer girls than boys being suspended was evident at La Fuente and Beacon. Table 4 displays the number of suspensions from Beacon during 1988–89 by reason, sex, and ethnicity; similar statistics were unavailable for La Fuente, but observation and interview data suggest that the gender pattern was similar. Excluding students suspended more than once, 9 percent of girls versus 32 percent of boys had been kept out of school for periods ranging from one day up to two weeks. No Filipinas or Latinas (particularly noteworthy given their numbers in the school) were suspended. Of those who were suspended, girls were most likely to get into trouble for fighting or threatening their peers (40 percent) and smoking cigarettes (40 percent), while boys were most likely to be punished for cutting (56 percent) and coming into conflict with a teacher (22 percent).

These gender differences are understandable if one considers Beacon's rules and how they were enforced as well as student misbehavior that went unnoticed or unrecorded because it was punished by means other than suspension. Individual students caught smoking, for example, could choose to perform some cleanup task at school rather than be suspended, and most of these cases went unrecorded.

Boys on the whole seemed more willing to flaunt school rules. For example, five of the six boys suspended for tobacco were caught smoking or lighting up in class. Girls were much more likely to sneak a smoke in the bathroom between classes. The four who were suspended for tobacco had been caught together—an unusual occurrence—and the girls assumed a more confrontational stance, culminating in the group choosing suspension over cleaning the sinks. The year before, the principal suspended (without choice) eight girls in a similar incident, according to an official incident report. In a discussion of whether disciplinary action differed by gender, he explained:

> I've even caught myself in some inconsistencies where I may have nailed some girls harder [for tobacco] than I would have the boys, whether it was because I was internally more upset that girls smoke than boys, I don't know if that's the case. But I remember nailing nine girls in the bathroom at once: [they were] making it a club house. (5/1/89 interview)

TABLE 4
Suspensions from Beacon, 1988–89, by Reason, Sex, and Ethnicity

Ethnicity	Females			Males		
	Other[a]	Latino	White	Other[a]	Latino	White
No. in sex/ethnic group (school total)	6	27	54	18	43	59
Suspension reason Individual						
Cutting class			1	2	6	23
Tobacco			4		2	4
Marijuana					1	2
Dangerous object				1		
Conflict w/teacher Disrupted teacher			1	1	3	2
Obscenity				1	2	1
Verbal abuse					1	1
Conflict w/peer(s) Fighting	1		1	1		1
Threat	1		1			
Totals	2	0	8	5	16	34
As percent of sex/ethnic group (school total)	33	0	15	28	37	58
As percent (minus repeat offenders) of sex/ethnic group	33	0	11	22	26	39

Note: If a student was suspended for more than one offense at a time, only the most serious one was tallied.
[a]Other includes 7 Asian-Americans, 6 African-Americans, 7 Filipino-Americans, 3 Native Americans, and 1 Iranian-American.

In this case, flaunting the rules ("making it a club house") seemed to prompt the more severe punishment rather than the act itself (smoking). In general, continuation girls seemed less willing to challenge authority directly, yet a significant minority of girls did resent institutional authority. They tended to look down on girls who, in order to avoid punishment, acted like "nice, sweet girls—ladies," as Annie (Beacon) put it. Instead, this defiant group of girls preferred to act "tough" (compare McLaren, 1986: 167). Selectively employing certain traditional masculine traits like aggression and stoicism, the tough girls swore, yelled, and otherwise refused to act submissive in the face of disciplinary action. Most had hit at least one teacher (always female) before coming to con-

tinuation school, usually, they said, after being provoked (the teacher
had grabbed or shoved them).

Tough girls complained privately that they got "busted" for swearing, using street language, and obscene gestures, whereas boys did not.
I observed teachers correcting both boys and girls for swearing, but their
comments to girls were frequently linked to what teachers considered
gender-appropriate behavior. One example from La Fuente:

> Ms. Wilson asked Shawna to remove her cap [in accordance with
> her classroom rule], which she did. Ms. Wilson then compli-
> mented Shawna on her cornrows. Appearing embarrassed that
> attention had been drawn to her personal appearance, Shawna
> announced: "I'm a tomboy," to which the teacher responded,
> "Why don't you be a tomgirl?" A minute or so later, Ms. Wilson
> caught Shawna and Gina swearing and reprimanded them: "It's
> not ladylike for girls to be cussing like that." (field notes, 2/9/89)

Thus, these girls' perception of bias may not have stemmed from their
getting "busted" more (although this might have been true, too), but
from school staff stressing the offense because it represented a violation
of gender as well as school norms.

Another instance of boys violating school rules more flagrantly involved cutting, which Beacon defined as leaving campus without permission. A subset of boys would leave campus in small groups, often to
smoke marijuana in a nearby apartment complex, and then occasionally
return to campus.[4] They obviously wanted to flaunt the rule because
attendance was checked in every class, and cutting was usually detected.

Other students, and girls especially, either never showed up at school,
came during third period (before the school reported the absence to
their family), or pretended to be sick and got a counselor to give them
a pass home. (At La Fuente, girls, even if they were not in the SAM
program, could often leave school by pretending they had business in
the SAM building, located outside the fence surrounding the main school
compound, while boys trying to cut had to jump the fence—and were
more often caught.) While these tactics may have hurt them in the long
run because they were not receiving credit, none was technically considered cutting and hence was not punishable by suspension. This, in

---

4. Apparently because boys would meet up in the bathroom to smoke marijuana during class, staff decided to lock the door and allow only one boy at a time to check the
key out from the office. The girls' bathroom door remained unlocked until December, when three girls were suspected of smoking marijuana there (field notes, 12/06/
88).

turn, put the girls less at risk of being pushed out through the APP system because, unlike suspended students, they had not forfeited the opportunity to earn credit or the chance to match credit through homework.[5]

A final instance where boys seemed more likely to confront authority directly—or at least be suspended for it—can be seen in their relations with other people. Only two boys (in one incident) were suspended for fighting their peers, but twelve (in separate incidents) either disrupted or verbally abused a teacher. In contrast, only one girl disrupted a teacher, but two threatened to fight—and two more actually did fight— their peers, in a total of three incidents.

Because, in general, boys tend to achieve academically at lower levels than girls, they may be more likely to express their frustration in school by challenging teachers' authority. Girls, on the other hand, report more frustration with the social status system in place in most schools, for reasons that I analyze in the next chapter, and this frustration may lead them into more conflict with their peers. As Duke (1978: 148) found: "For better or worse, teachers and administrators generally are less disturbed by problems among students than by problems between students and school employees," and this may help explain why girls who fight get into less trouble with school authorities than boys who fight.

During my field work at Beacon and La Fuente, I observed more girls than boys actually coming to blows with one another at school. Teachers and administrators seemed to notice, and take more seriously, tension between male students—perhaps because they were more physically imposing than most females—and then try to diffuse it. In addition, girls seemed less willing than boys to defer the fight, perhaps because in most cases of girls fighting girls that I knew about, girls were demonstrating their loyalty to friends who would not or could not engage in physical conflict. "My friend Mandy, when she got pregnant, I looked after her, cuz I knew exactly if the guy [the father of Mandy's baby] left her, she'd have to go to work after school to support her kid," Linda told me in an interview. "Looking after" Mandy included fighting a girl at school who had begun to date Mandy's boyfriend (La Fuente, field notes, 10/12/88).

Although competition related to academic achievement was reduced

---

5. Students at both schools agreed they were much less likely to cut than before, particularly due to the more flexible and compressed schedule that continuation programs offer. And because the major discipline problem for many, particularly girls, had been truancy, they reported spending much less time in the principal's office compared to when they were at the comprehensive school.

in the continuation school, boys still came into more conflict with teachers and administrators than girls, and school authorities still interpreted such conflict as a major act of misbehavior. Three factors contributed to this gender difference: (1) the boys' greater willingness to flaunt authority, (2) the higher profile of the relatively few defiant girls, and (3) the effect gender had on teacher-student interaction. Nearly all incidents of student conflict with school officials that resulted in suspension followed a similar pattern. First, the student violated a school or classroom norm and was corrected by a teacher or administrator. Second, the student tried to justify his or her action, while the school adult insisted on compliance. Third, the student yelled an obscenity at the teacher or administrator.

When girls do openly defy school authority, they may be punished more severely. None of the boys at Beacon was suspended more than two days for conflict with faculty members, and some simply got in-house detention for the rest of the day, were transferred out of the teacher's class, or both. The lone girl got suspended three days, and because she was on step II of probation, the suspension contributed to her being placed on furlough. Her harsher punishment seemed to result from the fact that she publicly told a man teacher to "fuck off." I then overheard this teacher denouncing the girl to teachers and students alike, announcing that she would never be allowed in his classroom again; he also insisted to the principal that she be dealt with severely. This, coupled with her high profile, convinced the principal she was a "troublemaker" (Beacon, field notes, 12/21/88).

For students seen as "troublemakers" or "nonstudents"—including girls but more often boys—the continuation schools had ways of disengaging or pushing students out, just as comprehensive high schools do (compare Fine, 1986, 1991). I have discussed how Beacon's APP system acted as a pushout mechanism. At La Fuente, school authorities used the same criteria (attendance, productivity, discipline) to assess a student's progress, but in a more informal manner. Further, La Fuente's climate encouraged a get-tough policy. At least three factors influenced this atmosphere. First, gang members and drug dealers, mainly boys, had a higher profile both in the school and districtwide. Second, La Fuente had to service feeder schools with a combined enrollment of more than 20,000 students, and the bigger demand to enroll their "misfits" put La Fuente under pressure to withdraw students who were especially truant, disruptive, or reluctant to work. Third, given its mini-comprehensive school philosophy and organization, La Fuente students had fewer effective advocates.

Administrators and teachers employed several means of implementing this unstated, informal mandate. First, incoming students had to attend a half-day orientation class for one to three weeks. Among other things, they were told what was expected of a good student. If after the first day they came to orientation class late or without a notebook, the teacher, selected for the job because she was well-liked by most students, motivating yet demanding, routinely sent them home.

> Barry appeared at the door around 10:00 saying he'd overslept. Ms. Wilson told him to go home. Barry: "At least I made the effort to come." Lance added: "Yeah, if you keep kicking us out, how are we gonna get an education?" Ms. Wilson explained that Barry had to take responsibility for being tardy, and Barry left. (field notes, 5/10/89)

If students were absent a lot or reluctant to complete in-class assignments or participate in discussion, they often had to repeat the class for another three weeks. These policies did discourage the most disengaged students: 18 percent of all eventual dropouts left after six weeks or less at La Fuente during 1988–89. Wrote one such student in his journal: "I just got some desturbing [sic] news that I might have to repeat the window. . . . I'm not going to go to the class. I will just get into the GED program." He did not do so while I was at La Fuente.

Another means of disengaging from students deemed marginal was referrals to what was euphemistically called the Responsibility Center. About half the teachers routinely sent tardy and disruptive students there, where they had to copy rules from the student handbook. In interviews, students and some teachers complained that the man in charge treated them harshly. He repeated his philosophy to me several times: "I tell the kids [who come to the Responsibility Center], 'It's like cancer and garbage. You cut one out, and the other you throw out' " (field notes, 5/31/89). More often than not, girls reported being shocked, upset, and inclined to skip future detentions, whereas boys were prone to swear, flee, or challenge the disciplinarian to a fight. As one teacher explained: "The kids [especially boys] who get sent to Mr. Zuniga are at risk of suspension because they're just not as equipped as adults to deal with his abrasive personality. They end up fighting him over piddling offenses like being tardy" (field notes, 5/10/89).

Other teachers and administrators fully supported Mr. Zuniga's approach and encouraged each other to deal with chronic absenteeism and other discipline problems through the referral system because this created an official record. At a certain point, students who had built up poor reputations were withdrawn under the code "other"—the largest but least explanatory category of dropouts/pushouts. Sitting in the office on numerous occasions, I witnessed students being quietly withdrawn under the "other" code for smoking marijuana, chronic absenteeism and failing grades, and fighting (field notes, 5/4/89, 5/11/89, 5/24/89, 5/31/89, 10/12/89).

One teacher referred a Latina to the office for chronic tardiness, saying she was "not a serious student" and "taking up space in the class." The counselor withdrew her from school that day. I then overheard the girl asking a secretary if she could appeal to the principal—apparently unaware that La Fuente had no principal at that time (field notes, 10/12/89). A similar pushout practice was observed at Beacon for a Mexican-American boy considered "too disruptive." His teacher-counselor asked that he not be sent registration information, and he was withdrawn under the code "over 18—not reenrolled" (field notes, 8/23/89).

Some teachers at both schools told me they were unhappy with these school-initiated, exclusionary practices. At La Fuente, a group of teachers formally complained to the acting principal that students were being withdrawn before they even knew the students were in trouble (field notes, 5/18/89). But they hesitated to push strongly for due process unless they felt a particular student had academic potential, was pleasant if unmotivated, or had participated in school activities.

The Influence of Gender and Sexuality on Teacher-Student Relations

Underlying the debate over how best to deal with the most disengaged students was a conflict over teaching philosophy and how teachers defined their work. Gender shaped this debate and influenced how teachers acted on their values and ideas as well as student responses to these practices. Gender and sexuality affected which teachers bonded—or failed to bond—with which students, a critical factor in the engagement process.

The split between traditionalists and developmentalists was mentioned in the previous chapter. At both schools, almost all traditionalists were men, and most developmentalists were women. There is some evidence to suggest that the patterns I detected are more widespread. Brophy (1985) reviewed the literature at all levels of education bearing on gender differences in general teaching styles and concluded: "In general, . . . male teachers tend to be relatively more teacher-centered and direct, and female teachers tend to be relatively more student-centered, indirect, and supportive of students" (136–37). In both formal and informal interviews I conducted, teachers and administrators drew from gender-differentiated experiences to describe their work, to explain their approaches to teaching and maintaining discipline, and to justify their stand on what to do about the most disengaged students.

The traditionalists were usually less explicit than developmentalists about their work as teachers, although a few compared themselves to coaches and even drill sergeants. One male teacher outlined the philosophy sharply:

> Being a biologist, my attitude is that when you go into a new environment, every organism is going to adapt, migrate, or die. When a kid elects to come here, that's his decision; he's got to really put forth. If a kid doesn't want to work at this school, he's not going to get his productivity point for that day. We don't cater to the kids, but we're there to help them in any way we possibly can. They have to accept responsibility for their actions. (Beacon, 5/30/89 interview)

Within the school hierarchy, teachers made decisions and resolved conflicts, and students were expected to "adapt" or "migrate."

For students who resisted, traditionalists took what one called the "hard hat" approach—the expression reveals not only a gender but a class orientation, an identification with a working-class, masculine style. Speaking in favor of the APP program which pushed some students out, a Beacon administrator explained:

> Some feel that you should keep trying to help these kids, while others say get rid of those who are really disruptive so you can concentrate on those who are left. Personally, I think you should let society deal with some of these kids out on the streets. (field notes, 11/15/88)

Most traditionalists advocated some trial by fire—suggestions included living on the streets, joining the military, or a stint in juvenile hall—to make disengaged students appreciate high school.

In contrast, developmentalists frequently compared teaching to being a parent. (The teacher-parent analogy may have seemed particularly salient within the continuation context because the small school size allowed teachers to get to know students better, and some concluded students needed a surrogate parent.) Most of the women teachers were mothers and had interrupted their careers to care for their children at home until they had reached school age; they told me this experience had made them better teachers. "I think teachers are more effective in any kind of school area if they assume a parental role," explained one. "If I present myself as someone who really cares about [students], they pick it up right away and they can respond to that" (La Fuente, field notes, 6/15/89). Hearing the complaints of some traditionalist men teachers that "lazy" students should not be "babied," one woman teacher-counselor said:

> [Like babies, students] have to learn to crawl before they can learn to walk and run. I had to be here [at Beacon] a long time before I saw that they really do progress, that they won't be hanging on forever. But some students have to be put through patterning on one stage before they'll ever learn the later stages of behavior. (field notes, 11/14/88)

In addition to helping students modify their behavior, developmentalists spoke of maintaining discipline through communication (for example, explaining the rationale behind a rule) and participation (for example, involving students in making classroom rules). They also saw their role as listening to students' psychological and family problems because these were seen to interfere with learning.

The contrast between styles was particularly evident at Beacon, where all but two of the teacher-counselors were women and the rest of the staff were traditionalist men teachers. An illustration: a woman teacher-counselor sent a male student to a man teacher to get a tally of his productive hours. According to the teacher, the "very sensitive young man" came at a bad time, and "I reverted back to my normal teaching routine where if a kid didn't do things my way, man, I'd bite." The student complained to the counselor about the way he was treated, and she later suggested to the teacher that he might have explained that he did not have enough time and then asked the student to come back later.

Granting that this approach may have been better, the teacher still maintained that this left the student less prepared for real life: "Hey, guess what, these kids are going to go out in the big, bad, mean world" (Beacon, 6/9/89 interview). In response to such comments, developmentalists argued that students should be "sheltered. That's how they gain their self-esteem. . . . And once you are sheltered so that you have enough knowledge about yourself, then you can go out and face anything" (La Fuente, 6/7/89 interview).

Several factors encouraged men to be traditionalists. First, many had had military and coaching experience, both of which promote adherence to the values of hierarchical authority and competition. Second, some aspired to move into school administration so were motivated to help maintain discipline outside their classrooms; a demonstrated ability to deal with behavior problems was at least an informal requirement of top administrative posts. I observed several instances of women teachers choosing not to punish students for inappropriate behavior outside the classroom at La Fuente (for example, two boys exchanging lewd comments during lunch, field notes, 5/11/89; visiting students smoking at a special event, field notes, 10/11/89); men teachers then called the women to task for it.

Third, like a number of their male students,[6] some men associated a developmentalist approach with femininity and homosexuality. For example, at a faculty meeting I observed a man teacher pretending to gag at a woman teacher's suggestion that they send home "good news" cards to parents instead of contacting them only about academic and discipline problems; another let his wrist go limp (La Fuente, field notes, 10/3/88). Another man teacher explained to me that he could not talk to male students about their problems as he did with female students: "I can't go up to a boy and say, 'How's your love life?' They'll think I'm some kind of a fruity guy" (Beacon, 5/1/89 interview). Indeed, I overheard several boys remark that one of the few developmentalist men teachers was homosexual. When I asked one to elaborate, he would only say, "[The teacher] acts like a fairy and has an attitude" (field notes, 3/17/89). (Some girl students thought this particular teacher was gay, too, but the possibility evoked more curiosity than hostility from them.)

This polarity between developmentalist-feminine and traditionalist-masculine styles affected the engagement process in several ways. First, some traditionalist men said they expected more out of boys because they saw them as the future breadwinners:

> I'm a little more lax with the girls. I'm really kind of tough on the guys only because I feel for them probably a little bit more because they got more responsibility to carry, seems like to me. . . . *Eventually, they're going to be providers,* so I try to really get them to be more serious with the things they do, to commit a little bit more. (La Fuente, 6/8/89 interview, emphasis added)

> They [male students] can't be carried for the rest of their lives. When they go to work, who's going to carry them? You're fired, you know, you don't get paid. (La Fuente, 6/9/89 interview)

---

6. Like many of the traditionalist men teachers, a number of male students associated a developmentalist style with femininity, something to be shunned. When a developmentalist teacher-counselor and I trained a group of students to go talk to junior high students about the transition to high school, a group of boys wanted to use what they called a "Scared Straight" approach. In the movie by that name, streetwise ex-cons talk tough to teenagers about what lies in store for them if they continue to use and deal drugs.

For their part, most male students said in interviews that boys were treated worse than girls in school (35 percent) or at least different (21 percent); no boys felt they had been treated better than girls. This may explain why two-thirds of the boys asked said they thought their experience *in school* would have been better if they had been born female. Fifteen percent of the girls interviewed agreed that girls were treated better in school. The most common reason students of both sexes gave for their answer was that boys were disciplined more often, more harshly, or both, although most girls and some boys qualified this: they reasoned that boys were more prone to act in ways that would result in punishment, not that teachers and administrators favored girls.

Second, the traditionalists' concern for maintaining hierarchical control, particularly in combination with individual men teachers' propensity for motivating students through teasing, sometimes seemed to interfere with the male teacher–male learner relationship. The following is a typical exchange from one such classroom:

> Mr. Lopez walked around the classroom, helping students. He noticed a boy apparently daydreaming and commented: "Adrian, you're a piece of wood. That goes for some of you others. Sheriff [Mr. Lopez's nickname for an African-American boy in the corner], you think you're real tough, don't you? You can't divide thirty-six by three." After a pause, "Sheriff" muttered to himself, "Anyone can tell you it's twelve." (La Fuente, field notes, 5/24/89)

Although most students seemed to recognize such comments were meant as playful teasing, others confessed in interviews that this approach discouraged them from asking questions. "If you don't get it the first time," one African-American male student said, "[some teachers] will say they don't want to have to repeat it. [Mimicking an authoritarian teacher]: 'You knucklehead' " (La Fuente, 10/20/88 group discussion). Such students seemed highly at risk of being sent out of class: frustrated or emboldened by the teacher's teasing, they infringed on the teacher's authority by refusing to work, for example, or coming to the defense of a classmate being disciplined (La Fuente, field notes, 5/17/89).

Adding to the traditionalists' propensity to "crack down," as one teacher explained, was the open-entry feature of continuation schools. He wanted to be "nice" at the start of a grading period because new students were present, but then "one of the students [who] has been here for awhile will show off in front of the new students. So they're flaunting this at me, and I really try to sit on them. But it comes out to the new ones as [I'm] a hard guy, not fair" (La Fuente, 6/8/89 interview).

Some evidence points to the fact that boys react differently for women and men teachers. In a conflict, certain boys were quick to assume a fighting posture (remove their jacket, hold their chin up, and so on) with men teachers and administrators (field notes, 10/28/88, 3/21/89, 5/11/89, 4/4/90). Just the implied threat of physical violence can feed intolerance for even minor challenges to their authority because, as one tradition-alist put it, "somewhere there has to be a cutoff." The dynamic was not lost on students:

> [Mr. Berg] has this teen phobia. . . . You hear about gangs, and Berg, I guess it scares him cuz I guess he hears, "Berg, you tell on me, I'll kill you," like that. It kinda scares you, especially if you're at the age of forty-five, fifty. (David, Beacon)

A woman teacher, who combined a traditionalist outlook with some developmentalist practices, voiced what I had observed in her classroom:

> Boys are easier for me [to teach], and I think part of it is be-cause they react to me differently. Here I am a little old lady type, grandmother type . . . and they're inclined to be very gentle with me. *When I give them what for, they'll take it.* Girls are more inclined to become defensive than the guys are. (La Fuente, 5/18/89 interview; emphasis added)

Another example: I observed a woman substitute teacher send a male student to the office for being disruptive, unjustly, he felt. Explaining his side of the story to me, he concluded: "I swear I would have hit her if she'd been a man" (Beacon, field notes, 3/27/89).

A third way the gender-differentiated split in teaching styles af-fected the engagement process had to do with the developmentalists' greater willingness to discuss their personal lives, admit to human frail-ties, and concede some of the inherent inequities in the teacher-student relationship. These factors seemed to encourage students to open up, a key element in the reengagement process.

> [Being a teacher] is like being a mother. I've got a lot of kids [of my own], and I always had the same feeling with them: *"You're going to have to take me for all my foibles just like I have to take you."* There's that mutual respect for humanness that becomes ex-tremely important, particularly in schools. (La Fuente, 5/18/89 interview; emphasis added)

Men, somewhat across teaching approaches, seemed to feel that too much openness about their feelings was unmanly. In a revealing exchange, a woman teacher-counselor, Mrs. Smith, told a man teacher-counselor, Mr. Ullmann, and me about an incident in which a boy counselee had made her cry. She had apologized to him over a minor classroom matter, but he had refused to forgive her and was verbally abusive. Mrs. Smith justified her action by stating her belief that parents should not always hide their feelings from their children and, further, that the student might learn to be more empathetic if he saw the effect his actions had on her. Mr. Ullmann strongly disagreed. He felt that students should never see school "personnel" cry because it signaled "weakness." Mrs. Smith replied that men expressed their emotions through yelling and aggressive posturing and that these modes of expression alienated students (Beacon, field notes, 2/7/89).

Although the two teacher-counselors did not discuss their differences further (in my presence, at least), they seemed to hold two different conceptions of power. For Mr. Ullmann, teacher-student power relations were a zero-sum game: what teachers relinquished in matters of top-down control could not be reclaimed and put in service of another goal. Rather than hierarchical domination, Mrs. Smith assumed a notion of power as "the ability to get things done, to mobilize resources, to get and use whatever it is that a person needs for the goals he or she is attempting to meet" (Kanter, 1977: 166). Her strategy risked overinvolvement, but Mrs. Smith believed that relative openness about her emotional relationship to students and building empathy were ultimately resources for getting students to learn more.

Fourth, given the developmentalists' broader educational goals (that is personal growth, not just knowledge acquisition), they were sometimes more keyed into issues like student choice in dress[7] and even in steady dating partners. Unless they were tactful and caring, teachers' comments could provoke angry outbursts from students. Traditionalists, who saw themselves only as subject-matter experts, felt such personal matters were illegitimate teacher concerns. When a developmentalist mentioned in the faculty room that she planned to talk with a boy student who was dating a girl the teacher considered promiscuous and not too bright, a tradi-

---

7. I heard only women teachers comment on students' dress. Comments usually focused on girls' outfits considered too revealing, although one woman teacher told her class that the lycra biker shorts many boys were wearing "leave nothing to the imagination" (La Fuente, field notes, 5/10/89). The women argued that risque outfits distracted male students. Perhaps some men teachers felt this way, too, but to comment would imply they had noticed and were perhaps lascivious. Besides discipline, the women teachers seemed worried about the type of boyfriends that girls would attract by "dressing to impress"—and type of boyfriend was a critical factor in how seriously many girls took school.

tionalist told her to mind her own business: "You're not his mother!" (La Fuente, field notes, 10/11/89).

Fifth, sexuality—influenced by the age, appearance, and personality of teachers—further complicated the effects of gender on teacher-student relations (compare Wolpe, 1988). Certain teachers used their sexual appeal, unwittingly it seemed, to motivate learning and maintain discipline. Students used their sexuality, too, to break the routine and bend the rules. This dynamic created opportunities for engagement as well as disengagement, as the following examples will show.

Relatively young, attractive teachers can be particularly appealing to students of the other sex. One woman teacher had a following of some male students, whom other teachers considered discipline problems, because she knew how to play to their egos. Her highest compliment for boys ("you guys are tough") linked a trait they valued—toughness—with academic achievement. "You're the only teacher I'd do homework for, Miz Wilson," a boy—otherwise concerned not to appear bookish—announced for all to hear (La Fuente, field notes, 11/16/88).

A man teacher a number of girls described as "sexy" explained how student crushes were a double-edged sword: he could use his appeal to motivate attendance, but it made discipline more difficult because a cross word from him could be misinterpreted as a judgment about the girls' attractiveness to all members of the other sex:

> I've got two girls first period, and we fight. It's really cute. I think they like me, and that's why they're still here [in school]. . . . I feel really concerned for them and at the same time, too, we've got to get the work done. So things don't really click, and then they go off on their own little bit of a hangup which interferes. And then I add more interference when I scold them because they get turned off." (La Fuente, 6/8/89 interview)

For this reason, older men sometimes had more success in drawing the most disengaged girls, especially the shy or isolated ones, out of their shell, as I observed was the case with a teacher at Beacon.

> I'll be the first to say I flirt cuz I don't think it hurts anybody. It's harmless because of my age. If I was twenty-four and flirting, I think I'd find myself in trouble cuz they get these crushes. No girl is going to get a crush on a sixty-year-old man. (Beacon, 5/1/89 interview)

Women, too, seemed to be able to employ their sexuality to maintain classroom discipline without disrupting the teacher-learner relationship. An example from La Fuente:

Lance and Patrick kept singing, trying to impress Ms. Wilson. Angry at the disruption, she told them, "You need lessons." A few minutes later, they both looked jealous when the teacher praised two other boys for the essays they wrote: "You guys are tough." Lance and Patrick did not disrupt the class again that day. (field notes, 5/17/89)

Under similar circumstances, men teachers seemed more likely to risk getting into a fight with girls that could result in the students being kicked out of class or to risk being perceived by other students, both male and female, as "perverts."

Gina enjoyed kidding around with Mr. Lopez. Like a number of tough girls, she enjoyed breaking gender stereotypes; they enjoyed riding motorcycles, physical fighting, and openly lusting after boys. Although she and her crowd shunned "dainty" or "prissy" mannerisms and dress, they often wore makeup and occasionally outfits considered sexually provocative.[8] (Depending mainly on their size and how "buff" [muscular] the tough girls were, other students considered them to be either "major sleazes" or "dykes.") Gina liked to call Mr. Lopez "the little man" and then offer to build him a stepstool to reach the chalkboard. In a seeming effort to bring her back into line, he would draw attention to her personal appearance by asking, "When are you going to comb your hair?" In response to her tougher style, he called her by her last name as he would the boys. One day Gina came to the defense of another student Mr. Lopez was disciplining, so he had her removed from his class. She was so upset, she dropped out for the remainder of the school year (La Fuente, field notes, 4/26/89, 5/17/89, and 6/9/89).

In student interviews, when asked the open-ended question "Do you think girls were treated differently than boys at your old school?", 13 percent of the girls and 24 percent of the boys mentioned that some male teachers were "perverts." Girls interpreted perversion to mean unwanted sexual attention:

I didn't like my first period teacher at all because he's our wrestling coach. Maybe he didn't see it as the type of way I'm going to say it, but this is the way I saw it, and this is the way a lot of girls saw it. He would come over to help us with our work, he

8. One particular type of tough girl was the "hair bear," so called because of the ratted out bangs piled as high as hairspray would allow. Most hair bears were Mexican-American, and though not all were tough, their leaders usually were. Heavy eye makeup, long permed—and sometimes bleached—hair, lycra biker shorts, and a love of high energy dance music were other shared conventions.

would hover over us and he would have to have his arm around us, and I just felt like, "OK, you're not my boyfriend. Get away. Get away before I hit you." I mean, I didn't like it. (Carmen, La Fuente)

Linda: Yeah, the male teachers are like perverts.

DK: Can you give me an example?

Linda: OK. My freshman year I used to do a lot of drugs, and I used to be like super, super skinny, and I used to wear a lot of sexy like provocative clothes, you can say. And they'd sit me right in front of their desk.

DK: Like assigned seating?

Linda: Yeah, but only for me. It was weird. . . .

DK: Did that make you want to come to class, or not?

Linda: No, that made me not want to come to class. That's when I stopped dressing that way cuz I realized . . . "God, I don't even want to come to school and have a bunch of eyes on me." (La Fuente)

Boys, more often, mentioned girls getting special treatment: "Say the teacher's in his forties or something, and the girl is sixteen and real pretty: he'll do favors for her," explained one (Taylor, Beacon). Such accounts failed to recognize that many girls considered the extra attention a form of sexual harassment.

No women teachers were described as "perverts," probably reflecting a wider cultural assumption that adult women are less sexually aggressive, particularly toward teenage boys. Even if that were assumed, the flirting of female teachers did not seem to strike male students as potentially harmful.

In summary, traditionalist, particularly men, teachers sometimes expected more from boys and interacted with them in ways that could interfere with the teacher-learner relationship. At the same time, certain boys reacted differently to men teachers, making them especially vulnerable to punishment by traditionalist men teachers and administrators. Although I observed that developmentalists were more likely to bond with students, they ran the risk of alienating boys and especially girls by getting too personal. Put another way, in attempting to resolve teacher-student conflict, traditionalists risked exerting power through domination, and because boys were more likely to resist this head on, they were more at risk of serious punishment. Developmentalists risked exerting power indirectly through manipulation, and students sensing this resented not being treated as responsible young adults.

Although some teachers succeeded in using their sex appeal to motivate and discipline students, this approach was hazardous, especially for men teachers and a subset of girl rule-breakers. These girls were sometimes encouraged to be impertinent because they could get away with it, but only up to a point, and were quicker to take offense at teachers' personal remarks. If men teachers touched the girls, as they did the boys, or expressed too much concern, students sometimes construed these actions sexually (compare Davies, 1984: 83–84).

5

REASONS FOR AND TIMING OF DISENGAGEMENT BY GENDER

The preceding chapter showed that, although there are significant exceptions, girls at Beacon and La Fuente generally disengaged in ways less likely to bring them into contact with school authorities and to get them suspended or expelled. Their symptoms and styles of disengagement sometimes differed from those of boys. This chapter discusses the prominent reasons for school disengagement identified by students. The symptoms, styles, and underlying causes of school disengagement were not always easy to distinguish. My purpose in this chapter, therefore, is not to establish causality or to determine the independent influence of sometimes very artificially separated factors, but to identify and detail reciprocal influences.

I draw upon what students said about their experiences in both the comprehensive and continuation high schools and weigh these formal interviews against what I observed them do and say informally within the continuation school setting. I found that most girls, like most boys, reported conflict with teachers and peers and said it was a fundamental reason for leaving the comprehensive high school (see table 5). In general, girls also disengaged for a few reasons that differed from those given by boys (for girls the reasons included a stronger reaction to institutional labeling practices, domestic responsibilities often associated with early mothering, and marriage; for boys, paid labor), although these were often symptomatic of the same underlying disaffection from school. The relationships (with boyfriends, girlfriends, family members) from which girls derived support, satisfaction, and status also contributed to their disengagement when they conflicted and competed for the girls' loyalty.

TABLE 5

What Students Disliked about Comprehensive High School by Ethnicity,
Sex, and School (In Percentages)

	Total	Ethnicity		Sex		School	
		White	Other	Boy	Girl	Beacon	La Fuente
	$N=82$	$n=24$	$n=58$	$n=35$	$n=47$	$n=39$	$n=43$
Teachers/staff	67	75	64	69	66*	72	63
Do not care	32	33	26	17	43	36	21
Misc. conflict	26	29	21	40	15	26	21
Are biased	13	4	9	17	11	5	9
Peer conflict	57	63	55	60	55	49	65
Jocks/preps	27	42	21	23	30	31	23
Ethnic	18	25	16	26	13	10	26
Bullies	12	17	10	20	6	10	14
Former friends	5	0	7	0	9	3	7
Gangs	4	0	5	6	2	3	5
Unclear	2	0	3	0	4	0	5
School rules/ bureaucracy	49	50	48	49	49	72	28*
Schedule	38	46	34	40	36	38	37
Homework	33	54	24*	31	34	59	9*
School work							
Boring	29	46	22	31	28	33	26
Too hard	17	17	17	11	21	18	17
Counseling	28	46	21	20	34	31	26
School or class size	27	50	17*	23	30	28	26
Tracking	20	33	14	14	23	23	16

Note: Columns do not add to 100 percent because most students cited several things they did not like about comprehensive high school. An asterisk indicates that the observed difference (either between sexes, ethnic groups, or schools) is statistically significant at $p < .05$, using the chi-square statistic.

After exploring these similarities and differences, I show that the timing of disengagement differed somewhat for girls. While a significant group of boys had already disengaged by the end of elementary school, most girls described the transition from junior high to high school as particularly critical. This reflects girls' responses to the changing organizational structure of school as well as the onset of puberty, given that girls seem to derive more status through informal social channels (participation in extracurricular activities, relationships with female peers and boyfriends) than through academic and athletic achievement. Low achievers aggressively pursued alternatives (sometimes resulting in entangling love relationships, early pregnancy, or both), while high achievers agonized over popularity and attractiveness.

FIGHTING

The two most common themes in student explanations of why they disengaged from the comprehensive high school revolved around conflict with teachers and administrators and with peers. In fact, the two types of conflict were sometimes linked. Some continuation students felt they had been blamed and punished more harshly for behavior that preps and jocks got away with only because school authorities saw the latter groups as contributing to the good reputation of the school through high scholastic and athletic achievement.

Conflict with Teachers and Administrators

Two-thirds of those interviewed complained about at least some teachers and administrators, and most linked conflict with school staff directly to their disengagement. About one-fifth of the students saw themselves as pushouts from the comprehensive high school. Across ethnic groups and schools, boys were significantly more likely to say that they fought with some or most teachers, up to and including physical confrontation. Girls were more likely to say, "Teachers don't care." Relatively fewer students of both sexes spontaneously reported specific instances of teacher and administrator bias, but boys were more likely to do so than girls (see table 5).

These gender differences were not manifest when, later in the interview schedule, I asked students to describe their favorite and least favorite teachers and what qualities they looked for in a good teacher. Boys were just as likely as girls to mention "caring"; indeed, this quality was universally valued (mentioned by 96 percent of those asked). And girls were just as likely as boys to say a good teacher should be fair (44 and 47 percent, respectively) and to protest prejudice based on ethnicity, gender, subcultural style, or ability. Only one-third mentioned that a good teacher should be knowledgeable, able to communicate ideas clearly, and other traits related to technical competence and pedagogy. These respondents did not differ by gender, ethnicity, or school but were usually students who liked to learn, were relatively academically engaged, and thus were considered intellectual within the continuation school setting.

These findings shed some light on the debate over whether the ethic of care should be seen as a category of gender difference; see Tronto (1987) for a review.[1] Carol Gilligan and her associates have found, for example, that women's moral statements are often expressed in terms of caring, as opposed to justice (Gilligan, 1982). At first glance, one might interpret my findings as supporting this. The fact that almost all students valued caring highly in a teacher, however, suggests that this ethic may stem from their secondary status. They occupied subordinate positions within society on the basis of their ethnicity, class background, or both, as well as their current social and academic standing within the schooling system. The boys seemed more reluctant to express the ethic of care when describing why they personally disliked school, preferring to emphasize their toughness by relating how and why they clashed with school authorities. In the context of describing a good teacher in the abstract, though, the mention of caring did not imply vulnerability (namely that they *personally* needed or wanted a teacher to be concerned or interested in them).

One-third of the students interviewed spontaneously cited various forms of prejudice—based on gender, ethnicity, academic ability, or subcultural style—as the source of their conflict with comprehensive school staff members and occasionally with continuation staff, too. More than one-tenth of the girls said they had encountered sexism in the classroom or elsewhere on campus; no boys mentioned this.

> The first day [of class], I was the only girl . . . who showed up.
> . . . I wanted to sit in the back, and he [the teacher] made me
> sit in the front. He kept puttin' down girls, puttin' down girls,
> sayin' that we're stupid, cuz he kept forgettin' I was in there. So
> finally I just kept sayin', "Shut up. Shut up." Ever since then,
> when all of a sudden girls started poppin' up, he slacked off.
> (Nancy, La Fuente)

Thirteen percent of interviewees said that some teachers were racially biased; for reasons discussed in the next section, ethnic minority and male students were more likely to report this. While I did not observe many blatant examples of ethnic prejudice in classrooms, a few white teachers I interviewed, both in the continuation schools and in the comprehensive feeder schools, held some negative stereotypes of ethnic

---

1. In addition to the debate over whether the ethic of care should be seen as a category of gender difference, feminist and other scholars have debated both the extent of gender difference with respect to moral development, the origins of such a gender difference if it does exist, as well as the adequacy of Lawrence Kohlberg's cognitive-developmental theory which informs the debate.

minority students. The most shocking example came in response to a question I asked about whether ethnicity affected the disengagement process:

> I would say the blacks, for example, they're more fun loving. You know, they just, if you get one in the class by himself, he's pretty good. If you get two, he's not as good. If you get three, forget it type of thing. They just go to school because they have fun. I think the Mexican tends to be more lazy. And, well, the kids we get here in the Oriental set, they're usually not with it. If an Oriental kid gets here, he's pretty bad off because . . . [usually] they are good students. (La Fuente)

Almost one-third of all students—across ethnicity, gender, and school—mentioned that teachers had pegged them as "troublemakers" based on surface appearances. In analyzing these comments, I found that half of the girls and none of the boys interpreted troublemaker to mean "dumb" (a low achiever), while all of the boys and half of the girls interpreted it to mean disruptive. This difference, statistically significant, seemed to reflect three factors.

First, boys were more prone to clown around and disrupt class to cover up learning difficulties, express boredom with the curriculum, or enliven regimented classrooms, which then got them into trouble. "It's OK for a girl to ask questions and to be dumb," Joan, a Beacon student, told me. "But the guys I know, they don't always ask the questions that they want, especially if they have friends in the class [because] they don't want to appear really stupid." This behavior pattern provides one explanation for the identification and placement of more boys than girls into alternative programs. In special education, for example, teachers play a key role in referring students out for testing, and they refer more boys to special education than girls (Butler-Nalin and Padilla, 1989: 4).[2] One naturalistic study found that teachers tended to attribute boys' school difficulties to unruly classroom behavior and "cast boys in negative terms," whereas teachers spoke of girls more positively and attributed girls' failure to a lack of ability (Mehan, Hertweck, and Meihls, 1986: 148–50).

Second, more girls appeared to have lower self-esteem than boys. Several of the girls made flat pronouncements in interviews like "I'm not a smart person" (Beverly, La Fuente). In an ironic exchange during

2. According to data from the National Longitudinal Study of Special Education Students, 68.5 percent of youth with disabilities are male, 31.5 percent female. Boys are primarily overrepresented among youth with learning disabilities, the largest special education category (Butler-Nalin and Padilla, 1989: 3–4).

a unit on self-esteem, the teacher asked a Latina to define self-esteem. "I don't know," she insisted. "What does that tell us about you?" the teacher persisted. The girl, obviously chagrined, replied: "That I'm an airhead" (La Fuente, field notes, 4/26/89). Simmons and Blyth (1987) review the literature on gender differences in adolescent self-esteem; their own longitudinal study found that white girls' self-esteem was significantly lower than boys' in grades six through ten.

Third, some girls held generally favorable opinions of themselves but displayed a greater willingness than boys to admit publicly to school failure even while rejecting the labels "dumb" and "troublemaker." Maria, a Beacon student, was one such girl:

> I would treat them [the teachers] nice. I would be just sitting there quiet sometimes and they'd be, "Well, what's your problem? Can't you sit up? Can't you do your work? Are you stupid, or what?" And it'd make me go off, you know, because I would listen to my mom [who advised the Golden Rule], but they would just treat you like you're some idiot that doesn't know anything because you're not on the student council or you don't get straight A's or you're not a cheerleader.

As Maria makes clear, exclusion from the three common sources of status within the high school (athletics, academics, and government) can inspire rebellion. Many of the subcultures that continuation students identified with formed partly in opposition to the schooling system that marginalized them. One-tenth of the students interviewed mentioned examples of teacher bias against certain subcultural styles. Still others were convinced that this occurred, although not to them personally:

> If you dress a certain way, they [teachers] tend to pay less attention to you. Say if you were a stoner or say if you were a thug off the street or whatever, they think that you're hopeless. They know that it—not that it necessarily will be harder—but they have an idea in their head that it'll be harder to teach this child and that he'll put you through this and that, so they just don't bother with him. (Mike, La Fuente)

Compared to one's gender, ethnicity, and academic ability, students exercise more control over their personal style and the friends they have. For this reason, some school staff members see subcultural style as a legitimate basis for discrimination and act on it, thus further alienating rebellious students from school and the opportunity to learn. In labeling theory, Lemert referred to this process as secondary deviance, whereby so-called deviants have had to form "their whole persona around the deviant role to cope with problems arising from the application of the label" (Davies, 1984: 186). Mandy, part of the stoner crowd, identified the last year of junior high as a time when she might have got back on track academically, given a caring teacher:

> I think that if the teachers would have tried to talk to me and say, "Well, you could do better," and tried to change—be more like a friend [in order] to change me—then maybe I would have got out [of being a stoner] and said, "Well, he really wants to help me, so I'll go and change *for him.*" But in the long run it would have been for me. (La Fuente; emphasis in original)

Mandy underscores the point that students need to relate to a teacher first as a person in order to be motivated to learn, especially when they are too young to connect schooling with employment possibilities.

Few students mentioned instances of teacher bias based on socioeconomic status, although I interpreted some of the examples students cited of ethnic and subcultural discrimination as partly involving socioeconomic status. Although students implicated teachers above all, most teachers I interviewed at the continuation and feeder high schools, with a few notable exceptions, cited the home environment and values as a root cause of student disengagement. In student accounts of conflict with teachers, I often read cases of submerged class and ethnic tension. Lorena describes a major fight with a teacher who questioned the way she dressed:

> I got kicked out cuz of my teacher. Me and my girlfriend, our pants, OK, they were kinda tight, but I had just washed my pants and you know how they shrink up? If I want to wear my pants like that. She's all telling me that I shouldn't wear pants like that, *how does our mothers dress and what do they think about it.* You know, getting off on our parents, I mean! If they're going to bitch at me for something, hey, that's me. But *if they don't like my parents, they shouldn't say nothing cuz I'm very protective of my parents.* We got in a big old fight about it. She pushed me, so I hit her, and I got kicked out. . . . It's just the way I am. I don't like anybody to put down my family. (Lorena, La Fuente; emphasis added)

In fact, Lorena's mother, and other women in her community, dressed very much as Lorena did, so Lorena interpreted the teacher's comment as a profound insult, whether intended or not.

Submerged class and ethnic conflict continued to fuel the disengagement process at the continuation schools. Nowhere was this more evident than in the disagreements over child-rearing practices that arose between school-age mothers (white, African-American, and Latino) and the teachers and administrators (mainly African-American and Latino) who promoted middle-class norms. Like the white working-class parents interviewed by Rubin (1976: esp. 126–27), a number of the young mothers favored tough discipline so that their children would learn more and do better than they perceived they had done in school and elsewhere. "I don't like the way I turned out as a kid, and I don't want my son to turn out like that," explained Mandy, a La Fuente student.

> She [an administrator] expects me not to scold my son [for "throwing a fit"]. I tell her, "I'm going to scold him. You can kick me out of the program. I'm going to scold him because when he gets home, he's going to think I won't scold him there either, and he's going to get away with it."

Inherent in most examples of child-rearing strategies I heard about and observed were conflicts between individualism and self-expression (fostered by middle-class staff members) and obedience to authority (fostered by working-class students).

Over such issues, I knew of one girl who was "kicked out of the [SAM] program" and another who quit; both eventually left school altogether, partly because they could not afford to pay for child care on their own (La Fuente, field notes, 9/20/88, 9/21/88, 10/5/88, 11/3/88, 12/7/88). Others had verbally sparred with teachers and risked losing SAM privileges. Nora complained about a teacher who had criticized her for spanking her eighteen-month-old daughter:

> She talks about her family all the time like they were the Waltons. She wants our families to be more like hers and less like they are. I've got my daughter in line. She's toilet trained and off her bottle. She was ready because she was talking and could understand. I don't beat her, but she needs the discipline. (field notes, 3/29/89)

In most instances, teachers assumed that the child-rearing practices of students like Nora and Mandy were born of ignorance, poor parental role models in their own lives, or both, rather than developed "as adaptive strategies that help people to cope with external constraints" (Lubeck, 1988: 46).

Peer Conflict

In *The Hidden Injuries of Class*, Sennett and Cobb (1972: 96–97) describe a boy's shame caused by a teacher not treating him as an individual because of his low academic ability. The boy responded in anger at the situation by attacking those not shamed, his peers whose ability had been rewarded (compare Schwartz, 1981: 107–8). (As he reached adulthood, the boy directed anger at himself, too, for lacking the inner resources to be successful.) I detected a similar dynamic at work— shaped not only by relations of class but of ethnicity and gender as well—in a number of student accounts. More than half mentioned peer-related conflict as one reason they disliked the comprehensive school, while 12 percent mentioned this as the decisive factor in getting them off track: either they were kicked out for fighting or decided they could no longer cope with peer conflict and stopped attending.

These figures are higher than those reported in national surveys of dropouts. For example, in the High School and Beyond survey, about 6 percent of the students, across sex and ethnic groups, said they dropped out because they could not get along with other students (Peng and Takai, 1983). There are at least two explanations for this difference. First, not all continuation students have or will drop out, but a number of them end up in an alternative setting because of fighting. Second, admitting to being unable to get along with other students is not socially acceptable. Students may be more willing to talk about this conflict in an interview with someone they know because they can provide a contextual explanation to justify their actions.

Girls were nearly as likely as boys to say that they had difficulty getting along with certain groups of students, though the reasons for conflict differed somewhat. The tough girls had often fought physically and had thus been pushed out of the comprehensive school. "At [my old school], the guys were more the bad guys; the girls were good girls. Here, everybody's created equal: the girls screwed up as much as the guys" (Matt, La Fuente).

Overall, the most common source of conflict was the high school social system that pitted numerous subgroups against the "high crowd," the jocks (athletes, cheerleaders, and their friends) and the preps (those in college preparatory classes, often involved in student government and other activities). But at La Fuente, slightly more students mentioned ethnic-based conflict than fighting with jocks and preps (see table 5). In fact, the two types of conflict were closely interconnected, more or less depending on the ethnic composition of the feeder high school a student had attended and which ethnic group was perceived to dominate the ranks of the jocks and preps.

In discussing their troubles at school, boys were twice as likely as girls to mention ethnic conflict (26 versus 13 percent)[3] and more than three times as likely to mention getting caught up in tests of power or strength (20 versus 6 percent), a category I have labeled "bullies" in table 5. In addition, almost half (46 percent) of the boys interviewed felt they had been "treated differently" by peers, teachers, or both at school based on their ethnicity, while only one-quarter (26 percent) of the girls mentioned this. An additional 13 percent of the girls versus 3 percent of the boys spontaneously mentioned the existence of ethnic prejudice, although they had not personally felt victimized by it at school.

Several factors might explain these differences. First, boys were more likely to belong to gangs or informal groups like car clubs which were usually ethnically and neighborhood-based. Six percent of boys and 2 percent of girls spontaneously mentioned gang fighting in the interviews. Seven percent of the 111 students surveyed anonymously at La Fuente cited gang rivalry as a common reason that high school students get into fights with each other, and peer pressure to create and maintain a tough reputation was mentioned by an additional quarter. "That has a lot to do with school," Matt told me. "Personally, I couldn't do my work knowing people are going to jump me. It's happened that way all my life" (La Fuente). These fears were real. In an orientation class at La Fuente, rival gang members exchanged insults. That night, one shot and wounded the other. He was arrested at school the next day (field notes, 4/25–26/89).

Second, boys reported experiencing more ethnic prejudice outside of school than girls did and this appeared to make them more sensitive to it while at school. Police stopped them in the street without reason, they asserted, and certain store owners and managers eyed them suspiciously and refused to consider their job applications seriously. David, a Filipino-Hawaiian, applied for several sales jobs at an upscale shopping mall with no luck. He concluded that "they only seem to hire whites that dress well. The minorities are only hired to work at fast food places or [as] stock boys" (Beacon, 4/26/88 group discussion).

A third reason boys were more likely to report ethnic conflict with peers involved interethnic dating. Boys more often took the initiative in

---

3. Twelve percent of the 111 students surveyed anonymously at La Fuente mentioned "racism" as a common reason for fighting. Only half of the respondents indicated their sex on the survey; of those who did, boys and girls were equally likely to mention ethnic prejudice.

asking girls out on dates—and were perceived as the initiator even in cases where they were not. Sometimes a boy dating a girl not of his ethnicity would be attacked by other boys who claimed to be "protecting their own." Daniel, an African-American student at Beacon, said he had "Harley-Davidson white dudes" at school calling him "nigger" and writing "KKK" (Ku Klux Klan) on his notebook, partly out of jealousy: "I was more friends with a lot of the white girls than I was the white guys." Girls occasionally fought other girls for similar reasons. Tanya, a white Beacon student, said a group of African-American girls beat her up because they did not want her dating a Mexican boy they liked, and I witnessed a Chicana being harassed by her former friends, mainly white, after her love relationship with an African-American man became known (Beacon, field notes, 11/15/88).

Girls who cited peer conflict as a reason for their disengagement most often mentioned the comprehensive high school's polarized social structure. While boys mentioned this second after ethnic conflict, their comments were usually less detailed and intense. Common examples included jocks wanting to fight them because their nonconformist style posed an inherent challenge to the established order. In contrast, most girls focused on the pressure to be popular. They rarely mentioned academics or athletics as direct sources of popularity, citing instead the few social sources: cheerleading, student government, and association with the in-crowd, both male and female. Each of these sources was influenced by academic standing because one could not participate in sports, cheering, or student government without maintaining a C grade point average, and the in-crowd was made up of fairly good students— but not "brains" or "nerds." Maria, whose grade point average prevented her from cheerleading, complained, "[I hate] the way they run everything over at [names old school]. Like I was asking my friend, 'Who made homecoming queen and everything?' There was no one who made it who was not either a cheerleader or on the Council" (Beacon).

While a number of continuation students had participated in school athletics, this did not translate into popularity for the girls as much as it did for the boys, given community and school focus on boys' sports. As one girl put it, "The girls are getting more involved in sports, [and] they get praise, too, but not like the guys. The guys—they're our school" (Jacqueline, La Fuente). Cheerleading was associated with popularity, but, in general, relatively few such positions were available compared with sports. Given that the paths to status are narrower for girls, it is not surprising that they expressed a more intense dislike of, and frustration with, the system.

Stinchcombe (1964) made a related argument. He posited that girls are more likely to key into informal status systems (based partly on family background),[4] such as the ranking of students by personality, because these bear more on their success in the "marriage market" than academic success. Boys stake their self-esteem more on the formal status system of academics because success in this area is perceived to be linked directly to future success in the labor market. In testing his argument, however, Stinchcombe found that participation in student activities (clubs, social affairs, and so on) was a confounding variable: girls participated in these more than boys, and this seemed to lessen their alienation from the informal social system. The girls who did not participate in student activities—and this describes a sizable number of continuation students—were even more rebellious than their disengaged male counterparts (ibid.: esp. 34–36).

Several types of data support the argument that girls were more likely to invest their self-respect in the (sometimes not so) future marriage market and thus to react more strongly against peers who seemed to threaten their prospects. In the La Fuente survey of why high school students fight each other, 17 percent (mostly girls) specifically mentioned girlfriend or boyfriend problems, usually fighting same-sex peers over a member of the other sex. In both the survey and in interviews, although boys reported fighting other boys, a vocal and misogynist subgroup ultimately blamed girls for the conflict. They argued that girls had "PMS" (pre-menstrual syndrome) and spread "rumors" that they had been cheating on their girlfriends. From these boys' perspective, rumors were rumors even if certainly true. The bigger wrong was not in their lying to girlfriends, but in girls stirring up trouble ("girls talk shit"). Matt, angry at his girlfriend for starting "rumors" that he was a "snake" because he was "seeing other girls," concluded: "Girls cause more gossip. A girl can be outside at lunch gossiping, but then she stops in class and does her work. The guy gets pissed off and takes it to class and gets in trouble for not working" (La Fuente). Boys like Matt did not acknowledge how the sexual double standard—which prescribes monogamy for women while condoning multiple sex partners for men—limited girls' sexual activity lest their reputations be tarnished.

A few girls reported—always in journal writing, never in interviews—dating boys without their steady boyfriend's knowledge. But as Beverly put it: "Boys it seems flaunt what they do. Everything they do they seem to flaunt. Girls, they seem to hide it. They feel they have a reputation to keep" (La Fuente). Carmen summed up the sexual double

---

4. Stinchcombe defined status system as "a socially established pattern of judgment of persons, with respect to their relative worth" (1964: 26).

standard this way: "If you're a guy, you have to sleep with a girl by a certain age or you're considered a wimp. And the girl, if you do, you're a sleaze" (La Fuente).

Occasionally, girls reported fighting their boyfriends over infidelities. But more often girls would fight each other, some in defense of their sexual reputation, others to hold onto their boyfriend or intended boyfriend. Dressing provocatively or flirting made girls particularly vulnerable to gossip, although simply having a voluptuous figure could spark rumors. Both boys and girls gossiped about "sluts," "hoes" (whores), "prick teases," or "players" (the latter term was also used to describe "scamming" boys). Some of the boys seemed motivated by jealousy or spite; either they wanted to date these girls, who, in turn, often preferred to go out with older men, or the boys wanted to hurt former girlfriends by damaging their sexual reputations.

Other girls disliked female "flirts" because they allegedly competed "unfairly" for boyfriends. As one Latina, herself the target of rumors, explained:

Some girls see it [a miniskirt] looks nice on you and they're jealous. So they go to the store and buy the same skirt, but they don't have the same body shape at all, so it doesn't look the same. And they want to have some attraction to guys, but they just can't because [of] their body. (Isabel, La Fuente, 2/2/89 group discussion)

When asked if they had been treated differently at school because of the way they looked, 13 percent of the girls interviewed said other students thought they looked "loose" sexually, while another 13 percent interpreted the question this way but said it had not happened to them personally; no boys mentioned this. (In addition, 11 percent of girls and 3 percent of boys interpreted the question of differential treatment in terms of negative physical characteristics such as being considered fat or ugly. I recorded more instances of girls being judged by peers along this dimension in field notes; both sexes were distressed by such judgments as they affected their dating—and later, marriage—opportunities.)

All but two of the girls who had been called "loose" attended La Fuente, and they stressed that their pregnancy or the mere existence of the SAM program on campus contributed to their sexual reputation. Explained Patricia: "I realized that when I was pregnant, they would look at me funny. 'Oh, she's easy.' 'Oh, look at her, she opened her legs' " (La Fuente). Despite their looks and style, some girls managed to avoid the reputation of being "easy" because they received good grades and demonstrated their competence in class. Anita, a Mexican-American student at La Fuente, was one:

> If you hang around someone [female] who goes out a lot, they think like you're easy or something. But I don't think they really think that about me cuz I'm pretty smart in class and stuff so they wouldn't think like a smart person would do something like that.

Thus, other students assumed that these sexually attractive yet studious girls would not have to be financially dependent on a male partner in exchange for sex; they were seen to be smart and motivated enough to pursue well-paying careers on their own.

Like sexual reputation, family background appears to bear on one's success in the marriage market. Stinchcombe (1964: 37–39) found that girls at school were more sensitive to perceived status threats to the family; Lorena's conflict with a teacher over how she and her family dressed and the school-age mothers' dispute with school staff over child-rearing practices, both previously discussed, lend support to this interpretation. With respect to peer conflict, then, girls frustrated with the high school social system might be expected to cite the unfairness of popularity being linked to social class background. Pressure from the "high crowd" to buy designer clothing particularly annoyed some continuation girls.[5] "If you don't wear Jordache or Reeboks and this and that, you're not accepted," said Mandy of her old school. Thorne (1990: 109–10), in an ethnographic study of several elementary schools, found that clothing and hair style "standards were more exacting for girls than for boys," and peers could more easily distinguish girls from low-income families who could not meet these standards and were then treated like pariahs. In interviews few continuation girls explicitly mentioned social class,[6] but

---

5. In the La Fuente survey on peer conflict, 6 percent mentioned that high school students fight over specific material possessions, while an additional 10 percent said "jealousy." One elaborated: "Some have money, others don't—jealousy."

6. I never pursued the topic of social class unless an interviewee broached it first. When a student did mention class bias, he or she sometimes commented on its subtlety. Joanne, a white Beacon student, remarked: "The people that have more money tend to look down on people [who are] less fortunate. It's not really noticeable. I mean, it's not like they're all saying, 'You suck. You don't have no money.' "

In trying to explain peer conflict, many students focused on immediate causes such as "dirty looks." They sometimes felt the underlying causes of conflict but found it difficult to articulate them. Joan said she disliked "people" at her old school: "I'd walk into my classroom, whatever, and people'd just give you dirty looks. You sit down, you give them a dirty look, and they're all, 'Are you mad at me? Did you give me a

they attributed standards of popularity—which were partly shaped by social class—to their conflict with the jocks and preps.

I analyzed the interview transcripts of all students who said they disliked some aspect of the high school social system, and boys were as likely as girls to relate their animosity toward jocks and preps to the fact that the high crowd came from rich families. But girls' comments seemed to imply a perceived threat to them personally and to their families. Rosa, a La Fuente student whose single mother received welfare, angrily described how the "cheerleaders" had "looked down" on her; she concluded with a maxim: "Just because you drive and she walks doesn't make you better." Boys, on the other hand, tended to emphasize that "rich kids" put down their ethnic group or neighborhood. I asked Kurt, a Beacon student, why he got into so many fights. He explained:

> In our neighborhood it's against the people on *that* side of school, all the rich people live over there. Everybody down here is just low class, that's what *they* think. (emphasis in original)

INSTITUTIONAL LABELING PRACTICES AND STIGMA AVOIDERS

Both girls and boys disengaged because of conflict with peers and teachers, although the underlying sources of, and ways of expressing, conflict sometimes differed by gender. Another reason for school disengagement, more prevalent among girls, was a dislike and avoidance of institutional labeling practices. Fine and Zane (1989: 28) have suggested that girls may be more likely to interpret in-grade retention "as an institutional message of their personal inadequacy." Evidence from a study of a comprehensive high school showed that although girls who had been held back a grade were as likely to drop out as boys, "they were far more likely [92 versus 22 percent] to leave school prior to age eighteen, and four times more likely to express a relationship between being retained and eventually dropping out" (ibid.: 28).

None of my interviewees spontaneously linked their dislike for the comprehensive school to having been held back; indeed, none mentioned that they had been technically retained, though most were behind in credits. Several factors explain this. First, at the time of the interviews, these students were still in school, and the most disengaged either never

---

dirty look?' It's like *they don't even know that they're giving you a dirty look when they look at you. They're like so high above you*" (Beacon; emphasis added). Fueling the conflict, I discovered, was a resentment of "rich people when they have a snobby attitude. . . . the ones who flaunt and flaunt and flaunt and . . . could go through their life living off mommy and daddy."

bothered with the continuation school or stayed only a short time; students who had been retained in kindergarten or first grade seemed to be overrepresented in the latter group based on information provided at screenings. Second, although most students were short on high school credit, they were not treated as though they had flunked a grade, and many did not see their academic failure as due to low ability but, rather, the result of absenteeism. Third, with one exception, students' ages matched their grade level, suggesting that even if they had been retained early on, later they had been socially promoted.

About one-fifth of those interviewed, however, blamed some aspect of the differentiated curricular program for their disengagement. Six students (four girls, two boys) said they had been placed in classes that were too easy for them and felt bored and stigmatized. Two girls felt that their placement in upper track classes set them apart from their friends and put them under too much pressure to achieve. The remaining students (five girls, three boys) did not question the validity of their placement, but argued that focused-service classes (special education, English as a Second Language), remedial classes, or informal ability grouping within classes had negative side effects. They created separations between students that carried over into social interactions, damaged students' self-esteem, and sometimes made it more difficult to learn because these classes could be more disruptive (compare Oakes, 1985).[7]

Girls were more likely to bring up tracking practices and the like, though the difference was not statistically significant. More striking was the quality of their comments. Girls reacted more strongly to school practices that resulted in labeling, as evidenced by the detail they gave, the amount of time devoted to the topic, and their willingness to discuss how they felt personally.

Compare the following: Renee, whose parents emigrated from the Philippines when she was a child, felt teachers should be more sensitive to differences among students and try to "involve everybody":

> Sometimes you feel left out, sitting in the back of the class. You see all the kids getting picked on. Like, "What's the answer? Oh, good, correct." And you're sitting there [thinking]: "That per-

---

7. Not included as critics of curriculum differentiation were students who said school work was too hard, mentioned by twice as many girls as boys (21 versus 11 percent, possibly due to girls being more likely to show vulnerability), or those who argued that school staff members distinguished students based on their grade point averages. As John, a Beacon student, put it: "Priority students: college prep. Probable graduates: C students. Dropouts: below C students."

son is better than me. I don't want to have any competition."
You feel really down.

She described the school practice of setting apart the top students and giving them privileges. "I guess you're supposed to work your way up there; that's what they're trying to do. But it doesn't help. It just makes you feel, 'Well, I'm dumb anyways. So why should I even try?' "

Rather than give personal examples, Ed, a "Star Trek" fan at Beacon, cited the televison show's motto: "The needs of the many outweigh the needs of the few." By adopting this motto, Ed did not have to admit to having experienced pain as a result of tracking practices, nor did he indicate whether he was one of "the many" or one of "the few"; he merely signaled his dislike of the current system and provided a rationale for an alternative.

Girls more often expressed the theme that tracking intensified subcultural conflict, which they found distressing. Joan, a stoner by appearance, had transferred from out of state. She claimed that the counselor wanted to place her in remedial math even before she had been tested. She successfully avoided this but found that the jocks in algebra class treated her as though she were "dumb" and "on drugs":

> This cheerleader sat next to me and this guy on the football team sat behind her. She was friendly and you could tell it wasn't fakey, so I'd talk to her every once in awhile. She wouldn't understand something, so she'd ask me cuz she knew I knew it. She'd look at me like, "I'm surprised that you're smart." But at the same time to her friends it was more like, "I'm acknowledging that she's smart, even though . . ." One day I was laughing with my friend (she's got long blonde hair and she's always wearing rock shirts), and that football player turns and he tells me, "What, are you having a flashback?" I got pissed off and I started a fight with this guy. (Beacon)

Sandra and Simone were a different type of stigma avoider. Both had been identified as gifted in elementary school, and although they enjoyed the pullout classes, this fact did not outweigh the added pressure from teachers and parents to perform or the painful separation from their friends. "I was the only one out of all my friends that was in the MGM [Mentally Gifted Minors] class" (Simone, Beacon). Later, in advanced classes, these feelings intensified:

> I remember that when I was in junior high and in high school, they always put me in advanced courses and they would kind of

set you above the other kids and say, "You're the one. You are the kids who are going to these colleges. You guys, you have this ability." And the whole time I'm thinking, "Well, what about everyone else? What do you have planned for them?" (Sandra, Beacon, 4/26/88 group discussion)

Together, these stories suggest that girls may be more concerned with minimizing differences among students. As Eder (1985: 163) has argued: "To surpass one's friends appears to have more costs for girls than for boys, because achievement is not a main avenue for peer status for girls and because the avenues that do exist for girls are more arbitrary and therefore less widely accepted."

COMPETING DEMANDS OF RELATIONSHIPS AND
THE RELATIONSHIP-ABSORBED

Girls were more likely than boys to report feeling "stress" or "pressure" from people and institutions competing for their time and attention. A number of teachers observed that girls were more inclined to get caught up in relationships, then feel "victimized" and "fall apart" emotionally, whereas boys were more apt to respond aggressively or violently to competing demands. This may help explain why girls were more likely than boys to spontaneously complain about inadequate counseling at the comprehensive high school (34 versus 20 percent).[8] In any event, continuation school, with its flexible and compressed schedule, emerged as one solution to the competing claims on their time, as Kris (Beacon) makes clear:

High school is like a soap opera. You totally get stressed out cuz you can't handle it. You've got to treat your boyfriend one way, your friends another way, your parents another way, your teachers one way. You've gotta separate all those things, and you've gotta think about what you wanna do, and you get confused. . . . School, of course, it's a big part of our lives. We have to go there. When we're there, we're not particularly thinkin' about what we're learning, or what we're supposed to be learning. Maybe we're somewhere else, you know? So to minimize

8. Late in the interview, I specifically asked students how they felt about the counseling they had received. More than one-half of the girls (51 percent) felt there had been too few counselors (versus 29 percent of boys), and more than twice as many girls than boys said the counseling had been poor, that is, unhelpful, coercive, and so on (23 versus 10 percent).

the time that we have to go to school to do what we have to do, it's better.

In the next two sections, I explore some of the categories identified by Kris and others—boyfriends, other friends, and parents or families (teacher-student relations are discussed above)—and relate these to disengagement from school. Unlike Kris, though, my focus is on the competing institutional demands that encroach on individual students—those I call the relationship-absorbed—as opposed to the psycho-physiological concept of stress.

Boyfriends and Girlfriends

Girls were significantly more likely to be in exclusive love relationships than boys; 45 percent of the girls interviewed had steady boyfriends, 15 percent were engaged to be married, and 9 percent were married, while 32 percent described themselves as single. Only 23 percent of the boys interviewed had steady girlfriends, 3 percent were engaged, and none was married, while 74 percent described themselves as single.[9]

One-fifth of all girls interviewed cited boyfriend problems as a primary reason they got behind in school; no boys cited major girlfriend problems (a point taken up below). For these girls, the school had usually failed to communicate its vocational relevance, and they sought an alternative safety net. Parents (usually mothers) blamed their daughters' boyfriends for their disengagement from school, which was only partially true. These girls argued that they "freely chose" to spend time with their boyfriend because they disliked school.[10] They resented their parents seeing their boyfriend only as a "bad influence"; hence the frequent complaint: "They don't even know him!"

Just before she turned sixteen, Jenny stopped going to classes. "I hated school," she stated. Her mother was convinced that her boyfriend, who had quit school two years earlier, had talked her into dropping out

9. The difference in marital status (single, going steady, engaged, or married) by gender was statistically significant. The chi-square $(3, N = 82)$ was 15.86 at $p < .001$; the phi coefficient was .440.

10. I recorded one instance in which a girl claimed to have always liked school, but when she moved in with her boyfriend, her mother went to her school and asked the registrar not to enroll her. Lilia could not sign up for independent study without parental permission nor would other schools in the district accept her once they discovered she was not really living with her father. Only when she finally did move in with her father was she able to enter the continuation school to make up for the three quarters she had been out. Concluded Lilia: "They always say that by law you have to be in school . . . [but] I was just having a hassle" (Willows).

because she would overhear him commiserate with Jenny about the overcrowding and the teachers.

> My mom was really mad . . . [She'd say], "You're telling her not to go" because he'd sit there and talk bad about [names home school], too, and say, "They're stupid; I wouldn't even go back." He'd tell me that, and it was true. Everything he said, I knew already. But she'd hear him, and she thought he was a big influence on me not going. . . . She was getting so confused, at one time, she thought I was pregnant. She didn't know what was wrong with me. She wouldn't talk to me. She tried to bribe me to get back in school. She said, "I'll buy you this and I'll buy you that." I said, "Mom, it's not 'buy me' anything. I don't want to go back there!" (La Fuente)

Girls who had since broken up with their boyfriends often explained that their parents had been right, and that they had been "naive." They had believed that their boyfriends were different, that they would take care of them. Those still in the middle of a heavy romance would, if confronted, deny that their boyfriends kept them out of school. In nonaccusatory discussions, however, these girls equivocated. For example, Louise made these unprompted statements (presented in order) in the course of a discussion about the influence of boyfriends: (1) "He really has nothing to do with whether I go to school or not" (complete denial of influence); (2) "Yesterday he let me not go to school" (partial negative influence); (3) "He'll usually push me to go to school" (partial positive influence); and (4) "In a way I think he had an effect on what my positions were [regarding school] because he lives on his own. He's out of school. He's older" (admission of influence) (La Fuente, 1/12/89 group discussion).

Like Louise and Jenny, most of these girls had older boyfriends who were out of school. Older men were appealing for several reasons. They usually had more money, a car, and their own apartments. They seemed more mature, both physically and emotionally, and thus more worldly. Older men were more able to project a caring attitude, up to and including providing an alternative place to live. For girls in combative, changing (especially through divorce and remarriage) or chaotic family arrangements, a promised refuge from such unpleasantness was particularly attractive. Older men could speak with almost paternal authority, easing the pressure to succeed in school by providing "an easy way out," an alternative route to security and purpose in life.

But older boyfriends had their drawbacks, as well. They sometimes expected girls to cook and clean for them in exchange for a place to live or consumer goods and urged them to bear children. Explained one who, at the time of this interview, had so far resisted:

> Older guys, they want to settle down and have a family, and that's the reason all these girls are pregnant. These girls are so in love because a twenty-five year old likes you. You're like, "Oh, my God, a twenty-five year old likes me." And they [the boy-friends] are secure with their jobs. And sometimes a lot of the guys are bums, but they're secure with their lives, and so they're messing up your life. (Linda, La Fuente)

By "bums" Linda meant not necessarily that these boyfriends were unemployed, but, like her boyfriend, some were addicted to drugs or alcohol and seemed emotionally unstable. Others dealt drugs and some-times behaved in ways that exposed the girls to violence or implicated them in illegal activities without their knowledge. For example, Dawn's boyfriend, in jail for selling drugs, had hidden crack cocaine in her par-ents' house without telling her (La Fuente, field notes, 5/4/89). For awhile, being involved with an outlaw figure might have seemed thrilling, even romantic:

> [Being with this guy] I felt like, "Now I'm at the top." He was buying me clothes and I was driving around in nice cars, fancy cars. I was on the other side of the law. [But] now when I think about it, I'd never be there again because I could have gone to jail for a long time for just being there. (Tanya, Beacon)

Regardless of how limited some boyfriends' horizons might have ap-peared, many girls cut to be with their boyfriends, not just those girls who felt they had really "messed up" in school because of the relation-ship. I recorded several instances of girls leaving or not showing up because they had fought with their boyfriends and said they were too upset to concentrate at school (Beacon, 4/26/88, 12/19/88, 12/20/88; La Fuente, 10/19/88, 11/16/88, 12/8/88).

Others said at first they especially liked the continuation school be-cause it allowed them to spend more time with their boyfriends (a fair number of whom had preceded them at the continuation school), toler-ated more open displays of physical affection (Beacon, 4/26/88 group discussion), and (particularly at Beacon, given individualized learning) allowed them to focus more on their relationship while getting credit. For example, I observed Joan reading a cookbook in English class, and she explained that she was planning a romantic surprise dinner for her boyfriend (Beacon, field notes, 4/10/89). Lupe, who felt her boyfriends had distracted her from her studies, told me in hindsight she wished she had gone to an all-girls Catholic school. "That's where you find your character," she concluded (Beacon).

Not all girls felt that their boyfriends, particularly those who were enrolled in college, had been a negative influence. Repeating her mother's advice, Erica explained, "If you don't go to college, no man'll want you" (La Fuente, 11/17/88 group discussion). Sometimes boyfriends who regretted dropping out could persuade girls to stick with school. And one sophomore boy told me that his eighth-grade girlfriend would not see him if she discovered he had cut school that day.

This admission of a girlfriend's influence was unusual. Only one boy mentioned seeing a particular girl the semester he cut a lot and got behind, and teachers argued that a failed romance was a primary reason another boy dropped out of Beacon (field notes, 12/6/88). Three other boys, when asked about the biggest problems facing them as teenagers, said they had difficulty meeting girls or finding a steady girlfriend.

Several factors may explain why so few boys associated love relationships with getting off track academically as well as emotionally. First, in line with cultural norms, very few boys established long-term love relationships with older women. This meant that the girls they dated were still in school, not yet driving, and less likely to be cutting more than just a few classes. Second, boys appear to have been less likely to admit that they were influenced by their girlfriends because of masculine pride.

Third, boys may not focus on and discuss relationships to the extent that girls do. A number of feminist scholars have documented how unequal male-female power relations are expressed in talk patterns (for example, Fishman, 1978). Girls tend to focus their social activities around a best friend and spend a lot of time discussing relationships, while boys play in larger groups centered around activities such as sports. Boys are more likely to use language to jockey for status and impart information, although this is not always the case (Thorne, 1986; Thorne, 1990). As men, they may be more likely to find talk about relationships to be vague. I saw evidence of this difference not only in interviews but in the type of music girls liked. I asked the students in my music class to bring in lyrics to their favorite songs. The following was typical of what the girls liked: "I want somebody to share the rest of my life, share my innermost thoughts. . . ."

Fourth, boys still envisioned futures in which they would be the primary provider for a family. Occasional jokes about marrying rich women seemed to fall into the same category as winning big in the state lottery:

wonderful if it happened but highly unlikely. Therefore, boys did not see establishing a relationship with a woman as an alternative safety net.

A fifth and final reason has to do with the nature of subcultures. If girls are marginal to, or occupy subordinate positions within, largely male-dominated subcultures, they do not build their self-esteem through participation. This is because the alternative definitions of success that subcultures can offer, such as fighting prowess, sexual conquest, or guitar playing, frequently favor boys. This may not seem that important to girls who are infatuated or in love with their boyfriends, but in the wake of a failing (or failed) relationship, some girls reported feeling severely isolated and depressed. "When I was going out with [my boyfriend], I had tunnel vision; I didn't realize that other things were going on around me. . . . I was just totally being brought down so low I couldn't even stand it anymore" (Joanne, Beacon).

Girls who had been financially supported by their boyfriends felt so dependent that they suffered an identity crisis: "I just feel like I don't even know who I am anymore; I kind of lost myself somewhere down the line" (Erin, Beacon). Contributing to this feeling was the fact that most girls' identities began to derive from their boyfriends, regardless of the nature and extent of their own participation in a subculture, as Peggy's comment makes clear:

> The thing about that [getting labeled by what you do] is, even if you don't ride a skate board, I hung around with all the skaters last year, Joe and Donovan and everybody, and they always called me a "skate betty." And it was like: "No! I'm not." But that's just the label you get. (Beacon, 4/26/88 group discussion)

A "betty" was used derisively and implied dependence and vanity; the term may derive from Betty Crocker, an icon of the traditional housewife. Similarly, I heard non-stoner males refer to female stoners as "stoner bitches," implying their main activity or worth was sexual.

Even when girls participated marginally in the subculture, they were more known through their boyfriends. For example, although Sandra was an athlete in her own right, she did not feel this was why others called her a jock: "Mostly it was because my boyfriend was a jock so everyone considered me one" (Beacon, 4/26/88 group discussion). Similarly, Jacqueline liked to rap, but at her home school rapping was considered "a taboo for the girls to do." She, like the girlfriends of gang members, got respect because the males she hung around with would protect her: "I've got people behind me" (La Fuente).

In sum, boys rarely became so absorbed in love relationships that they completely cut themselves off from their other friends. Plus, they continued to participate in subcultural activities that provided them with a sense of worth and success. So if and when they broke up with their girlfriends, the boys seemed much less likely to feel devastated.

Same-Sex Friends

Teachers argued, and I observed, that girls seemed more concerned than boys about their relationships with same-sex friends. At least one interviewee explicitly left the comprehensive school after she had a falling out with her best friend, who, in turn, dropped out altogether. "We were like sisters, and it seemed like right when we got to [names home school], . . . everybody else was coming in between us. We didn't talk, and I had to look at her every day, to see her face. She stopped coming to school, and so did I" (Sylvia, Beacon).

As Sylvia hints, competition for boyfriends and status (strongly associated with one's subcultural identity) seemed to increase once the girls entered high school. Used to confiding their secrets to one another, girls found that some people they felt were their friends could no longer be trusted. Hence, a number of girls made initially cryptic remarks about coming to the continuation school to avoid "former friends." They cited "knowing who your true friends are" as a major problem facing teenagers. More girls than boys argued that belonging to "a big crowd" contributed to their disengagement from school. Elena, for example, had fallen behind while cutting with her crowd: "They weren't really friends. I only have one best friend, but she doesn't live here. They'd only use you. Like if you had a car or money: 'We'll be your friend' " (La Fuente).

As a defense against this, even the most outgoing girls said they only had a handful of "really close friends" and only one best friend. Mc-Robbie (1978: 106), who studied the friendships of a group of working-class white girls, suggested that best friends may be boyfriend substitutes. In formal and informal interviews, girls did talk about their best friend relationships in terms usually associated with romantic relationships. Joanne (Beacon), for example, explained that she felt as "possessive" of her best friend as of her boyfriend. Girls sometimes wrote the names of their best friends on their class folders alongside declarations of love for their boyfriends. Boys rarely did this, although they often wrote the names and logos of their favorite musical groups, gangs, or both.

Almost every girl who mentioned her best friend in any detail, however, also had a steady boyfriend, so the relationship was not necessarily a substitute. Further, the presence of a steady best friend sometimes helped girls to weather stormy relationships with boyfriends and to stay focused enough on school to graduate. Ingrid, for example, boosted Megan's morale when her fiance left her for another girl, tutored her in math, and urged her to do homework. Joanne introduced her best friend to boys and helped bring her out of her shell, while her friend, in turn, talked Joanne out of her bouts of depression and calmed her down when she got angry at a teacher or classmate.

By the same token, fights over the shifting balance of affections within a small group of female friends or over a boy who introduces competition among the girls for his attention can affect a girl's decision to stay in school or not.

To illustrate both sides of this dynamic, I draw on my knowledge of one group of female friends at La Fuente. I got to know these girls through my year-long involvement with the student council (open to all students) and related activities, and I subsequently interviewed four of the five. Three of the girls dropped out eventually, for reasons both directly and indirectly related to the changing fortunes of their friendship network. In turn, these relationships affected each girl's relationship with her steady boyfriend and her family, and vice versa.

Linda (of Puerto Rican and Mexican descent), Gretchen, and Mandy (both white) all entered La Fuente at about the same time, a year before I met them. Linda and Mandy became best friends and helped each other with their personal problems. Linda helped Mandy confront her boyfriend and the father of her child when he started dating another girl and, later, as a show of loyalty, fought the girl for Mandy, who did not want to risk getting caught and losing her child care privileges. In turn, Mandy comforted Linda as she tried to cope with a new stepfather and a suicidal boyfriend addicted to cocaine. Linda, though, found herself turning more and more to drugs and alcohol to forget her troubles, something that Mandy, with a child at home, did not want to do anymore.

Linda found a ready party mate in Gretchen, who was not getting along with her financially struggling single mother. Mandy felt "pushed aside" but tried to remain philosophical:

> I said, "OK, that's what friends are for, and I understand." So I just went on with my life. I didn't just sit at home and say, "Oh, Linda forgot about me." . . . But I told her she was going to get hurt because that was the wrong kind of girl to be hanging around with. So she did get hurt and everything and got into a lot of trouble and I had to come to her rescue. And then she was kind of drunk that night, and she goes, "I love you. I'd never hurt you." And I [said]: "Unhuh, shut up and go to sleep,

Linda." And then we became best friends again, started hanging around and doing everything [together].

Meanwhile, longtime friends Kathy (half white, half Pacific Islander) and Jenny (white) decided they would both attend La Fuente and there became acquainted with the other three girls. Jenny particularly enjoyed Linda's company, and Kathy, who felt somewhat excluded, pursued a closer relationship with Gretchen. In what she saw as a show of loyalty, Kathy reported back to Gretchen some derogatory remarks Mandy had made to the group (compare Mandy's characterization of Gretchen as "the wrong kind of girl" cited above). This confirmed Gretchen's growing feeling that nobody liked her, and she decided to drop out (field notes, 1/19/89). This decision, combined with the rest of the group's anger at Kathy for breaking a confidence, seemed to touch off a long string of absences for Kathy, who claimed to be ill.

During this period, Linda decided that life with her stepfather was intolerable. At the same time, Jenny's mother had been demoted from supervisor to assembly line worker because of her company's decision to automate and thus was in need of some extra cash. So Linda moved in with Jenny and paid rent with social security money she had been receiving since her real father's death. At first, the two got along well. As a lark, they both flirted with a boy they knew from one of Linda's classes, even though Jenny had a steady boyfriend. When the boy returned their interest, Jenny spent time at school writing him love letters and won him over. Linda felt jealous, stopped attending school, and finally moved back in with her on-again, off-again boyfriend.

Once more, Linda turned to Mandy to be her best friend. But Mandy, who felt she had "been dropped again" when Linda and Jenny became so close, was skeptical. "I told her, 'You know, Linda, you have to find time for yourself, who your real friends are. And your boyfriend's not much of a boyfriend'" (Mandy, La Fuente). Indeed, Linda told me her boyfriend was insisting she accompany him on a vacation to Mexico while school was in session, and he and his family were urging her to marry him and have a child, hoping this would prompt him to stay off drugs. Linda then missed three weeks of school, and La Fuente withdrew her with no option of returning because she had just turned eighteen.

Jenny began to see more of Kathy, urging her to attend school and picking her up every morning. Kathy did begin to attend more, but her mind was on her new boyfriend, who wanted her to move in with him. Kathy wanted to, even though it would mean dropping out to go to work, but she feared that her parents would refuse to see her ever again. At this time, Kathy joked: "I wish I could just have a baby." Because of her erratic attendance, Kathy could not graduate with Jenny and Mandy, both of whom had steady boyfriends still in school and were on relatively good terms with their families. Although Kathy returned the following fall as a fifth-year senior, she dropped out about a month later to be with her boyfriend, claiming she no longer had friends at La Fuente and life at home had become intolerable (her father beat her, her parents locked her in at night to keep her from running away, and she was expected to care for her younger brother daily).

This complicated, real-life soap opera shows the important role that girlfriends played in the engagement process. The five girls entered La Fuente with similar backgrounds and attitudes about academic learning, teachers, extracurricular activities, and the importance of a high school diploma. At the time Gretchen and Kathy dropped out and Linda was pushed out, all three had significant problems at home and with out-of-school boyfriends, and their relationships with close girlfriends at school had become strained or were nonexistent. Jenny and Mandy, the two eventual graduates, had both experienced family and boyfriend problems in the past, although not simultaneously, and they had always cultivated at least one close girlfriend at school who helped them survive the bad times and motivated them to attend classes.

What about the boys? Somewhat ironically, a number of girls mentioned that boys seemed to be more influenced by their male friends. But they meant influence mainly as pressure to engage in behavior that took the boys out of school such as fighting, doing drugs, and hanging out with the gang. For example, Sylvia (Beacon) said, "Guys, I think, if their friends push them, [will say]: 'OK, I'll do it.' Girls sometimes [will say], 'No, I'm not going to do that just because you say.' But guys, they feel like they have to look like a man." Although boys were less likely than girls spontaneously to cite peer pressure as a major problem (20 versus 36 percent), those who did reinforced this perspective. Tim (La Fuente) explained: "I like coming to school, but the people I hang around with don't like to come to school. They pick me up and say, 'We're going to school,' and then they drive to the mountains [instead]." He complained that his friends would put him down if he insisted on going to school, and he hated to risk taking drugs with them because he was on probation. Still, he did not mention the possibility of finding new friends, not an easy task in any event, as I discuss in chapter 7.

I have argued that for girls, relationships with girlfriends provided support that helped them stay in school but, if destabilized, could contribute to their leaving. In formal interviews no girls described themselves as "loners," but three boys (9 percent) did. Indeed, in current usage the word almost implies a masculine subject; a loner "prefers" not to associate with other people, so the term betrays little vulnerability.

EARLY PREGNANCY, PARENTHOOD, AND MARRIAGE

Research has clearly demonstrated the link between early marriage and childbearing and dropping out, the magnitude of which is much stronger for youths of low socioeconomic status (Rumberger, 1983). In the High School and Beyond survey of dropouts, females were more likely than males to cite marriage (31 versus 7 percent) or pregnancy (23 percent) as the reason for leaving school (Ekstrom et al., 1986: 59). Analysts often categorize these reasons as personal rather than school-related.

More often than not, pregnancy and marriage were partly symptoms of, and attempts to deal with, disaffection from school. As Fine (1986) points out about pregnancy, "having a baby at least offers a full-time job and a sense of purpose and competence." This seemed to be especially true for girls in my study from low-income and working-class backgrounds, whose expectations (as opposed to aspirations) for further education were low compared to middle-class girls due to lack of money, role models, and encouragement.

Of the twelve pregnant or mothering girls I interviewed formally, only two reported liking school and doing fairly well in college prep classes prior to pregnancy. Both Molly (white) and Jacqueline (African-American) came from middle-class families and neighborhoods. They, along with April (Mexican-American), were the only ones to feel that pregnancy alone was responsible for their presence at the continuation school. In support of this belief, these three girls had the three highest grade point averages of all my interviewees, excluding Brenda, who had been in special education classes before La Fuente, and Anna, who began ninth grade at La Fuente. Molly had never missed any school, came to La Fuente so she could breast-feed her baby, and graduated ahead of her class. Jacqueline, embarrassed, dropped out after her pregnancy became obvious and missed over a semester of school before a relative talked her into attending La Fuente.

Besides Molly and Jacqueline, the other girls, according to ninth-grade transcripts, had been placed in general or remedial English and math courses or were in special education (Carmen [Mexican-American] and Brenda [African-American]). Although most had passed state competency tests by the time I interviewed them, their basic skills seemed low. This and the fact that they came from families of low socioeconomic status are factors associated with early childbearing. One-half of low-income teens have poor basic skills, and one in five low-income female

teens with poor basic skills—whether African-American, white, or Latino—are teen mothers (Children's Defense Fund, 1987).

Anna (Filipino-American) and April became pregnant just prior to
or a few months into ninth grade so never really experienced the comprehensive high school, while the others reported already cutting classes.
Some like Rosa (Mexican-American), Berta (Puerto Rican and Mexican-
American), Mandy (Polish-American), and Patricia (Puerto Rican) got
into trouble for fighting or substance abuse. Some interviewees, particularly the three low-income African-Americans (Brenda, Beverly, and
Denise),[11] insisted at first that they liked school, but then proceeded to
paint a portrait of disengagement, though none had officially dropped
out. Faced with this contradiction, at the end of such an interview, I
asked girls directly whether they disliked school first and then got pregnant or liked school all along. Brenda's response was typical: "For me, I
was always cutting, and my boyfriend is older than me and I was stupid,
stupid enough to cut school and go see him and it [getting pregnant]
just happened."

Three girls had actually dropped out (Mandy, Patricia, and Rosa)
and another had been suspended (Berta) so were out of school when
they got pregnant. Mandy, for example, had not gone to classes for six
weeks: "I wasn't interested in school at all, then I got pregnant and I
felt, 'Well, I've got to do something.' So I went back to school. It's not
like I liked school a lot, and *then* I dropped out" (emphasis in original).
These findings confirm recent research that has shown that a substantial
minority of young women dropouts or pushouts become pregnant after
they leave school.

Further, this pattern is more common among whites and Latinas
than it is among African-Americans.

Data from the High School and Beyond Survey of 1982 (the
sophomore cohort) revealed that for 28% of the girls who had
experienced both a conception and a school dropout, the dropping out had preceded the conception. This sequence of events

---

11. Though generalizing from such a small sample is not advisable, my sense was
that the low-income African-American girls were under even more pressure to stay
in school; their elders, particularly parents and African-American women teachers I
observed, held up education as doubly important for them because they would face
ethnic discrimination in the workplace and could not count on connections to land
good jobs. Further, their partners would not likely earn enough to support a family
alone. These girls were thoroughly convinced that they needed an educational credential, but since their academic experiences had not often been pleasant, they felt
coerced.

was particularly likely for white girls: A full 35% of these girls, compared with 14% among blacks and 23% among Hispanics, experienced the pregnancy after leaving school. (Polit and Kahn, 1987: 134, citing Morrison, 1984)

The SAM program seemed to address effectively the special needs of the pregnant and mothering girls. For those behind on credits, the program provided both incentives (free child care, special transportation, and extra counseling and tutoring) and sanctions (withdrawal from the program if a participant failed one course) to keep them on track once at La Fuente. Similar programs have been shown to reduce the incidence of dropping out among this group (Polit and Kahn, 1987). A number of interviewees also said that being responsible for another human being renewed their interest in graduating so that they could get a better job, avoid welfare, and make their child proud. Nevertheless, several factors seemed to hinder the reengagement process, all centering around competing values and attitudes about early motherhood and its alternatives, abortion and adoption.

First, considerable peer pressure was brought to bear on the few girls in the SAM program who had originally intended to put their babies up for adoption. I knew of two girls (both white) who changed their minds and decided to keep their babies, and SAM staff members were convinced that their classmates were responsible (La Fuente, field notes, 5/31/89). Working-class African-American and Mexican-American girls were the most outspoken against adoption. Brenda's attitude was typical: "I felt [adoption] was wrong because it's your body and it would be stupid for you to carry it for nine months if you really didn't want it in the first place." SAM teachers argued that caring for an infant caused more absenteeism than pregnancy. So keeping a baby versus adoption may hinder reengagement and contribute to complete disengagement: a ninth-grade girl who later decided to keep her baby did subsequently drop out of La Fuente.

Second, peer and teacher attitudes contributed to the embarrassment pregnant girls experienced, the same embarrassment that helped convince other girls not even to try the SAM program let alone remain at the comprehensive high school. If they became pregnant, they were vulnerable to being seen as "easy lays" or as "stupid" for not protecting themselves or obtaining an abortion, the right to which was favored by most girls, regardless of ethnicity and social class.

Both boys and nonpregnant girls occasionally expressed embarrassment and frustration at having to attend a school associated with a SAM program. Several boys said they liked to come to school to meet girls but felt that La Fuente girls were either pregnant or had steady boy-friends. Thus, girls not in the SAM program who were interested in meeting boys sometimes felt compelled to disassociate themselves from girls in the SAM program and the stigma attached to teen pregnancy (for example, field notes, 10/5/88). These fears and frustrations—hurtful to pregnant girls—came out most often during orientation, a critical time for students wondering whether they really wanted to return to school:

Juan: That's embarrassing, to be six or seven months pregnant. I'd be embarrassed to go to school.

Jeff, sticking his hands and belly out: They get this big, as big as a basketball.

Ms. Wilson asked Jeff to move to his own table . . . and said: Most La Fuente graduates are SAM girls.

Juan: Fuck! You say you go to La Fuente, and people say, "Oh, that's that school where all those pregnant girls are." There's no after school sports. They could go into labor at school. It's so embarrassing. (field notes, 12/8/88)

Teachers generally discouraged these types of remarks in the classroom, but during breaks and nonclassroom activities, they were not uncommon.

Teachers not directly involved in the SAM program sometimes resented having to deal with pregnant bodies in their classrooms and the issues they raised (see also McDade, 1987). Others, particularly recent or single mothers themselves, were very supportive and openly gave girls in the SAM program extra attention (for example, La Fuente, field notes, 9/20/88). This displeased many other students, who argued that girls in the SAM program should not get privileges, such as being let out of class early, "because it was their choice to have a baby" (Jenny, La Fuente).

Even the most sympathetic teachers worried that by treating the girls in the SAM program differently, they were sending the "wrong" message to girls about getting pregnant, either the first time or subsequently (Beacon, field notes, 11/21/88, 12/21/88; La Fuente, 1/9/89, 4/27/89). They sometimes found themselves not bringing up birth control and related topics for fear of hurting the pregnant girls' feelings or of not being able to prevent boys from making insensitive comments.

Others went so far as to argue that the SAM program itself promoted teen pregnancy because it provided girls with free child care, meals, diapers, and transportation (La Fuente, field notes, 2/15/89, 2/21/89). "There should be a stigma attached to teen pregnancy," said one teacher I interviewed. Stated another: "School-age mothers, they come here because they get their welfare check." These teachers' argument that school-age mothers must face "reality" sooner or later and that the sheltered atmosphere of the program simply postponed their eventual failure is reminiscent of what traditionalist teachers said about continuation students in general.

Some parents agreed with the traditionalists. "My parents are old fashioned and figure once [a girl] gets together with those [SAM] girls, they'll talk about it and she'll end up having a baby, too," Lorena told me. "I was like, 'No. I don't want to have babies. Not 'til later.' " Whenever a girl became pregnant after coming to La Fuente, as was the case with two of my interviewees (Carmen and Rosa), some took this as evidence that the SAM program caused it. The school-age mothers I asked about this, however, tended to ridicule the argument. The SAM program, responded Molly, is "not a teenage pregnancy cult!" A counselor worried that "a lot of aspersions in the classroom from some students and staff" had created a poor "learning environment for pregnant girls."

Third, although pregnant girls received extra services in the continuation setting, this could not always make up for the criticism or withdrawal of support—emotional and financial—from family members, prompted by news of the pregnancy. Tamara, a Latina at Willows, said her parents lost interest in her education because she had a child. Nicole's mother kicked her out for, among other things, refusing to get an abortion, and she was living in a room without heat or electricity (La Fuente, 4/25/89 essay). One study found that the strongest factor preventing early childbearing for whites was a good relationship with their parents (Abrahamse, Morrison, and Waite, 1988). This held true for all but one of the pregnant white girls I got to know. Sandra, a Beacon student, said she "hated" most of her family and, though this was not her only reason, she saw keeping her baby as "a chance to prove my parents wrong. It [child rearing] can be done better."

A fourth factor that sometimes hindered the reengagement of girls in the SAM program was early marriage. School-age mothers married older men, most of whom were already in the work force full-time.[12] Three of the SAM girls I interviewed were married (Beverly, Brenda,

12. The fathers of babies born to teenage mothers are generally no longer adolescents themselves. Brindis and Jeremy (1988: 26) report that for California in 1986, only 28 percent of such fathers were teenagers at the time of the birth, and most of these fathers were between the ages of eighteen and nineteen; 48 percent were between twenty and twenty-four years, and the rest were more than twenty-four years old.

and Anna), the latter two to the fathers of their babies; all three had married after their babies were at least a year old. Despite their husband's steady employment, continued family support (especially free child care), and a good relationship, these girls felt that marriage made staying in school even more of a struggle.

Although Anna said her marriage was positive, she argued regularly with her husband about caring for their child while she tried to do her school work. Because of babysitting costs and transportation difficulties, Beverly could not afford to attend both La Fuente and a vocational program, so consequently attended neither consistently.

> Then when I get home, I'm cooking dinner and I'm cleaning and I'm washing clothes. I'm doing whatever I have to do, and my son goes to bed and it's like me and my husband have no quality time together. It's really hard. . . . [My husband] has [said], "If you have [another] baby, you can stay home." And I said, "I'm not staying home!" I go crazy staying home.

Isabel got pregnant again two months after her first birth, but managed to graduate shortly thereafter. Of the other seven girls at La Fuente I knew who were married, only one had graduated as of October 1989, and she was in the process of a divorce, while another was still enrolled. One had run away from an arranged marriage, another had to drop out to support her child after her husband was jailed, yet another wanted to devote more of her time to her husband and twin daughters, and the remaining three left for reasons unknown.

At Beacon, four childless girls got married during 1988–89, one right before she graduated. Two dropped out, ostensibly to work so they could pool their resources with their husbands' and move out of their parents' homes. The fourth enrolled in independent studies in order to accommodate her work schedule but dropped out the following year. Once married girls leave school, they are less likely to return than their male counterparts. Borus and Carpenter (1983) found that marriage rather than the presence of a child is what hinders returning to school, though they could not explain this with their data. My findings suggest that young unmarried mothers tend to live with relatives and may get welfare benefits, while their married counterparts choose to work and take on more domestic responsibilities in order to maintain a separate residence with their spouse.

FAMILY AND WORK RESPONSIBILITIES

Significantly more girls than boys reported family problems (45 versus 17 percent), and more than twice as many (23 versus 9 percent) cited trouble at home as the major factor pushing them off track at school.[13] Family problems included divorce, alcohol and drug dependency, incest, financial difficulties, death of a parent (because of illness, accident, drug overdose, or suicide), and physical and verbal abuse. As Fine and Zane (1989: 27) put it, "family complexity" seems to disrupt girls' schooling more than it does for boys. For example, using High School and Beyond data, Barro (1984, cited in Earle and Roach, 1987: 9) found that dropout rates tend to increase as the number of siblings increases, particularly for low-income whites. The dropout rate increases faster for girls with three to five siblings (11.2 to 20 percent) than for boys with the same number of siblings (14.7 to 17.6 percent).

In my study, family complexity affected the disengagement process in at least three ways. First, girls faced increased domestic responsibilities, particularly caring for siblings or elderly relatives, cooking, and cleaning. In a special survey I did at Beacon,[14] girls reported spending twice as many hours per week doing chores (an average of 26 and a median 16.5 versus an average of 13 and a median 8.5 hours for boys). Latinas spent just over 40 hours per week (as measured by the median and average), more than any other group.

At La Fuente, a content analysis of daily journals, in which students were asked to comment about domestic chores, showed similar patterns. Girls mentioned doing chores 61 percent of the time versus 28 percent for boys. Further, as in the Beacon sample, boys were expected to do traditional male tasks (taking out the garbage, mowing the lawn, cleaning the garage) that are typically performed much less often and take

---

13. White students were also significantly more likely than nonwhites to cite family difficulties (50 versus 26 percent). I believe this is partly a school-related phenomenon since more white students attended Beacon, and the teacher-counselors there dealt with issues such as divorce openly and regularly. Other students may have been more apt to consider such matters private and were therefore less likely to confide in me, particularly given my white, middle-class background.

14. Every student present in an English class the day of the survey was given an anonymous questionnaire regarding domestic responsibilities (types of chores, hours spent, effect on ability to study and attend school regularly). The sample size was seventy (60 percent male, 40 percent female; 54 percent white, 46 percent nonwhite or mixed ethnicity). I went over the questionnaires as I collected them to make sure they were complete and, in some cases, asked students to elaborate on comments or unusual answers.

less time overall than traditional female tasks (cooking, babysitting, house cleaning, laundry).

At Beacon, few students of either sex felt that their duties at home made it very difficult for them to study or attend school regularly, but more than one-third of the girls (36 percent versus 14 percent of the boys) said domestic chores "sometimes" interfered. The girls with the heaviest home responsibilities, from what I observed in La Fuente's orientation class, did not last long in the continuation school.

Sara, a Mexican-American who never even made it onto the official roll, was a prime example. In her journal she wrote that she had not "fit in" at school since the sixth grade. But encouraged by her father and boyfriend (who already attended La Fuente), she decided to resume her educational career after a long absence. Her mother, isolated at home with younger children, "got use [sic] to having [me] with her all the time." Sara described taking her sister to the doctor, washing and ironing the family's clothes, fixing dinner. But her mother began to complain that she was not getting her work done at home. "All that really happened yesterday was a lot of arguments between me and mother. I went to bed early just to get away from her." At the same time, Sara hoped for a late schedule once she began her regular classes: "I'll have more time in the morning with the kids. They miss me when I'm gone all day." Reading between the lines, Sara seemed to drop out again because she no longer could complete her chores (and thus keep her mother happy) or spend as much time with her boyfriend ("my favorite past time [sic]") and her siblings, despite agreeing with her father that "to get some kind of edjication [sic] would make my future a little better than his."

Second, because some families monitored girls' activities more closely, they had to stay close to home and had fewer opportunities to escape stressful situations. Boys were more likely to be sent on errands, were not as closely watched—partly because there was no concern about them getting pregnant—engaged in more physical activities, and could respond to tense situations with aggression (including fighting and yelling) with fewer negative repercussions. At school girls "stressed out" by family problems often either became preoccupied and withdrawn or lashed out in anger at teachers and classmates who tried to engage them. Patricia was one:

> I never yell at my mom.... I've always kept it inside, and I guess that's why I used to get into a lot of fights cuz all my anger would just go out at one person. I almost killed a person.

> So [now] I like letting everything out on my own time, talking
> to somebody instead of taking it out on someone. (La Fuente)

Indeed, talking about their problems was one of the few acceptable ways
for girls to express their frustration and elicit support. Boys, with more
outlets, could better afford to make stoicism a virtue. This point was well
illustrated in an episode of "The Power of Choice," a television special
shown at La Fuente, in which high school students discussed how they
dealt with personal and family problems. One boy explained that solving
a problem on your own "makes you stronger," and another boy agreed
that to do so was a "victory." The girls strongly disagreed. Responded
one: "But you build up scar tissue on your heart."

Third, girls who could not cope with family problems, usually in
combination with the demands of school, sometimes directed their anger at themselves or ran away from home. About 10 percent of the girls
interviewed said they had attempted suicide, some more than once; no
boys did so.[15] "Teachers were putting pressure on me, my mom was
putting pressure on me, my dad not being there, having problems with
things, that's the main reason I tried it [suicide]" (Patricia, La Fuente).
About one-fifth of the girls interviewed—and no boys—lived with people who were not relatives, usually with a boyfriend or husband, occasionally with friends or in a group home. Both responses (attempting
suicide and leaving home) often led to major detours in these girls' educational careers.

Somewhat in contrast with girls, boys may cope with the combined
demands of family and school by choosing to enter the paid labor force
full-time. In the High School and Beyond survey of dropouts, males
were more likely than females to cite job offers and choosing to work
(27 versus 11 percent) and having to help support family (14 versus 8
percent) (Ekstrom et al., 1986: 59).

When asked if given the choice whether they would prefer to be at
home, in school, or at work, 35 percent of the boys in my study versus
24 percent of the girls selected work.[16] In the special survey at Beacon,

---

15. Nationwide, boys' suicide rates exceed girls', suggesting that when they attempt
it, they more often succeed in killing themselves. According to U.S. Dept. of Health
and Human Services statistics, white males between the ages of fifteen and nineteen
have the highest suicide rate (18 per 100,000), followed by nonwhite males (10 per
100,000), white females (almost 5 per 100,000), and nonwhite females (3 per 100,000)
(cited in *Newsweek*, "Special Issue—The New Teens," Summer/Fall 1990: 15).

16. Other responses (besides "at work") to the hypothetical question, "If you had the
choice, would you prefer to be at home, in school, or at work?" were as follows: "at

similar proportions of boys and girls said they "sometimes" thought they should go to work full-time rather than attend school to help their family pay the bills (32 and 31 percent, respectively). But more than twice as many boys said they thought about it "a lot" (17 versus 7 percent). Only a few indicated direct family pressure. The eldest child in a Mexican immigrant family commented: "My parents keep telling me to work, because they say they cannot handle the bills, but I know they do." Others felt that working would allow them to gain their independence or that they were a drain on their parents. Ironically, the juvenile justice system that forced one white boy to attend continuation was also contributing to his desire to leave school to work: "The bills my mom has to pay are due to me. I was in the Ranch [a residential school for students in trouble with the law] for about eight months. That costs $1,000 a month. Juvenile hall is about $10 a day, and I was in there a month. My mom is still paying [for that]."

Originally, continuation schools served mainly low-income youths who had to work out of economic necessity. This seems to be less true today. Now these youths may be concentrated in independent studies where they only have to attend school one hour per week, or they may settle for a GED. In addition, even families in desperate financial straits (except undocumented immigrants) can usually apply for government assistance, on condition that their children remain enrolled in school.

More often, students were tired of school, and working was a relatively socially approved reason for dropping out. Ramona, age sixteen, had dropped out for a semester to work at an electronics firm with her mother for $7.50 per hour. At an orientation class, she insisted she really wanted to continue working rather than reenter school (and she did drop out again), and an outspoken handful of boys argued her case with the teacher. They pointed out that teenagers need money for movies, dates ("impressing girls"), clothes, food and drink, and cars. In what they felt was a contradiction, parents urged them to pay for their own entertainment and so forth, but when they said they wanted full-time jobs, their parents responded, "You'll be working all your lives. Enjoy life now" (La Fuente, field notes, 2/21/89).

In some ways, there is a parallel between those who dislike school and want to work and many of the pregnant and mothering girls who were disengaged before conceiving a child but will cite pregnancy as the reason they dropped out, unless probed for details. Likewise, boys who get girls pregnant sometimes leave school to help support their future

home" (15 percent of girls, 21 percent of boys); "at school" (46 percent of girls, 38 percent of boys); unable to choose (15 percent of girls, 6 percent of boys).

child, but in all cases I knew or heard about, the boys already disliked school and jumped at the chance for a face-saving reason to leave:

> When my boyfriend found out I was pregnant, [he left school]. He was going to drop out anyway, whether I said anything to him or what, because he didn't like school to begin with, so there was nothing I could do. (Brenda, La Fuente)

The point deserves emphasis, if only because I observed a number of educators blaming the "traditional values" of some families—typically low-income Mexican and Portuguese immigrants—for the disproportionately high dropout rates among these groups.[17] From interviewing students and talking with parents informally, I sensed a different family dynamic at work, perhaps having more to do with class than ethnicity. If a student is not doing well in school and gets into trouble a lot, middle-class parents will typically place the student in a private school or hire a tutor. For families who cannot afford this and may be more accepting of the school's judgment concerning their child's future academic career, the reality of hard labor seems like one of the few ways to convince their child of the importance of discipline. Reinforcing this view is the knowledge that their child will at least be contributing to the family's financial well-being rather than continuing to be a source of grief. The one interviewee (an undocumented Mexican immigrant) who said his divorced mother was pressuring him to leave school had, until recently, been a gang member. Although Alejandro and his teachers felt he had turned around academically and had college potential, his mother remained unconvinced.

In sum, adherence to traditional gender roles—work for boys, family for girls—seemed more symptomatic of school disengagement than a cause of it.[18] When responsibilities conflicted, both girls and boys appeared to draw on these cultural norms to justify their choice and give

---

17. One teacher-counselor, who prided himself on being sensitive to cultural differences, found that family-related excuses for nonattendance were frequently "scams" among a group of Latino males he counseled. He described the case of a boy who told him: " 'Well, I didn't come to school because my grandmother's sick.' So you [the teacher] could very easily say, 'OK, there's more of a devotion to family than to school.' And that may be true, but then I find out in fact grandma was sick, but someone else was taking care of her, and there was no reason [for him] to be home at all."

18. Fine and Zane (1989: 29, citing Ekstrom et al., 1986) also link adherence to traditional gender norms to disengagement from school: "Of the High School and Beyond respondents, young women who ultimately dropped out were more likely to agree that 'most women are happiest when making a home' and 'it is usually better if the man is the achiever and the woman takes care of the home.' "

it meaning. More fundamentally, these students were responding to negative schooling experiences, limited opportunities, and societywide discrimination.

TIMING OF DISENGAGEMENT

The timing of disengagement differed by gender, across ethnicity. Almost one-fourth of the males interviewed (24 percent) versus 4 percent of females said "things began to go wrong in school" for them in the elementary grades.[19] Junior high (grades seven and eight) was seen as problematic for both boys (24 percent) and girls (30 percent), with the transition (grade nine, the first year of high school for some and the last year of junior high for others)[20] being especially difficult for girls (34 versus 21 percent). One-third of both males and females (32 percent each) saw their problems in school as fairly recent (grades ten or eleven).

Some researchers (for example, Johnson, 1985: 208–9) have argued that, at least at the elementary level, classroom culture and society are biased toward females because the ideal student is quiet, orderly, conformist (all traditionally feminine traits). (For a critique of this argument, see Robertson, 1992.) African-American boys, whom researchers have described as being more kinesically expressive, active, and so forth (cited in Irvine, 1985: 344), may find their elementary experiences particularly discordant. In my sample, a significant group of white and especially Latino and African-American boys, as early as third grade, but usually by grades five and six, had started to skip classes. "I was cutting in elementary school. . . . My uncles were in high school and they used to cut, and I used to just stay with 'em" (Tim, La Fuente). Dennis (Beacon), for example, said he cut because he felt that "most of the time [teachers] come down harder on Mexicans":

> Even in elementary school, my teacher used to make me stay in
> the class until everybody else went out. I was the only Mexican

---

19. The difference in timing of disengagement by gender was statistically significant, with a chi-square (2, $n = 81$) of 7.09 at $p < .05$; the phi coefficient was .296.

20. Most Beacon students had attended junior high in the unified district, which had, in response to declining enrollments, shifted ninth grade to the high school in 1987–88. Beacon students were significantly more likely to cite junior high as the time things went wrong for them in school; the chi-square (2, $n = 81$) was 6.561 at $p < .05$; the phi coefficient was .285. La Fuente students, in contrast, attended grades seven and eight in another district, and, with the exception of boys who had early bad experiences in school, they were more likely to perceive that they had gotten off track beginning in grade nine or later.

in my class. Actually, there were a couple guys, but they were the smarter students and it's like, I was just a little punk.

By junior and senior high, the supposed bias towards girls may shift, although the results are not necessarily reflected in aggregate measures of academic achievement by sex. On the average, girls in the United States earn higher grades than boys do in elementary and secondary school. Much of the research to date has shown that boys score higher on tests of math and visual-spatial ability while girls score higher on tests of verbal ability and that these gender differences become significant in early adolescence (Goetz, 1978: 5), although they have been declining in recent years (Sadker, Sadker, and Klein, 1991: 307–14).

Several factors emerged from the educational histories I recorded that help to explain the shift in the student role, perceived by many of my informants, that had seemed to favor more girls in elementary school. First, the organizational features of many junior highs anticipate high school: departmental structure, with its emphasis on teachers as subject matter specialists, larger school size, individualized scheduling with classes in discrete fifty-minute time periods. Teachers have fewer opportunities to connect with students, while at the same time, they expect students to be more verbal. Academic competition intensifies. Although boys are more likely than girls to be reprimanded in elementary school, they may also "learn to live with criticism and to become less dependent on approval from authority figures" (Robertson, 1992: 54), thus easing their transition to junior high.

About one-tenth of girls versus 3 percent of boys pointed to this change in school organization, with its attendant increased expectations and stress, as the biggest factor pushing them off track. Some felt uneasy about these changes in junior high, particularly those who attended in Beacon's district because it encompassed some wealthier neighborhoods and was more competitive academically than La Fuente's district. One-third of the girls and one-half of the boys had already begun cutting in junior high. Tardy and truant students were punished with detention and suspension, and these disciplinary procedures further contributed to the disengagement process for some (compare Larson, 1989).[21]

---

21. Larson (1989) identified students in sixth-grade classes considered at "highest-risk" of dropping out and compared them to a stratified random sample of others considered merely "at risk" over two years. Both groups had poor attendance, but it got progressively worse after the first quarter of seventh grade. She noted that year, a major reason for classroom removals and suspensions was tardiness or prior nonattendance (11 percent of all cases).

Most, however, perceived the transition into high school itself as the decisive moment in their educational careers. Nancy's description is typical in that the organizational analysis is implicit and concrete:

> I started cutting when I was a freshman in high school cuz the teachers, they didn't care. Some of them did, . . . but [most] teachers these days don't like students. They figure they're just there to teach and get the money and then go on about their business. In junior high, they would push you to do the work: "Come on, you could do it!" In high school, they're like, "If you do it, you do it; if you don't, you don't." (La Fuente)

Or as Carla (La Fuente) put it, "It made you realize you gotta either go down or go up. And I went down."

Second, as discussed earlier in this chapter, peer status groups begin to form in earnest during junior high, partly in response to organizational changes. Developmentally, early adolescents are experimenting with social identities:

> Junior high was my hardest time. It really was, cuz you're going through your identity crisis, trying to find who you are, what kind of people you hang around with. . . . When I first started going there, I hung around with some of the people that are cheerleaders now, like really smart people. But I was always different from them. . . . So I started finding other friends. I was with stoners for awhile. Then I got into the sports thing kinda, . . . and then I met this one girl that was all Duran Duran New Wave and . . . I knew right then and there, that was it. (Joanne, Beacon)

For girls, who have fewer routes to status, their identity is strongly associated with their appearance and social success. "Whether you're going to have a boyfriend, girlfriend, school, a job, it's all judged on your looks," explained Mandy. At a time when many girls feel awkward about their changing bodies, their appearance seems to matter most.

A third and related explanation for girls' declining success in school has to do with the onset of puberty, which starts earlier for girls and—given the sociocultural context just described—is associated with a drop in self-esteem (Eder, 1985: 154; Simmons and Blyth, 1987). At this time, girls seem to get more distracted by romantic relationships and close friendships with other girls. High-achieving girls may be considered less attractive and popular; low-achieving girls may seek alternative ways to feel good about themselves.

Not coincidentally, of the twelve pregnant or mothering girls I interviewed, five had conceived at age fourteen and three had done so at age fifteen (about ninth grade). At this age, Kris explained, "You're kind of a little girl, but you're not a little girl." Boys at the same age, "are into something else. They don't think about having kids. They don't think about meeting somebody and falling in love and having one relationship with one person and having it be forever" (Beacon).

6

WHAT DO CONTINUATION SCHOOLS CONTINUE? LEARNING GENDER AND CLASS

> My boyfriend is talking about leaving in the summer. He's talk-
> ing about me leaving with him, and I want to graduate from
> Beacon [next year]. But I really can't say anything. He wants to
> go to Folsom [to find work].

Blonde hair feathered and permed and eyes carefully made up, Joan
was wearing a Doors t-shirt and jeans this day and musing aloud about
the most important decision she had ever had to make. Her troubled
expression changed into an impish, skeptical one. "He wants to go to
Folsom. I'm going, 'Good, go visit Charlie [Manson] for me.' "

Joan is what some Beacon students refer to as Heinz 57, with three
main ingredients: Italian, Ukrainian, and Scottish. At the time of our
formal interview, she was sixteen and a junior. She met James the year
before, not long after moving from Boston on the heels of her parents'
divorce. In the transfer, she lost enough high school credits to put her
behind and found herself out of place among the children of high tech
managers and engineers. "Around this area, there's lots and lots of rich
people. I mean, you have to be at least upper-middle class to be living
here, and even then, you know, you're just scrounging."

At school, Joan felt people "looked down" on her. "I don't like to
put up with it, [but] you start a fight with somebody and they don't
understand that you're starting a fight with them either," she said,
laughing at the thought. "The rich girls, they acted dumb, real dumb.
All they talked about was their new clothes, their new hairdo, the surfer
dudes they met at the mall. It's like, I wanted to go to school just to get
my education."

Shortly after her sixteenth birthday, Joan asked to come to Beacon in order to make up credits and get away from the jocks and preps. She quickly landed a fast food job to help her mother—on maternity leave and later laid off from her clerical job at an electronics firm—pay the bills. Beacon's secretary worried that Joan was missing a lot of school to care for her new sibling. Joan's experiences informed her critique of the comprehensive high school: "Some teachers give a lot of work with really short deadlines, and they don't think about the fact that lots of kids have to go to work or do stuff for their parents."

Joan felt more positively about Beacon and its teachers:

> Like Mr. Thorndike [a science teacher] was talking to me [and] using my engagement ring so I could relate to it. He's like, "All right, see your ring? Now, how much do you think that would weigh up in space?" . . . So every time I had a problem, I'd look at my ring and remember what he said [about gravity].

Yet Joan's attendance remained erratic. As she liked to remind her friends, she was in love, and she spent time in and out of class writing letters to James and planning romantic outings.

James, two years older than Joan, stopped attending high school at age fourteen—too young for Beacon. The vice principal had accused him of a drug problem and alienated James's family in the process. "I've had more schooling than my boyfriend, yet I feel he has so much more knowledge than I do about so many different things," Joan commented.

When I asked about her goals, she replied: "I'd really love to write. It'd be real hard, though, and I'd need something else stable to be giving me money while I was trying to get established writing." She wanted to attend college but worried, "Am I going to have enough money to pay for college schooling, and am I going to be able to get in?"

Joan's joking defiance about following James to Folsom receded and she turned serious:

> See, I don't like some of the things he has to say to me about my work. I've talked about going into writing. What am I going to do? He goes, "You can get a job waiting on tables." Oh, for the rest of my life—no way! No way. . . . Sometimes he does [have high expectations for me]. But then when it comes down to it really, see, he just wants to make his money setting tile, doing what he does, and wants me along for the ride.

As Joan spoke, I thought of the words to one of her favorite songs, "Should I Stay or Should I Go?" by the Clash: "One day is fine, the next is black." Ultimately, James decided against moving to Folsom, and Joan graduated from Beacon the next year. High school is supposed to help students with the transition to the working world, but at Beacon and La Fuente, girls were not encouraged to think broadly and imaginatively about what that work could be. Often boyfriends like James were a more profound force shaping these girls' future employment possibilities. Beacon counted Joan a success story because she received a diploma, yet she left still engaged to James, and Beacon and the rest of her schooling had provided no well-grounded framework for analysis to help her sort through the dilemmas she faced.

Girls and boys anticipate futures that still diverge by gender. This fact bears directly on the disengagement process, as students evaluate the importance of school compared to work and family responsibilities. Therefore, it is important to examine how the continuation school challenges or, more often, reinforces prevailing gender relations. My evidence shows that the continuation school helps prepare students mainly for working-class, sex-segregated jobs. Through its formal and informal curriculum, the continuation school helps define and legitimize the separation of public (for example, paid labor) and private (for example, sexuality, childbearing, and child rearing) spheres which has contributed to an ideology of male dominance. This ideology minimizes the importance of women's work outside the market economy, underpins men's superior access to paid work, and justifies women's limited access to wage labor by emphasizing procreation and socialization of the young as their primary responsibilities. Individual teachers and students within the continuation school challenged this ideology, but their responses were isolated and unsystematic and therefore limited in effectiveness.

The institution was largely passive with respect to peers' informal enforcement of traditional gender identities. The relatively few students who resisted "business as usual" risked their sexual reputation and were hindered by an underdeveloped alternative ideology and vision. For example, working-class boys who did well in school or even cared about doing well sometimes risked being labeled "gay." Girls who excelled at sports and other extracurricular activities or were outspoken in class and elsewhere risked being labeled "dyke" or "slut," depending on their style and appearance.

Finally, the consequences of dropping out altogether versus receiving a continuation diploma seemed more severely negative for girls. With or without a high school diploma, girls faced higher unemployment rates. Girls were also informally excluded from construction and other jobs sometimes open to boys who left school early. Current economic and social conditions that tend to confine women to lower-paying and less prestigious occupations suggest that girls, even with the diploma, will be placed at a relative disadvantage compared to boys who leave without graduating.

My impression, from visiting the feeder schools into Beacon and La Fuente, is that what continuation schools continue is not that different from what goes on inside the comprehensive high schools, particularly for working-class students. It is precisely this low-income group of students who disproportionately receive the message that they do not fit into the mainstream high schools. Rose (1989: 9), for example, eloquently and from personal experience describes the "environmental messages of defeat" as well as "the commonalities in working-class lives":

> the isolation of neighborhoods, information poverty, the limited means of protecting children from family disaster, the predominance of such disaster, the resilience of imagination, the intellectual curiosity and literate enticements that remain hidden from schools, the feelings of scholastic inadequacy, the dislocations that come from crossing educational boundaries.

CONNECTIONS BETWEEN THE CONTINUATION SCHOOL
AND STUDENTS' FUTURES

Dramatic changes in the structure of work and families have taken place since the end of World War II. Today, according to government statistics, 73 percent of women in the prime childbearing years (ages twenty to thirty-four) are in the work force, compared to 35 percent in 1950. Many work out of economic necessity: nearly 60 percent of women in the work force are either single, divorced, widowed, separated, or have husbands who earn less than $15,000 a year. Further, the traditional nuclear family (made up of a sole breadwinner father, a homemaker mother, and children under eighteen) comprises only 8 percent of all households today (Nine-to-Five, 1989).

These realities had begun to encroach on the romantic dreams of many of the girls interviewed for this study, who as early adolescents had hoped to become full-time homemakers (compare McRobbie, 1978 on the "culture of femininity"). (Their views on the relationship between future work and family life will be explored below.) All girls expected that they would have to work out of economic necessity. Their work aspirations were often extensions of domestic interests and skills. The girls mentioned cosmetologist (20 percent), nurse or dental assistant (20 percent), fashion designer or model (7 percent), and child care worker and teacher (7 percent). These and most other jobs mentioned were traditional women's occupations: secretary (7 percent), paralegal and court reporter (10 percent). Two girls mentioned wanting nontraditional jobs (air traffic controller and electrical engineer), yet they were scholastically unprepared to achieve their goals.[1]

No boys mentioned a job that was nontraditional for their gender, although some had high aspirations (psychologist, for example). They most often mentioned carpenter or construction worker, airplane pilot (via the military), auto mechanic, and businessperson (each 15 percent). With the exception of some professional and partial-fantasy occupations (rock star, professional athlete, model), the jobs both boys and girls mentioned reflected the work done by parents, who were also the most often cited influence on students' work plans.

Beacon and La Fuente, through their formal curricula (including the work experience program), linkages to vocational training, and informal curricula, helped prepare students to set their sights on "realistic" goals. Girls were subtly encouraged "to blur the distinction between family and work for themselves" while accepting as natural the work-family division for men (Arnot, 1982: 83). Of course, girls always interpreted the sometimes conflicting messages through reference to their own experiences and in light of structural constraints (Gaskell, 1985).

Formal Curriculum

The formal curriculum offered in both schools was largely remedial. Almost two-thirds of students interviewed felt that what they were studying at the continuation school was easier than regular school fare; the rest saw the curriculum as comparable, occasionally more relevant, but not harder. Only one-third felt they were learning less as a result, yet few academic standardbearers existed to challenge other students to put forth as much effort as they seemed capable of expending. This situation increased the odds that those capable of, and interested in, higher education would get sidetracked in remedial community college courses, become bored and discouraged, and eventually drop out.[2] Girls were more concerned about the level of academic learning at the continuation school: more than one-tenth of them spontaneously mentioned wanting more college preparatory courses; no boys did so.

---

1. A nontraditional occupation for women is defined by the U.S. Dept. of Labor as one in which women comprise no more than one-quarter of the total number of workers.

2. About 35 percent of students entering high school in California eventually enroll in community colleges, but less than one-third (28.5 percent) of those who enroll earn an associate degree; even fewer transfer to four-year institutions (CSDE, 1990a: 45).

Reminiscent of lower-track classrooms (Oakes, 1985; Page, 1987), many of the continuation classrooms I observed put a premium on attendance, punctuality, and productivity rather than academic content, on developing good work habits and conformity rather than critical thinking and creativity. Earning credit (based largely on attendance) as opposed to learning became the students' overriding goal. At La Fuente, if students missed too many days of a three-week grading period, some teachers wondered aloud why the students bothered to come to class because they would receive no credit anyway (for example, field notes, 4/5/89).

The most routine aspects of schooling were continuously likened to what future employers would expect of students: bringing paper and pencil would prepare students to wear a uniform, grades were paychecks, and so on. The analogy of school to work became strained when it came down to punishment for noncompliance. Several teachers wished aloud that they could fire tardy or disobedient students, and there was always at least one student to reply: "I wish I *could* be fired" (La Fuente, field notes, 9/8/88, 3/16/89, 5/24/89, 6/2/89). Seen from these students' perspective, they sought to minimize unpaid labor, to obtain the credits necessary for the diploma. They worked for the scholastic paycheck with no pride of craft.

The situation had been similar for many students while at the comprehensive high schools. But they sometimes witnessed different standards being applied to college preparatory students. A teacher at a Beacon feeder school, where all tardy students were supposed to be locked out of classrooms and sent to detention, gave this example:

> We have some teachers teaching high level math, calculus and trig, and chemistry saying, "I don't want students missing my class." Versus somebody else with a class of kids that are discipline problems and for them not to be there that particular period would make their class run a little smoother. (3/8/89 interview)

Thus, those aiming for professional careers were taught that learning is most important, while those expected to fill blue- and pink-collar jobs were taught that punctuality takes precedence.

I did not systematically examine formal curriculum, including textbooks, for gender (and within that, class and ethnic) biases, but I found little evidence that women's experiences and accomplishments were given more than superficial treatment (compare Sadker, Sadker, and Klein, 1991: 272–80). In all the classes I sat through, only one teacher explicitly organized a lesson around a gender issue (sex stereotyping) (Beacon, field notes, 2/6/89). She was prompted to do this in part because of the gender-typed literature her English students chose to read as part of an individualized course. Girls tended to read romance novels and popular psychology books, while boys selected stories about gangs, the Cold War, and drug culture. Although few of these texts challenged stereotypes, two "self-help" psychology books encouraged at least one girl to develop a liberal feminist analysis. Erin, a Beacon student, credited *Women Who Love Too Much* and *Co-Dependent No More* with helping her break up with a domineering boyfriend:

> I was reading books on co-dependency, but I was making my own interpretations about it. Like when I read that book *Women Who Love Too Much*, it says you can't change anyone; the only thing you can do is change the way you feel about it, or change yourself. . . . They mention a lot of the myths in the book [like] . . . "A woman's the caretaker of the family—the wife—she does everything for her husband, for her children, and her own needs are put last," which makes her actually crazy.

The general lack of emphasis on gender contrasted with the attention paid to ethnicity at La Fuente, where the majority of teachers were either African-American or Mexican-American. The school sponsored several ethnic pride days and events, teachers encouraged students to organize a Black Student Union, displayed posters, led discussions on racism, and suspended students for "racial slurs." While inequality based on ethnicity was routinely challenged, sexism and classism were not (compare Grant and Sleeter, 1986). Although most teachers treated girls fairly equally at the two schools, they did not teach students about institutional forms of sexism. Without such knowledge, students tended to interpret their problems as only personal ones.

Although academic classes were not sex-segregated, most electives were; this tended to reinforce, and perhaps foster, sex-typed work and family goals.[3] At Beacon, only girls enrolled in home economics; they got credit for cooking, sewing, or "talking about boyfriends or sex in a group" (field notes, 9/12/88). The fact that the class was all girls did allow more opportunities to discuss issues of sexuality, but when the

---

3. Gaskell (1985) found that working-class girls within the vocational or general track tended to take classes that prepared them for sex-stereotyped jobs (typing, business courses) or domestic work (home economics, family life courses), whereas the primarily middle-class girls within the college track preferred language and literature courses over math and science.

teacher tried to formalize the discussions (in combination with an all-female work experience class), some girls argued that boys should be able to join and the teachers shelved the project (field notes, 10/6/88).

Only boys enrolled in woodshop at Beacon. Typing was composed almost entirely of girls. Kris disliked typing so tried woodshop for a week. She dropped the class because she felt uncomfortable being the only girl (Beacon, field notes, 9/13/88, 5/1/89). The teacher explained that girls "are usually very good at woodshop," but he got more boys because "the boys have an option and many do go into construction. Especially in this area, there are a lot of companies that aren't union and you can get a job [as a carpenter]" (5/8/89 interview). Although he treated girls well, this teacher did not apparently encourage them to link their interest to nontraditional job plans.

At La Fuente, drafting was all male, and merchandising seemed to be predominantly so (field notes, 11/10/88). Boys were almost as likely as girls to participate in business classes at La Fuente because students learned to type only on computers, a male interest. The home economics course also enrolled a fair number of boys, for two reasons. First, the course was offered by the orientation teacher who recruited boys early, playing up past male students' accomplishments in home economics and asserting that "95 percent of tailors and chefs are men" (field notes, 9/6/88, 4/27/89). Second, other boys joined to meet girls (at Beacon, this was done in art classes). The boys often did little but flirt in these classes, causing one Latina to complain aloud that she had "to do all the work" (in this case, baking rolls; field notes, 10/11/89).

Girls in the SAM program were required to take a child development class and participate in a period-long child care lab. Most also took a course entitled Independent Family Living where they were taught to do such things as balance a checkbook and communicate more effectively. One in four girls not in the SAM program at La Fuente had elected to take such courses, either at La Fuente or previously; no boys had. Throughout the school year, I observed only one school-age father enrolled in a class at the SAM building; he always sat with his girlfriend and seemed well accepted by the other girls (field notes, 9/7/88, 9/21/88). More than one-fifth of the boys interviewed at La Fuente had or were expecting a child (though their girlfriends were not necessarily enrolled in the SAM program). Based on my participant observation, this proportion seemed representative of the school as a whole. Thus, there would have been enough school-age fathers to fill two or three fatherhood training courses. Yet the school made no visible effort to enroll them. A SAM program administrator told me it would be difficult to get boys to enroll and that, given limited resources, classes aimed at pregnancy prevention at the junior high level would be more effective.

I posed the idea of fatherhood training to three sixteen-year-old boys; two had girlfriends who were pregnant and one was the father of an infant. At first they laughed and wondered if it would consist of changing diapers and coping with crying babies. In the end, all three said they would "check it out" if it were available. Several barriers stand in the way of recruiting boys for such a program. First is the assumption that girls will assume most of the responsibility of child rearing, even if the couple stays together. (Only one young father interviewed was still with his girlfriend; a few others said they tried to help cover the expenses associated with the pregnancy and child care.) Indeed, many boys assume that contraception—and thus pregnancy—is a girl's responsibility. At Beacon, most boys were therefore reluctant to contact an obstetrician to ask about the costs of prenatal care and childbirth, one of the assignments for all students on furlough (field notes, 12/13/88). Second, the school has no way of knowing which boys are fathers. Third, many of the fathers are older and already out of school (Brindis and Jeremy, 1988). Fourth, teachers working in adolescent pregnancy and parenthood programs are typically women, reinforcing the idea that child rearing is mainly women's work.

One of the goals of continuation education is "to help the student develop principles for home and family living, including preparation for marriage" (CSDE, 1973: 1). It is difficult to see how this goal is being achieved for the boys. In a revealing survey (Schmidt et al., 1975) of continuation students (240 boys and 183 girls) in eight schools, girls strongly agreed that the continuation school was helping them "in preparation for marriage," whereas the boys were nearly evenly split.

Work Experience Education and Vocational Training

Another continuation education goal is to enable students to work while completing school. Although girls at La Fuente and Beacon, as well as statewide (CSDE, 1990b: 6), were as likely to participate in work experience programs as boys, almost all students held sex-typed jobs. In 1988–89, 50 percent of Beacon students obtained work permits, 19 percent full-time and 31 percent part-time; 35 percent participated in the work experience program. Half of the work experience students held jobs in restaurants, and of these, all line cooks, kitchen helpers, and delivery personnel were male; girls were waiters or cashiers, a job performed by two boys as well. In other industries, boys were stockers, security guards, and janitors; girls were data entry clerks and clothing salesclerks. At La Fuente, 30 percent of students were issued work permits, 14 percent full-time and 16 percent part-time; 6 percent participated in the work experience program at similarly sex-typed jobs.

One part of work experience classes is career planning, but this was made difficult by the fact that few jobs held by students had potential for advancement. Though most students were employed in fast food jobs, they routinely scorned these as "teenager jobs" that would not "pick up the bills" even if one became a manager (La Fuente, field notes, 11/30/88, 1/12/89). Drug dealing emerged as a lucrative, exciting alternative to "flippin' the greasy patties" (La Fuente, field notes, 2/21/89). Boys more often dealt drugs and engaged in other, more legitimate entrepreneurial activities such as disc jockeying. The going rate for disc jockeys was $35 an hour for house parties, $45 an hour for dances, and $200 an hour for concerts (La Fuente, field notes, 5/11/89). Girls had fewer such employment options.

Nontraditional careers received little emphasis in work experience, orientation, or career planning sessions. Beacon's efforts seemed limited to displaying a poster showing women police officers and brochures on sex discrimination in employment in the career center; the career counselor asked students if they knew what nontraditional meant (field notes, 9/16/88). At La Fuente, the career center person usually confined her remarks to students' expressed (largely traditional) interests, but once she commented, "Ladies commonly don't have experience in mechanics and using tools. You may need to pursue it if you want to do that" (field notes, 11/9/88). Nothing was said about how this might be accomplished.

The orientation teacher occasionally asked boys to consider nursing and secretarial jobs (La Fuente, field notes, 5/18/89) and girls to think about careers in the armed forces: "Ladies, the military wants more of you, too. I think it would be an exciting life, personally. If I hadn't gone to college, I'm sure I would have joined the military" (field notes, 11/17/88). Some girls responded positively to the military, prompting negative comments from some boys ("Girls are too weak!") and support from some girls ("Girls can do anything guys can do!") (field notes, 12/8/88).

Vocational training opportunities were often presented in a sex-segregated way. For example, the orientation teacher at La Fuente described the skills offered through the Regional Occupational Programs or Center (ROP/C) in this way: "For guys, there is construction, body finishing, welding. For girls, there's home ec, cosmetology, nursing, dental assistant" (field notes, 9/6/88). Few students (6 percent) at either La Fuente or Beacon enrolled in ROP/C, and those who did pursued traditional, sex-typed careers. At Beacon during 1989–90, for example, five girls enrolled in cosmetology, one in retail sales; one boy enrolled in cosmetology (then moved), five in electrical maintenance, and three in retail sales. At La Fuente, girls took dental assisting, cosmetology, and court reporting, whereas boys took mainly auto shop, air conditioning and refrigeration, and carpentry.[4]

I sensed no dissatisfaction on the part of students regarding the sex-segregated nature of most vocational training. They took it for granted and enjoyed the company of same-sex friends as well as the opportunity to develop their interests in a direction that might lead to paid employment. One girl described her day at "vocational" in this way:

> When I leave here [La Fuente] at 11:51 I'm going to go home and get ready to go to cosmetology. I usually leave my house at 12:30 and arrive at cosmetology at 12:50. I check in and go to the breakroom and smoke with my buddies until 1:00. Then we all go into the theory room and take notes on our operation for today. At 2:00 we have our break until 2:15. Then we get out our maniquinn [sic] heads and practice haircutting, perms, colors and roller sets. At 3:30 we start clean-up. Everyone gets assigned to a clean-up. At 4:25 they hand out the time cards and at 4:30 we leave to go home. (5/11/89 essay)

By the time most students reach the continuation school, they are at least sixteen years old, and although few have hard and fast career plans, most are considering traditional sex-segregated (or at best, mixed) occupations. The U.S. Department of Labor's Women's Bureau has identified nontraditional job training and placement as a major strategy for reducing the occupational segregation of low-income women. Little was being done to encourage this at the two continuation schools under study, however, despite a seeming endorsement of the approach. Extra counseling by staff supportive of the goal, presentations by—or internships with—nontraditional role models, selling employers on the idea (starting with those who provide work experience jobs), and recruitment to achieve

---

4. Statewide in 1986–87, 7 percent of continuation students participated in job training in ROP/Cs (CSDE, 1988: 29). One study found that the ROP/Cs were ineffective in retaining would-be dropouts or giving students any relative advantage in finding jobs after they graduated (Stern et al., 1986).

Further, enrollment by skill is largely sex-segregated, although the state funds a Sex Equity/Single Parent–Homemaker Program to counter this (CSDE, 1990b). Nationally, according to 1980 data, girls "represented 91 percent of students training as nursing assistant, 87 percent of those training for community health workers, and 92 percent of students in cosmetology and secretarial sciences. Similarly, 95 percent of students enrolled in electrical technology, 90 percent in electronics, 94 percent in appliance repair, 96 percent in carpentry, 95 percent in welding, and 96 percent in small engine repair were males" (Burge and Culver, 1990: 160–61).

non-sex-segregated enrollment in vocational electives are some ways the schools could have demonstrated a strong commitment to the strategy.

Hidden Curriculum

The hidden or informal curriculum refers to the implicit messages conveyed by teacher expectations and presentation of lesson content, the school's system of rewards, and staffing patterns (Kelly and Nihlen, 1982). Very rarely did teachers challenge traditional ideas about gender, or if they did, they sent out mixed messages. For example, Ms. Lopes instructed her class to "ask mom to pick you up a notebook when she's at the store," implying that women are responsible for such chores (La Fuente, field notes, 9/9/88). In an interview, she said she advises girls in her class: "I tell them, 'Housewives are dinosaurs; in another generation, they're going to be extinct. . . . You will not have the luxury of staying home and raising your own children' " (5/24/89 interview). Yet she herself chose teaching because it allowed her to quit work in order to care for her children until they entered school (as did all the other women teachers with children interviewed for this study, with the exception of one who divorced). More than once, Ms. Lopes and her colleagues remarked on the advantage of a job that allows women flexibility in balancing work and domestic responsibilities.

Consideration of social class was absent from teachers' comments about how work and family would mesh in the future. Most women teachers had married professional men (school administrators and teachers, corporate managers, lawyers, and engineers), acquired material and social resources, and established careers before bearing children. Their class position allowed them to withdraw from the labor force and then reenter. For the predominantly working-class continuation girls—a number of whom had a child or a steady boyfriend or husband, also working-class, or both—this scenario seemed remote. So perhaps a more accurate statement would have been that working-class housewives will soon be extinct dinosaurs, while the middle-class has evolved an amphibious animal, able to exist alternately as housewives and full-time workers. (Petchesky [1983] has noted two other possibilities: high-fertility middle- and upper-middle-class women whose husbands earn enough so that they do not need to work outside the home for pay at all and working-class women in poverty or on welfare. Recently, however, some states have linked receiving welfare to mandatory work or job training for women with young children. Thus, this type of low-income or working-class housewife also appears to be an "endangered species.")

Teachers and administrators sometimes conveyed gender-differentiated expectations. In reviewing school rules, Ms. Wilson occasionally highlighted different standards for boys' and girls' conduct. Example: "Maybe parents can accept the son cutting and messing up, but the daughter: it must be embarrassing," she noted, glancing at two girls who had boasted about cutting classes (La Fuente, field notes, 1/18/89). Other teachers catered to boys' reluctance to do certain tasks considered feminine. Example: Two boys in Ms. Hensley's class asked for a girl to be in their project group, arguing, "We need a secretary," and she obliged without comment (La Fuente, field notes, 3/30/89). Or adults unreflectively transferred traditional practices to the school setting. Example: a male administrator, who gave students caught smoking the option of performing cleanup tasks in lieu of suspension, usually asked boys to pick up litter. In contrast, he more often asked girls to do such things as clean sinks or vacuum, thus reflecting a common sexual division of labor regarding domestic chores (Beacon, field notes, 5/19/88, 10/10/88).

Less obvious than what school staff actually said and did were missed opportunities to challenge the gender status quo. Example: During an open discussion of careers, Bernard expressed surprise at how little his aunt earned as a secretary (La Fuente, field notes, 12/15/88). This provided an opening to discuss occupational segregation by gender and ethnicity, yet the teacher merely acknowledged the point and moved on. Example: In a self-esteem exercise, the teacher asked students to go around the room and state a talent they had; most responses were gender-typed: girls most often mentioned cooking, caring for babies, and listening or advising, whereas boys said sports, mechanical repair, and music. Two pregnant girls refused to admit they had a talent. The teacher remarked, "I'm surprised at you two who are expecting children. Christina, you keep your hair and makeup real nice. Don't you think that's a talent?" (La Fuente, field notes, 4/27/89). Girls were thus at once encouraged to consider cosmetology as a career, to focus on their personal appearance (perhaps with an eye toward pleasing men), and to see themselves as treasured objects (de Beauvoir, 1953).

Teachers regularly challenged the boys' most common job goal, construction. In part, they were responding to boys who questioned whether such occupations as carpentry logically required a high school diploma. Construction work, teachers argued, is dangerous and seasonal (Beacon, field notes, 5/16/89; La Fuente, field notes, 9/6/88, 12/15/88, 5/18/89). In contrast, I never heard school staff members discourage girls from cosmetology, child care, or office work. They seemed satisfied that the girls had work ambitions at all.

One reason for the differential expectations was the widespread acceptance of the sex-role socialization model (for a critical analysis of this theory, see Connell, 1987: 47–54). Many teachers assumed that students came to school with values and attitudes about what men and women are and how they should behave, that were formed in childhood and difficult to change. One in five teachers interviewed specifically mentioned that Mexican and Portuguese immigrant parents often had low educational aspirations for their daughters; "to marry and raise children is the objective," said one teacher (Beacon, 4/25/89 interview). While a few Latinas agreed that their parents had lower expectations for them than for their brothers, all said their parents wanted them to graduate and in a number of instances they credited parents with motivating them to persist. "My dad'd do anything to have me finish school" (Becky, Beacon). "My parents are the ones that pushed me. I think if they wouldn't have been pushing me, I don't think I would have stayed in school" (Sylvia, Beacon).

Stories by teachers who had encountered resistant parents (usually fathers) further contributed to low expectations for Latinas and may have convinced other teachers not to stir up trouble. One teacher had taken a girl from a strict, patriarchal family under her wing. The father, a Portuguese immigrant, would not allow the girl to date, drive, or work. All her purchases had to be approved by him in advance. The teacher noticed that the girl had picked up typing quickly and wanted her to get some office work experience, but the father refused his permission. Ultimately, however, the teacher located an office job on campus for the girl and succeeded in obtaining the father's blessing.

Besides teacher expectations and presentation of content, a school's system of rewards can convey implicit gender lessons to students. Because neither of the continuation schools had athletic teams, a common source of status that disproportionately rewards boys had been eliminated. Both schools rewarded good attendance and academic improvement through monthly recognition of one boy and one girl. The rationale behind the gender distinction was unclear, as was the message it conveyed. To some it implied fairness, but it also signaled that boys and girls were not in direct competition with each other, only with their same-sex peers. It also represented a specific instance of how some staff members took gender as a natural division, that is one based on biological differences and not linked to power relations. A number of teachers gave little thought to dividing classes into debating teams by sex (La Fuente, field notes, 3/9/89), to shaming one gender into greater academic effort by praising the other (La Fuente, field notes, 2/21/89) or to addressing part of an academic lesson to only one gender in the presence of the other (Beacon, field notes, 4/11/89), but to have done so by ethnicity would have been unthinkable.

Staffing patterns comprised a third aspect of the hidden curriculum. In terms of academic and vocational subjects, there was an obvious division by gender at both schools. Women tended to teach language, history, art, home economics, and child development classes, while men taught math, science, woodshop, drafting, physical education, and merchandising classes; social studies classes were mixed. Women also supervised student governance and social activities. Men held all top administrative posts (principal, head counselor, teacher in charge; on the underrepresentation of women in educational administration in general, see Sadker, Sadker, and Klein, 1991: 280–82). All teacher aides and clerical support staff were women, and all custodians were men. Thus, the schools did not present students with an alternative model to the wider, occupationally gender-segregated world of work.

PEERS' INFORMAL ENFORCEMENT OF
TRADITIONAL GENDER IDENTITIES

Peer groups played a major role in reproducing, and sometimes challenging, traditional gender identities at both continuation schools (compare Eisenhart and Holland, 1983, who reached a similar conclusion in a study of fifth- and sixth-graders). In order to challenge these norms, school staff would need an analysis of gender relations and a willingness to prompt students to think critically about the attitudes and values they held. But like many people in U.S. society today, they seemed ambivalent about gender-related issues such as sexuality and family arrangements. To introduce a feminist perspective into the curriculum requires changing priorities and focusing attention on subordinated groups, particularly women, and this remains difficult (see, for example, Weiler, 1988: esp. 131–43). Thus, many teachers and administrators preferred to minimize controversy, and resistance to prevailing gender relations was relatively rare and fragmented.

A Continuum of Male Dominance and Female Resistance

In my field notes, I recorded numerous attempts at male dominance, ranging from stereotyping and sexist remarks to sexual harassment and physical abuse. Girls and effeminate boys were devalued, and the negative stereotypes about these groups were used to justify the less common instances of physical violence. I never witnessed any girl attempting to dominate a boy (though the possibility exists), although once provoked, girls often returned an insult, sought protection, came to each other's aid, lashed out physically, and otherwise tried to exert control; girls were not simply victims (compare Wolpe, 1988: 37).

The most common and tolerated form of male dominance was the stereotyped or sexist remark. Example: In my music class, a day was set aside for a discussion of women in popular music. Before I was able to lay out some recent accomplishments by women musicians and set the tone, Cliff, the elected student body president, announced that "women rockers are posers. They should be at home doing housework." Rich added, "Women look good in spandex. That's about it." Even if they were "half kidding," their comments served to delegitimize the lesson and quash discussion, especially the girls' participation (Beacon, field notes, 1/19/89). The girls in the class respected Cliff's opinions about music, and his sexist comment helped undermine their confidence in this area. Joanne, for example, wanted to join a band. When I asked her why she did not start one of her own, she told me, "Guys put down girl groups as not good enough" (field notes, 4/4/89).

Certain boys regularly denigrated some girls as "airheads" or "blondes," referred to girlfriends as "bitches," and told others they were fat and ugly. At a meeting to discuss raising funds for senior activities, one boy suggested to the girls around him that they become prostitutes and participate in a wet t-shirt contest (La Fuente, field notes, 4/26/89). Although not impressed, many teachers either regarded such comments as a cute manifestation of the battle of the sexes or rolled their eyes and ignored them. One male staff member even participated, calling one girl in the SAM program "blondie"—who then brought her father to campus to confront him—and allegedly asked another, "How's the whoring?" The latter comment prompted several women teachers to complain to the principal on the student's behalf (La Fuente, field notes, 5/10–11/89). Noreen, a Beacon student frequently taunted about her weight, sometimes preferred that adults, myself included, refrain from interceding because help from school authorities seemed to reinforce Noreen's "goody goody" image, another label she struggled against (for example, field notes, 5/16/89).

Boys often drew inspiration from the sexist practices of their favorite music groups. The level of sexism, racism, and homophobia in rap and heavy metal rock music, the two most popular musical forms among the boys in this study, has received publicity of late. Some examples: During the fieldwork, a popular album by Guns 'n Roses featured a woman apparently raped by a robot on its inner jacket. Concert t-shirts bearing the playboy logo were popular at both Beacon and La Fuente, and I noticed one boy at La Fuente writing the title of a song by Slayer, "Speak English or Die," on his folder and the brim of his cap; the message, he explained, was aimed at "the Chinese" (field notes, 1/25/89).

This same boy was later, in a separate incident, suspended one week for a "racial slur" (La Fuente, field notes, 3/30/89).

Sexual harassment was less tolerated than sexist remarks but not dealt with as harshly as ethnic slurs. Some boys continuously annoyed individual girls, either with lewd remarks, pinching, cornering and "hitting up" on them. School adults did not often witness these incidents. One boy told his friends a man teacher "lectured me hard" for grabbing a girl's breast at lunch (Beacon, field notes, 11/1/88). Girls were reluctant to report such harassment because they felt that teachers could do little to prevent it, that it would be their word against the boy's, and that they might suffer retaliation (Beacon, field notes, 2/14/89, 3/27/89). Instead, girls preferred to hit the offender or get a boyfriend or brother to fight him. This response risked suspension for both parties (for example, Beacon, field notes, 12/5/88, 5/14/90) but was probably more effective in dealing with the problem given the schools' lack of formal support.

A special category of harassment was what Sandra, a survivor of assault, referred to as "couple abuse." The term, which Sandra heard from a counselor, allows for the possibility that a few girls hit and verbally abuse their boyfriends, though it obscures the fact that overwhelmingly the abuse comes from males. Sandra's boyfriend beat her regularly, and when a teacher at her old school finally reported the case as one of suspected abuse, Sandra said it was "treated the same as if I got into a fight in high school—not a big deal. I feel that the schools could take a bigger step as far as getting counseling programs, educating teachers more" (Beacon, 4/12/88 group discussion). Most girlfriend battering occurred off campus, but friends discussed individual cases in and out of class; I never heard a student except Sandra, however, analyze these as a social problem. Several girls said in interviews that boyfriends had physically assaulted them, and one student had to get a restraining order against her ex-boyfriend (La Fuente, field notes, 10/13/89).

The practice was not stigmatized enough to prevent several boys from publicly boasting of using physical force or intimidation. Ricardo announced during class that he had found his pregnant girlfriend smoking crack, "beat the bitch up," and had not seen her since. Two boys next to him turned to shake his hand in congratulations, while the girls looked uneasy, and after a pause one offered, "You could have just slapped her" (La Fuente, field notes, 9/6/88). Dennis told my music class, "If my girlfriend got pregnant and she didn't want to have the baby, I'd slap her" (Beacon, field notes, 11/28/88). I was talking with a group of Beacon students at lunch about the SAM program at La Fuente, and Paul commented: "That's sick when girls bring their babies to school. If

I got my girlfriend pregnant, I'd force her to get an abortion" (field notes, 6/14/89).[5]

These and other examples show that some boys feel they can justifiably dominate women physically. Other boys felt uncomfortable with this but, at the same time, found it difficult to understand why women would stay in abusive relationships. When the Joel Steinberg/Hedda Nussbaum case was in the news, for example, several boys concluded that "women love abuse" (La Fuente, field notes, 12/15/88), and a man teacher wondered aloud why abused women do not "migrate" (Beacon, field notes, 2/27/89). Some women teachers at both schools perceived a need to educate students and staff, particularly the boys and men, about domestic and dating violence. At Beacon, a male administrator responded, "That would be good for the girls to hear," thus missing the point entirely (field notes, 5/14/90).

At La Fuente a teacher invited a speaker from a battered women's shelter to address the orientation class after a new student confided in an essay (excerpted below verbatim) that she had been almost raped by her ex-boyfriend:

> I was suppose to get married to him but I broked it off cause he use to hit me. . . . He tried to force himself on me. I was hella scared. I didn't know what to do. He messed up my neck pretty bad. . . . I'm really upset from what happen yesterday. I can't write no more.

The guest speaker focused on how wife abuse is learned behavior and on factors that constrain women from leaving abusive situations (field notes, 5/11/89). Issues of family violence, defined by the larger society as private—but which affect students' ability to focus on school work—were given public voice within the classroom.

In one of the few frank discussions of gender relations I witnessed, both boys and girls acknowledged the prevalence of domestic violence and took seriously the dynamics that lead to it. Boys and girls participated equally in developing the following list of reasons women might stay with abusive men: fear of physical harm, concern for the children's

---

5. Abortion was the single most popular topic selected by students for written and oral class and school debate at both La Fuente and Beacon. In reviewing all student opinions recorded in field notes, only a handful of Mexican-, African-, and Filipino-American boys opposed abortion rights. Virtually all girls and most boys supported abortion rights, although some said they personally would not choose to have an abortion. At least a few boys felt entitled to the final say, by physical force if necessary, in whether or not their female partners would have an abortion.

well-being, love, lack of economic security, and sympathy for the abuser if he had been abused as a child. The speaker then showed a video that featured a white, middle-class family in which the husband repeatedly abused his wife, who ultimately found refuge in a battered women's shelter. I overheard generally positive comments about the video's messages, and in the discussion that followed, a number of boys opened up about why they came into conflict with girlfriends. The most common reason was girlfriends telling them, "You can't go out with your [male] friends and leave me at home." The speaker, who was street wise in a way admired by the toughest boys, explained why girls might feel that way and urged the boys to communicate their feelings and engage in "constructive problem solving" as an alternative to violence. Nobody, however, raised the feminist question of why women are disproportionately the targets of male violence or explored the connection between wife abuse at the personal level and the reality of women's subordination in the wider society (Yllo and Bograd, 1988).

Insecurity over Sexual Identity and Reputation

Peer groups often played on individual students' insecurities about sexual identity and reputation which, in effect, promoted adherence to traditional gender roles and homophobia (hatred and fear of gays and lesbians). Boys feared the homosexual label, while girls had to steer a course between lesbian on the one hand and "slut" on the other. In avoiding these pitfalls and trying to portray themselves as attractive to potential long-term companions, students would rarely challenge the current play of gender relations unless part of a group. The heterosexual-homosexual dichotomy was entwined with how students defined themselves publicly as "feminine" or "masculine" and also with the power relations between girls and boys and among groups of boys.

Most boys were quick to call any boy who displayed traditionally feminine behavior or interests a "fag" or a "girl." They seemed to fear, at base, the loss of privilege rooted in the traditional order or masculinity. Repeating what they had heard from some men bosses, family members, and teachers, boys used gender-baiting tactics to bring peers into conformity. Example: Three continuation boys were alone (with me observing in the distance) with a group of eighth-grade boys. They wanted to counsel them about the transition to high school outdoors, rather than in the classroom. When the younger boys resisted the move, they were brought into line by such comments as: "You guys, don't be women!" "You can hang in the sun—your hair spray won't melt" (Beacon, field notes, 5/26/89).

Quite a few of the boys at both schools had long hair, which for them symbolized rebellion. But some teachers and other adult men called them "sissies" (La Fuente, field notes, 5/11/89; Beacon, field notes, 5/23/89), sometimes implying that they were trying to make themselves sexually attractive to "real" men or "dykes" (Beacon, field notes, 2/7/89). Heavy metal and thrash rockers continuously put down the more mainstream glam (short for glamour) rockers as "gay." This, in turn, prompted the glam rockers to justify the long, styled hair and makeup of their idols as a way to get "chicks," "pussy," and "more sex" (Beacon, field notes, 2/7/89, 3/28/89, 5/9/89, 5/23/89).

Peers ridiculed tough girls as "dykes," "wannabe boys," or "sluts" because of their propensity to fight, get drunk, have sex, and be aggressive. Some tough punk girls dressed androgynously (in baggy layers of clashing patterns and second-hand fabrics, for example) and were seen as asexual. Most boys did not find the style sexually attractive, including the punk rockers. Sympathized one Latino punk at Beacon: "It's not *as* bad [to be a boy punk] as it would be for a girl, who's supposed to be pretty and everything. That would make a lot of difference." Tough girls who hung out in a group commanded some respect. Amy, a punk girl with a black mohawk, noted: "Boys are treated with respect [at school] because they supposedly deserve it. Girls are treated with respect [only] out of fear." Girls could create fear by banding together, flaunting their sexuality, or inverting traditional notions of feminine beauty. Ed, a physically imposing heavy metal headbanger, said he was afraid to attend Beacon at first: "I thought, 'Oh Jeez, it was going to be eight or nine pregnant girls with mohawks.' "

Tough girls who kept to themselves were subject to harassment and further isolation. I overheard a boy warning another away from one such girl: "She talks like a man. I don't trust a woman with a big butt and a smile, especially when she talks like a man" (La Fuente, field notes, 5/17/89). Other continuation girls benefited somewhat from the presence of the tough girls because they stretched the traditional conceptions of femininity. They challenged the stereotype, as Ingrid put it, "that women are a lazy bunch of bags. They don't want to do anything: they just want to sit around, have babies, and knit." Girls who did not feel a need to impress boyfriends found less pressure from their working-class, female peers at Beacon and La Fuente to wear makeup, get dressed up, speak and act daintily, and otherwise conform. "A lot of people don't expect you to dress up here. You're just coming to school. You can come in sweats, and they won't say, 'What, didn't you do your laundry?' " (Peggy, Beacon, 4/26/88 group discussion). Mandy explained, "People at La Fuente don't really worry about the way they dress," whereas at her old school, "Girls would tell me, 'Well, if your boyfriend went to this school, you would dress up.' " One girl jock at Beacon often wore expensive outfits and sported elaborate hair styles and professionally painted fingernails, and many other girls treated her as union members would a "rate buster." She confided in an interview that other girls judged her, saying things like: "Oh my God. I know how much she pays for those clothes. She must be stuck up." This girl eventually dropped out partly because, as one teacher put it, "she never fit in" (field notes, 4/12/88, 4/26/88, 5/20/88, 6/2/88, 9/15/88, 10/4/88, 5/1/89).

Those who violated gender norms most were singled out for unrelenting ridicule. Jess, an African-American, practiced ballet, attended cosmetology classes, and planned a career in fashion design: activities and interests that typed him as gay. Shunned by other boys, his upbeat and outgoing personality made him popular with a group of vocally loyal girls. On a daily basis, Jess coped with comments like "fag," "Jess, you count as a male?" (La Fuente, field notes, 11/9/88), and "Gays should all be lined up and shot to get rid of AIDS" (3/30/89). When Jess would get angry, his tormenters would call him a "crybaby. Why don't you put a pacifier in your mouth?" (11/23/88).

Teachers usually ignored these exchanges, on one occasion speaking out against labeling in general and on another sending the offender to the office (11/23/88). Many teachers seemed uncomfortable with gay sexuality. When I expressed sympathy for Jess, one teacher said, "Yes, but he should learn to control his life-style. It's fairly obvious he's gay. Why doesn't he keep it in the closet?" (11/23/88). I never saw any physical violence toward Jess on campus. But a few boys at both schools expressed gay-bashing sentiments (Beacon, field notes, 2/28/89, 5/22/89; La Fuente, 3/30/89, 6/7/89), and one Beacon student was convicted of beating up a gay man during the school year.

Nancy was physically bigger and stronger than a number of boys at La Fuente and her previous school. She had played intramural football with an all-male group and wanted to try out for the football team, but she met with resistance from the coach and most players.

> If there is a girl bigger than a guy, they call her "dyke." I'm not in for that. I know I was playing football better than some of those guys, and they got mad at me and didn't want me to play. It's like, "If you can't handle it, you get off [the team]." (La Fuente)

To counter the "dyke" label, Nancy often wore provocative outfits, which prompted some students and teachers to see her as a "slut."

The desire to please current boyfriends or attract new ones some-times led girls to play up stereotypically feminine traits, yet if they were not getting results, they would encourage each other to abandon the strategy. An example involved the student council (composed of volun-teers, three boys and fifteen girls at the outset) at La Fuente. At the teacher's suggestion, students elected one girl (Jenny, white) and one boy (Gary, white). Most girls considered Gary exceptionally "cute," and later several confided that they voted for him on that basis. Almost im-mediately, Gary's boasting about his post and refusal to help Jenny earned him the reputation of "conceited jerk." Working together, Jenny and her friends staged a coup and ousted Gary two weeks later:

Linda (Latino) stood up immediately after Jenny left the room: We need a new chair. Jenny is doing all the work, and she needs time to spend with her boyfriend and on homework. Gary is not doing anything.

Benjamin (African-American): We can't have two girls [as co-chairs]!

Marsha (Mexican-American): Why not? Girls do all the work anyway. Angelina is willing to do it; let her do it.

Gary: I quit. I didn't want to do this in the first place. I didn't vote for myself.

Linda: You're not resigning, Gary. You're getting the boot.

Benjamin then said he wanted to run, and Gary nominated Chico, a Filipino-American.

Benjamin: Chico—he's shy like a girl. No offense, Chico.

Shortly thereafter, Angelina (Mexican-American) was elected over-whelmingly. (field notes, 10/12/88)

The girls, unwilling to let Gary rest on his laurels, skillfully assumed the top student leadership positions, despite male resistance. Benjamin tried two tactics in a bid for power, both of which the girls rejected. First, he drew on the sponsor's original rule that the council should be run by one boy and one girl. Second, he accused the only other eligible male, Chico, of behaving like a "girl," which for him was a self-evidently de-valued category. Benjamin's use of the phrase "shy like a girl" was all the more striking in that Gary had just been outmaneuvered by girls who were, in this situation at least, far from timid or lacking in self-confidence!

Girls also collectively challenged male dominance in the midst of the collaborative dropout reduction project at Beacon. In the beginning, students were still getting to know each other, and the group discussions flowed freely, with me interjecting only to ask an occasional question. In reviewing the transcripts from earlier discussions, I noticed that almost every boy had made at least one sexist remark, which the girls let pass until the seventh meeting. They broke their silence when Pete announced: "I've been going with my girlfriend for two years, and I'm not going to marry her." The three girls present agreed that this was "cruel" and "rude."

From this point, they let no sexist remark go unchallenged. Example: The advisory group decided we should interview students about their future plans, and David volunteered, to laughter from Pete, that he planned to get married and "squeeze puppies" out of his wife. Annie and Sandra called David a "chauvinist," who responded that he was "just kidding." Example: Joe said, "I don't mean no disrespect, but I don't like teachers who are constantly on the rag," which prompted Sandra to ask why he said he meant no disrespect. Kris pointed out that men teachers couldn't be "on the rag" (menstruate), and yet they could "get on your case," too. John commented that Joe's remark was only a figure of speech. After an awkward silence, Joe apologized, and tensions eased a bit (5/5/88 group discussion).

Lack of a Well-Developed Alternative Vision and Ideology

Small victories such as the student council coup help empower girls to challenge in thought and deed their subordinate social, political, and economic position. Yet the lack of a positive, alternative vision and ideology—developed and backed by a strong women's movement—limited them. What Weis (1988) has called the Domestic Code—the centrality of home-family life for women, with wage labor secondary—still seemed to guide many continuation girls, despite misgivings on their part.

When I asked students about "certain goals" in formal interviews, 30 percent of girls versus 11 percent of boys spontaneously mentioned marriage and children. The number mentioning marriage as a goal would no doubt have been much higher if I had specifically asked students about marriage plans, as I did in some group discussions. A significant number of girls mentioned wanting to live with their boyfriend before marriage, and some already were. "I feel that if you love somebody, you should be able to just move in with them. If you don't get along, you can pick up your stuff and leave. You don't have to go through an annulment or divorce" (Jenny, La Fuente). "It's much cheaper to live together. You get married, they [the government] take all your money [through taxes]" (Kris, Beacon).

Boys were more likely to joke about marriage being too constraining, but in the end they generally planned on it. "It's like your normal life ends right there. I'm gonna get married when I have about six months to live," said Pete (Beacon, 5/5/88 group discussion). Like the white, working-class girls in "regular" classes (generally not university-bound) interviewed by Weis (1988: 194), a number of continuation girls felt strongly about waiting to get married until age twenty-five or at the latest thirty because, as Kris (Beacon) put it, "we women should have a backup and have something for ourselves." Girls who spoke of postponing marriage reasoned that this would give them time to finish high school and perhaps college, land a decent job, or both. Lupe (Beacon) predicted that were she to marry, her husband would work full-time while she worked part-time and went to school. "Then finally, you guys [the husband and wife] will say, 'Hey, you can't make it [financially],' and then he'll give you a choice: 'It's either school or your work.' I don't think that's right, so I'll stay at home until I get out of school."

Unlike the girls in "regular" classes interviewed in Weis's study, however, most continuation girls did not consider wage labor primary (1988: 202). (The contrasting economic contexts of the two studies may provide one explanation for this difference. Weis's research was set in a de-industrializing city with high male unemployment rates where girls had lost faith in the idea of a steadily employed, male provider, whereas girls in the relatively prosperous, high technology setting where Beacon and La Fuente were located had not.) All girls interviewed said they planned to work, but few envisioned jobs that would allow them to support children without a companion's paycheck to supplement their income. Some were unhappy about the need to work for pay. Simone (white), a newlywed, wished that she could be a full-time homemaker like her mother had been before she got divorced:

> It's different now. Now everybody has big jobs and are successful. It's either one way or the other, I think. People look at you for what you have, instead of you. "What kind of car do you drive?" Or: "What kind of job do you have?" I just got married, and I just want to have a happy life. I don't want to be poor; I want to have security and a home, but I don't want all that other stuff. I don't want to go to school for five [more] years and get some [high paying] job. It's too much pressure for me. (Beacon)

Simone shunned competition in the wage workplace as she did in school and wished that her aspirations to be primarily a wife and mother were accorded more status by her college-bound friends and society at large.

More commonly, girls argued that they would feel bored if home full-time with children. They wanted to earn money to maintain independence to buy things for themselves. Explained Jenny: "I don't ever want to have to be with somebody because I have no choice." Her scenario was representative for girls:

> I probably wouldn't work while the kids were little. . . . If [my husband] has a nice house and can afford it, I will stay home while they're young. When they start kindergarten, then I'll go to work. I mean, I like staying home, but that's boring. And even if I went to travel agent school, I wouldn't be making that much money. But if I had kids and they were going to school, I could have some flexible hours. I wouldn't have to work full-time. (La Fuente)

Valli (1982: 214), in an ethnographic study of an office education program, found, similarly, that girls imagined futures of "double subordination, in domestic labor and in wage labor."

A few continuation boys said they were looking for a girl of equal intelligence, with work plans of her own. In a group discussion of alternative futures, Gerardo said he would consider caring for his children at home if his wife earned more money, although he conceded that given the present economic structure, this possibility seemed unlikely (La Fuente, 5/18/89). By and large, however, the boys saw a more traditional arrangement as ideal, with wives taking primary responsibility for domestic and child-rearing duties and working for wages only out of necessity. Stan, for example, nostalgically hoped for a family like the one in "Little House on the Prairie." "I feel a wife would be better with the children because, you know how the role model is: dad is a mean, grumpy person who gives you money only on the weekends, and the mom's always there to tell dad to give you money on the weekday." Reversing those roles "basically would cause stress between the husband and the wife" (La Fuente).

Few students spoke of sharing home and work responsibilities equally, or changing family and economic institutions to accommodate alternative futures, or the collective actions required to bring about such changes. Although vaguely troubled by boyfriends who had low aspirations for them (like Joan's fiance, James) or who expected them to do most of the cooking, cleaning, and in some cases child care, few girls spoke of finding a different sort of mate. Over time, some may individually challenge male partners to assume more responsibility for domestic labor (Luxton, 1990; Stacey, 1990). At least a few girls had already become disillusioned with the reliability of a sole male breadwinner because they had seen their boyfriends put in jail or drinking heavily, families suddenly thrust into poverty by the death or departure of their fathers, uncles, and male cousins:

> I've seen this in my family: a guy might take you and support you. Later on in life, there's going to be another young girl that [he] is going to come across. And so when you're divorced, what are you going to do? You've been a housewife all your life, you've got three kids: what are you going to do? There's nothing for you to do. You have to either fight for alimony or child support. And that's not always enough, either. Or stick with the guy until the kids grow up, and then what are you going to do after they grow up? You don't have nothing. (Linda, La Fuente)

> A lot of my cousins, they got married early because they got pregnant, my friends too, and they ended up in divorce. They told me that I made one mistake [getting pregnant], don't make another by getting married. My baby's father dropped out of school . . . and like for three or four months, he was locked up in the Ranch. Now he's out . . . and he thinks we should be together for the baby. But if I'm not happy with him, why should I be with him, you know? (April, La Fuente)

Linda, April, and other continuation girls had become skeptical of earlier romantic desires for a husband willing and able to take care of them. Yet given their presence in the continuation school and current financial circumstances, even their hopes of running a child care center, owning a beauty parlor, or landing a well-paying secretarial position and gaining a measure of economic independence seemed remote at times. Given these structural constraints, when the most skeptical girls found new boyfriends, their willingness to believe old promises was not altogether surprising. Lupe, for example, dropped out of school when she fell in love with a boy at age sixteen. That relationship soured, but she had since met a new boy she had been dating for a year. Her sister, who married young and divorced shortly thereafter,

> always tells me, "I don't want you to get married. You don't need men" and stuff. And that's a matter of opinion, because he makes me happy. . . . He's there for me all the time, and I really do love him. It's just not puppy love because I found out what puppy love was before. (Beacon)

Teachers were sometimes reluctant to question the girls' renewed dreams:

> They still have the Cinderella complex. Even the ones that are
> school-age mothers, they're all going to have the white wedding,
> and the guy's just going to show up and they're going to have a
> house with a little white picket fence. And that's not reality. . . .
> But, you know, I don't blame them in a way because I think
> that if they didn't hold on to that dream, their lives would be
> real super depressing. (La Fuente, 5/24/89 interview)

My reading of the girls' renewed dreams of heterosexual romance dif-
fers somewhat from the interpretation prevalent among teachers. Although in their early teens, girls recalled fantasies of romantic rescue,
in their late teens, they had generally begun to take divorce and other
realities into account, even if inadequately.

Teachers rarely encouraged students to think of acting collectively
to change institutions that rest partially on the economic, political, and
social subordination of women as a group. Economic arrangements, for
example, were taken as given; to suggest otherwise perhaps would have
stirred up too much controversy. More often, some teachers suggested
students take individual action. Anna's English teachers, for example,
told her to ask her husband to be responsible for child care while she
attended an evening conference (La Fuente, field notes, 11/9/88). Teachers also tried to persuade girls to conform to middle-class norms of dress
and self-presentation, seemingly in the hopes that they might attract a
"better" class of husband (Beacon, field notes, 12/21/88; La Fuente, field
notes, 11/2/88, 4/5/89, 5/18/89). Ms. Smith, for example, coached Janis
to keep her legs together when standing in order to appear more "la-
dylike" (Beacon, field notes, 6/19/89). When I interviewed Ms. Smith,
she expressed concern about the girls' immodesty and overt expression
of sexual desire:

> I see girls as being much more forward, of being less modest
> and shy than years back. . . . This kind of stuff where you would
> picture men at a construction site whistling to women, these lit-
> tle girls are doing it to guys. In class, girls are not afraid to talk
> about it's their time of the month. (4/25/89 interview)

Finally, some teachers tried to make students aware of gender
stereotypes. Yet this implied that the root cause of women's subordinate
societal position lay in biased attitudes. No attention was paid to other
interpretations of women's oppression. Because students learned to think
of gender issues in terms of attitudes and equality under the law, I was
not surprised to discover that boys frequently felt that girls and women
already had as much equality as was warranted; today, argued Rich

(Beacon), some women "are trying to overextend" liberation; they feel they are "better than men." Girls, in contrast, often felt, as Jenny described, "that even though the world is like that now, *it's equal, but there is something there that guys are dominant. . . .* They have more freedom before girls have freedom; they're their own bosses sooner than girls are" (La Fuente; emphasis added).

Although many girls felt uncomfortable identifying themselves as feminists, they tended to support in principle women's rights to political and economic equality and to control their own sexuality. Yet in practice, personal, social, and economic forces were primed to prevent them from laying full claim to these rights. In part because girls did not fully realize that women are still disadvantaged institutionally, they tended to interpret personal misfortune as solely the result of individual choices they had made. Joanne (Beacon), trained and employed as a cosmetologist, chose that occupation because it interested her but earned so little she did not know when she could move out of her mother's apartment. Beverly (La Fuente) did not complete her court reporting class because the cost of child care became too burdensome; she did not like feeling dependent on her new husband, but most jobs she could find with or without a high school diploma seemed barely to cover child care, transportation, and clothing expenses.

CONSEQUENCES OF DROPPING OUT VERSUS
GETTING A CONTINUATION DIPLOMA

"Guys Think of Construction, Girls Think of Housewife"

I asked students to imagine what advice they would give to a friend considering dropping out of school and how, if at all, their advice would differ if the friend were male or female. For most, the question was not hypothetical because, they explained, they had relatives and friends who had done just that. They also drew on what significant adults and peers had told them in order to encourage their persistence in school. Virtually all felt that a diploma was critical for both boys and girls, though individual circumstances for dropping out might be compelling: a dislike of, and failure in, school combined with the need to support a family for boys or pregnancy and a stable, financially secure relationship for girls.

Most used an economic rationale to justify obtaining a diploma: those without one would be hired last and paid least; the decision would virtually bar them from further training and education that would lead to better job opportunities. Another prominent theme involved the pride in achieving a long-term goal and the knowledge that "if you're not ed-ucated, people will put you down" (La Fuente, 6/13/89 essay).[6] Pregnant and mothering girls often added an additional reason, echoing what teachers and other adults told them:

> [I tell my friend]: "Think about your baby. Your son's gonna grow up and ask his mama, 'Did you graduate?' and [he's] gonna ask for your diploma [and] make sure you're not lying to him. And he gonna wanna drop out: 'Well, since you dropped out, mama, why can't I?'" (Brenda, La Fuente)

Thus, girls were more likely to couch the decision to stay in school in terms of an obligation to family members rather than to themselves.

Although students considered their advice "the same" for both gen-ders, they based it on a belief that girls and boys dropped out to pursue gender-differentiated futures, each with its own pitfalls:

> Guys think, "Oh, I'll just go into construction." [But] you need brains for construction, too, not just muscle. Girls think, "Well, I'll just be a housewife." But what if your husband leaves you? You're going to have to have some kind of skills and some kind of high school diploma because people won't hire you without that. (Mandy, La Fuente)

Students of both genders tended to agree that it was easier for boys to drop out: "I think it would be easier for a guy to make it without a diploma than a girl cuz guys know all the hand skills. How many girls can go out and get a construction job?" (Sandra, Beacon, 4/28/88 group discussion). Whereas some boys might succeed, girls were more likely to end up victims. "[A boyfriend] could easily dump you like that. And you'd have nothing after that" (Maria, Beacon). Ed (Beacon) put it this way:

> If a guy drops out, he can maybe work on cars and stuff—and he'll be doing it the rest of his life. He might get good money at it. But if a girl drops out, all of a sudden [she thinks,] "It's hard for me to get a job. It's hard for me to do this. Maybe I'll

---

6. As Sennett and Cobb (1972: 24) have argued, "The word 'educated' . . . is a 'cover term'; that is it stands for a whole range of experiences and feelings that may in fact have little to do with formal schooling." As a certificate of social mobility and job choice, a high school diploma and later a college degree provide "more chance to develop the defenses, the tools of person, rational control that 'education' gives." Without this, working-class people fear they will not be respected.

see if I can find a guy." That's no way to think because if he splits, that's it [for the girl].

Government statistics show that the economic and educational consequences for girls of dropping out are more severely negative than for boys. Across ethnic groups, female dropouts and pushouts are much more likely to be unemployed than their male counterparts (Borus and Santos, 1983: table 1-6). They are also more likely to be out of the labor force altogether (U.S. General Accounting Office, 1986), but it is unclear to what extent this is by choice or a matter of disguised unemployment due to would-be workers becoming discouraged.

Regardless of marital or maternal status, according to Current Population Survey data, white, black, and Hispanic female dropouts (aged sixteen to twenty-four) have significantly lower labor force participation rates than their female counterparts who graduated from high school but did not go on to college. Of young women with children, Latina dropouts are less likely to participate in the labor force than white and African-American female dropouts and particularly women who ended their education with a high school diploma (21 versus 36, 36, and 60 percent, respectively). Without children, 60 percent of white and Hispanic women dropouts participate, whereas this factor hardly affects the labor force participation of African-American women dropouts (Markey, 1988: 39).

Of those who work for wages, women high school dropouts are much more likely than graduates to be low-paid operatives, laborers, private household workers, and other service workers (Reskin and Hartmann, 1986: 63). Whether dropout or graduate, African-American women (aged twenty-two to thirty-four) are two to three times more likely to live in poverty than white women, and four times more likely than white men (Fine and Zane, 1989: 25, citing U.S. Dept. of Labor statistics).

Once women drop out, they find it difficult to return to school, particularly if they assume domestic responsibilities. As discussed in chapter 5, this seems to explain the finding, using National Longitudinal Survey data, that women were not more likely to return, despite having reached higher grade levels before dropping out (Borus and Carpenter, 1983: 502). In the High School and Beyond survey, Kolstad and Owings (1986) found no sex difference in the return rate for sophomores who had left school and did not expect to go on with their education (26 percent) or for those dropouts who expected to go on to college (61 percent). Among those who had an intermediate level of educational expectations, that is junior college or vocational/technical school—and this describes the majority of continuation students interviewed—male dropouts were more likely than female dropouts to return and complete school: 51 percent compared to 44 percent for those who expected vocational/technical training, and 64 percent compared to 46 percent for those who expected to attend junior college. Overall, males, particularly whites from families with higher socioeconomic status, were more likely than females to return and complete high school (Kolstad and Owings, 1986: 17–18).

In short, female dropouts, particularly teen mothers, face economic and social hardships difficult to reverse. Continuation students had only a vague sense of this reality.

Uncertain Value of a Continuation Diploma

Women's lack of education does not explain their low earnings. Women with high school diplomas, for example, earn less than men who dropped out of high school (U.S. Dept. of Education, 1987: 283). Although evidence is lacking concerning whether employers treat the continuation and conventional diplomas as equivalent credentials, at the time of this study, the Marine Corps did not and was not accepting even full-time continuation high school girls as recruits; presumably the quota for women was smaller and could be filled easily with comprehensive high school graduates (La Fuente, field notes, 9/30/88).

Based on my informal knowledge of the educational and occupational paths that Beacon and La Fuente leavers (dropouts and graduates) have followed, I would predict that girls may be penalized more for having not been exposed to a college preparatory program while at the continuation school. Although the study is dated, findings by Elder (1969b) support this argument. In a follow-up survey of continuation graduates, most of the unmarried girls (one-third of the sample) were employed full-time in clerical and sales jobs. Girls were generally more critical of the school in retrospect, particularly with regard to its academic and vocational preparation. Few girls relative to boys felt that continuation education had been very helpful in developing basic skills in reading, writing, and spelling (15 versus 39 percent), in math (12 versus 47 percent), or job skills useful to the work they did (26 versus 42 percent) (ibid.: 332). Elder did not venture to explain this gender difference, but the type of jobs the girls held required more basic skills. Of employed boys, most were either in the military, semiskilled and skilled blue-collar jobs, or low-status white-collar jobs that presumably did not require as much academic preparation.

In part reflecting a profound, societywide, ideological conflict over the proper place for women, Beacon and La Fuente were failing to challenge the idea that the family sphere is the primary domain of women.

In effect, this makes unemployment an accepted social role for women but not for men and may explain why much of the concern over high youth unemployment seems focused on males. Disengaging girls—who came disproportionately from working-class and ethnic minority backgrounds—took home economics, child development, and family living courses that reinforced traditional roles and did not encourage them to continue their schooling or provide them with valued job skills. The most prevalent vocational education classes offered tended to orient girls toward low-paying clerical, sales, and service jobs.

Schools, apart from society, cannot change the job opportunity and reward structure. But given the increasing proportion of women householders living in poverty, it is time that schools begin early to challenge the idea that a girl's future monetary and status position will depend on association with a man rather than on her own, direct participation in the economy. School staff must address, directly and indirectly, the role played by peer groups in maintaining prevailing gender relations, especially among students who are skeptical that their futures depend on mastering academic skills.

Disengaging, early adolescent girls who ended up at Beacon and La Fuente had often clung to fantasies of romance and rescue and got derailed. By age seventeen experience may have taught them they were naive to believe that a man would take care of them financially and otherwise. But by then their usually poor academic achievement records and other immediate situational factors (such as a promising new boyfriend) seemed to effectively thwart their progress, sometimes despite plans and values to the contrary. This helps to explain why academically capable, though often underprepared, continuation girls failed to obtain more education and skills and participate in the booming sunbelt economy at levels aspired to by their better educated, middle-class, often white female counterparts. Quite a few did succeed, however, in obtaining the continuation diploma. The next chapter examines who achieved this goal and how.

7

REENGAGEMENT: WHO AND HOW BY GENDER

A second chancer:
I just decided I'm not going to be in that lower group. I just don't want to fight my whole life to have to pay my bills. . . . And the only way I'm going to be able to do that is to go for something and do as much as I can, the best that I can, because it'll look good later on. I mean, these transcripts that I have now, the grades I have, and my attendance record and everything else, they're going to look fairly decent. Even if it is in continuation school, it'll look fairly decent on a college application.
—Ingrid, age eighteen, a high school "stopout" for two years, on the eve of her graduation from Beacon

A push-through:
I'd rather be home if I had a good job and had my education [laughs]. Um, you really can't stay home if you have a job, so that's totally out of the question cuz I don't have the education, and I don't have the job. So, OK, I'd rather be in school learning. Sounds crazy cuz I cut so much, but I really would. I want to learn and I want to go to school—I just get so bored by it. I think about it: I can't stand being here [at La Fuente]. I might as well get out [fast or] else I'm going to be here for the rest of my life!
—Carla, age seventeen, responding to the question, "If you had the choice, would you rather be at home, in school, or at work?"

A pushout-dropout:
The teacher dropped me from first period and all that, and I wasn't getting anywhere here [at La Fuente]. And then when I

got dropped, then I just stopped going [altogether]. . . . There's a bunch of mess-ups here, and we hang around them. We mess up with them, you know? You don't get any better here.

—Steve, age seventeen, on his decision to leave La Fuente and enter the GED program

While boys were more polarized in their response to the continuation school and girls more ambiguous, this alternative setting was more successful overall in reengaging girls than boys, according to several measures taken at both schools. The most accurate statistics were longitudinal dropout and graduation rates that I collected for the Beacon should-be class of 1989 (whoever would have graduated that year whether they enrolled at Beacon in the tenth, eleventh, or twelfth grade). I tracked this cohort through June 1990, the end of five years in high school for those still enrolled. While this would seem a useful measure of school success, few schools or districts, Beacon and La Fuente included, monitor such student flows. Therefore, I had to construct them from data such as enrollment lists and individual transcripts. My extensive search shows no similar research tracking a cohort through continuation school to dropout or diploma. (For a fuller explication of my results, see the appendix.)

My findings show that across ethnic groups, Beacon girls were less likely to have dropped out than boys (45 versus 68 percent) and more likely to have graduated (36 versus 25 percent) or possibly to be enrolled still in school (19 versus 7 percent).[1]

Cross-sectional data—the only type available at La Fuente—showed that counter to expectations built up in the popular press, pregnant and mothering girls were more likely to graduate than other girls at La Fuente, who in turn were more likely to receive a diploma than boys. Of those students in their fourth year or more of high school, 16 percent of boys, 24 percent of girls not in the SAM program, and 48 percent of girls in the SAM program received a diploma.[2]

Several interrelated factors explain girls' relative success within the

---

1. Filipino males proved to be the only exception to this pattern. Their dropout rate was lower and graduation rate higher than one would expect given their numbers in the student body.

2. Girls in the SAM program who reached their fourth year in high school had higher graduation rates, but younger girls in this program may have dropped out at rates equal to or greater than girls not in this program and boys of the same age. I did not have the longitudinal data to test this idea, suggested by the finding that the younger a teen is at the time of first pregnancy, the more likely she will not graduate from high school (Moore, 1981).

continuation school. Overall, Beacon and La Fuente seemed more adept at reading and addressing the symptoms and reasons of girls' disengagement. This chapter will discuss these factors, drawing together previously mentioned findings as well as some new ones and grouping them by the four major components of engagement identified in chapter 1: the credential, academics (including teacher-student relations), extracurricular activities, and peer relations.

THE CONTINUATION CREDENTIAL

One explanation for the gender difference in reengagement is that the girls exercised and perceived more choice in transferring to the continuation school. They were more likely to want an alternative learning environment than to have been pushed out for disciplinary reasons as many of the boys had been (see tables 2 and 3). All pregnant girls were technically voluntary transfers. Although some reported that they had been coerced,[3] most agreed that the SAM program supported them materially and emotionally in their choice to have a baby in an environment away from peers and teachers who might have ridiculed their pregnancy. They tended to see less stigma attached to the continuation diploma; half the girls and only one-quarter of the boys described it as an equivalent credential.

Boys who felt pushed out of the comprehensive school into a devalued program were more likely to keep right on disengaging. Their presence in the continuation school seemed to mark them as incorrigible troublemakers. Manuel, like Steve who was quoted at the beginning of this chapter, said this was why he dropped out: "I just looked at my environment and the people around me, and I seen we weren't going anywhere. There were a lot of burnouts" (Willows). For this group, paid labor instilled more of a sense of competence than earning a credential considered second-rate; compare Fine and Rosenberg (1983: 266) who found that dropouts were less depressed than those still in school.

Girls, when presented with the hypothetical possibility that no continuation schools existed, were twice as likely to say they would have dropped out altogether. In contrast, boys were more likely to say they would have stayed at the comprehensive school or were unsure. This

3. An Equality Center survey of twelve geographically and demographically diverse schools revealed that nine of the schools may have been violating the rights of pregnant girls. A common violation was channeling pregnant and parenting students into specific courses of study (cited in Snider, 1989). Title IX (legislation passed in 1972 that banned sex discrimination within educational programs receiving federal funds) requires schools to allow pregnant students to stay in regular classes if they so desire.

may indicate that boys tended to be more unrealistic about their options, given no change in either their behavior or treatment by conventional school authorities. More girls seemed to be clear that the continuation school was their "last chance," as many put it, and they were relatively committed to making it work.

This commitment, in turn, appeared to reflect girls' reading of the gender-segregated labor market. As discussed in the previous chapter, significantly more girls realized that they would need a high school diploma, including college preparatory classes, and some college in order to get a decent job. The jobs that boys were planning, on the whole, required less education.

ACADEMICS: SECOND CHANCERS, PUSH-THROUGHS, AND PUSHOUTS

Many students at both schools made an informal distinction between liking to learn (evidenced by student-initiated questions and discussions with teachers and peers, extra time spent on academics) and liking school (notably, teacher and peer relations, extracurricular activities). Those who liked academic learning most comprised the greater part of students I came to know as second chancers. This group valued the chance to come from behind and responded enthusiastically to the incentives the continuation school held out through the variable credit system. Second chancers were intellectually capable and fairly well prepared but had got derailed from school, usually because of a personal or family crisis, rebellion against the nonacademic aspects of schooling (student cliques, petty school rules), or both. Many second chancers attributed their turnaround to increased maturity and "real life" jolts more than anything teachers or parents had told them: being beaten by a boyfriend and left in a crack house alone (Tanya), driving drunk and killing or injuring friends (Javier, Alejandro), being put in jail (Anita, Estelle, Lorena), being given an ultimatum by a boyfriend (Janet), being forced to live on their own (Ingrid, Lilia), and having a baby (Mandy).

Other continuation students saw the value of a diploma but felt bored with most classes and academically unmotivated. At the comprehensive school, they had cut classes to avoid looking unprepared and steadily got behind on credit. Many had been, and often still were, "into partying" with friends, and once at Beacon or La Fuente, they became interested in informal social activities and getting to know their teachers on a more personal basis. Those who connected with school adults, did not fight with peers, and participated in school activities were virtually pushed through the program. To them, academic work was often bad medicine, which they took to please teachers and out of a recognition that it was good for them. The continuation school's more varied and individualized teaching methods, easier and more relevant curriculum, compressed schedule, and credit system (with its short-term goals and more immediate payoff) sugarcoated the medicine and seemed to engage the push-throughs most.[4] They liked the fact that learning at the continuation school seemed much less coerced; they "chose" to do it.

Continuation teachers recognized this distinction between push-throughs and second chancers. They found that the low student-teacher ratio reduced their classroom discipline problems, but they were disturbed that many of their students did not necessarily make more academic effort. Indeed, I observed, and a number of students told me, that they had actually learned to put forth less effort than they remembered making at the comprehensive school. David, a Beacon student, reported:

> Like the first time you come to this school, you work hard cuz that's how you were doing at a normal high school, and then you look at other students: they're always kicking back, and you get irritated with that cuz they're not working. . . . Then the next year, you'll be slowly kind of slacking off. Then later on, you'll be talking the whole period, and you won't even recognize it.

Complained Ingrid: "A lot of the kids could be getting credit, they could be reading and writing something, but instead they just yak, yak, yak" (Beacon). Sometimes too late, these students realized they were not making up the credits they needed to graduate. "Actually," one teacher told me, "it is a fairly small group of people who are smart enough, motivated enough, and goal-oriented enough to benefit" from individualized instruction.[5]

Teachers' concern about the push-throughs manifested itself differently at Beacon and La Fuente, given their different overall philosophies and structures. At Beacon, with its emphasis on counseling and individualized learning, teachers worried that few of their students liked academic learning. I overheard two teachers agreeing that they were "connecting" with only a tenth of their students; another put the figure

---

4. Phyllis Bravinder, a former continuation teacher of eight years, suggested the term *push-through* to me in conversation.

5. Individualized instruction is a method often reserved for the lowest or remedial tracks (Oakes, 1985: 210). In an ethnography of "additional needs" classes at a middle-class high school, Page (1987) found that teachers used work sheets so students could work at their own pace, but little individualized instruction actually occurred and the content was not very academic.

at half, but added that she did not include liking to learn in her definition of connecting (Beacon, field notes, 10/10/88).

At the more traditional La Fuente, the tension between caring for students (addressing their emotional and social as well as academic needs) and maintaining relatively high academic standards was not so much felt as an internal conflict. Rather, the staff itself was split, and those teachers with a reputation for caring sometimes resented that they spent extra time, while those with high standards got the most work out of students. The comprehensive school teachers I spoke with experienced a similar conflict. One teacher felt that counselors had "earmarked" her "as more nurturing and understanding than others" and thus assigned the most needy or difficult students to her classes.

> So it's almost like a double-edged sword. [Students] feel like, "I know she likes me, and if I fail her class, she knows I like her . . ." But you put them in another situation where the teacher demands a certain standard and does not interact with the students, . . . then the student reverts back to "I'm going to have to do this and this and this," or they just throw it in and say, "forget it." (3/10/89 interview)

Girls were more likely to fill the ranks of the push-throughs and especially the second chancers. On average, girls entered Beacon and La Fuente slightly more prepared and on track academically. They had marginally higher grade point averages and thus more credits at entry.[6] At La Fuente, the median district proficiency exam scores for students interviewed showed girls scoring above boys on reading (78 versus 74 percent) and writing (77 versus 75 percent) and below on math (76 versus 80). At Beacon English teachers felt that more boys entered with poor literacy skills, and this put them at a disadvantage because the school's individualized learning approach was reading-intensive (Beacon, field notes, 11/21/88). But girls may be better at masking learning disabilities. Educators and psychologists have long assumed that dyslexia afflicts mostly

---

6. I examined the transcripts of my La Fuente sample, which included cumulative high school grade point averages. Girls in the SAM program had a median grade point average of 1.6 (or D+/C-), followed by girls not in the SAM program with 1.1 (or D), and boys with .9 (or D).

At La Fuente during 1988–89, 46 percent of males versus 43 percent of females entered during 1988–89 with less than fifty credits, while 5 percent of the boys versus 11 percent of the girls had more than 150 credits. At Beacon 31 percent of all males versus 23 percent of females enrolled with fewer than fifty high school credits earned; in contrast, 6 percent of boys versus 15 percent of girls entered with more than 150 credits.

boys. Recent studies, however, have shown that girls are just as likely to have the reading impairment, despite the fact that teachers are more likely to diagnose the condition in boys—perhaps because they are noisier—and refer them to special education classes (*New York Times*, 8/22/90).

In any event, the smaller school and class size allowed girls to connect better with teachers, which seemed to be more important to girls generally.[7] "The relationship with your teacher, that's the best part about Beacon," Trina told me. "That's what I love." Those who had previously employed a classroom withdrawal strategy (see chapter 4) or felt stigmatized by comprehensive schooling practices (see chapter 5) were sometimes less shy about asking for help. Continuation teachers were then better able to challenge these quiet students at a pace commensurate with their basic skills. Individualized teaching methods, an easier curriculum, an emphasis on attendance and credits over tests and grades, and few formal social activities all seemed to reduce the pressure of competition felt by the stigma avoiders, girls and boys alike. But to the extent that boys had transferred to the continuation school involuntarily and felt stigmatized by it, too, they found it especially difficult to reengage.

In addition, the compressed, flexible schedule of Beacon and La Fuente enabled the relationship-absorbed—again, mainly girls—to manage domestic responsibilities (which increased with early mothering and marriage) and to work on relationships that sometimes competed with school work for their attention. A curriculum more tailored to their interests and (in the case of Beacon) improved school-home communication and counseling also helped reengage the relationship-absorbed. In the short-run, these features helped girls stay in school but did little to set their sights on education beyond high school and instead inadvertently accommodated the idea of early marriage and pregnancy.

To recap, Beacon and La Fuente addressed organizationally the main reasons some students—girls more than boys—had previously disen-

---

7. In the only study I have seen that systematically examined gender differences between dropouts and graduates (done in Australia), Poole and Low (1982) found that both female stayers and leavers rated their chances of success in life low yet both achieved higher grades; they were both likely to conform to school values, to be influenced by their teachers, and to be introverted. The opposite findings were true of both groups of males. The factors that distinguished early leavers from stayers among the girls all seemed related, directly and indirectly, to social class: socioeconomic status, academic achievement motivation, organizational skills, verbal ability, and frequency of discussing job prospects with parents.

gaged (to avoid institutional labeling practices, the competing demands of relationships and family problems) as well as their styles of disengagement (classroom withdrawal, challenging school authorities in a nonphysical manner). With the exception of some second chancers, most of whom entered the continuation school relatively academically prepared and engaged, continuation success stories were mostly push-throughs. That is, they reengaged most at the level of establishing a rapport with teachers; they did not dramatically increase their academic effort or improve their attitude toward learning.

Still others—mainly boys and tough girls—remained vulnerable to pushout. They continued to behave in ways—validated and encouraged by subcultural styles—that got them into trouble. Normally, teachers would intercede for push-throughs based on three factors. One, they could point to knowledge of a student's personal or family problems and argue that these were the real cause of the violent or unpleasant behavior; boys, as previously discussed, were less likely to confide this information to adults. Two, teachers could cite a student's interest in the school, as indicated by participation in extracurricular activities; girls were more engaged by this measure. Three, they could argue that a misbehaving student, while occasionally a "jerk," generally had a pleasant or amusing personality (class clowns, usually boys, fell into this category). The most effective limit on such student advocacy was the opinion of fellow teachers and administrators, who tended to associate teachers with students and hold them responsible for student misbehavior (compare Metz, 1986: 42–43). When this limit was reached, students were then pushed out, as chapter 4 showed.

In contrast, the "good student" status of second chancers within the continuation school prompted teachers to plead their case to the administration when they engaged in behavior that probably would have landed them in trouble otherwise, and certainly so at the comprehensive school. I observed Ingrid and Megan—both second chancers—climbing on a scooter in the parking lot after school. Against district rules, Ingrid lit up a cigarette and, as she drove off, blew smoke in the general direction of the principal, who had just walked up behind me. Shaking his head, he noted: "It's a good thing I like those girls. At [names comprehensive high school], I would have suspended kids for doing something like that" (Beacon, field notes, 12/14/88).

EXTRACURRICULAR ACTIVITIES

Both Beacon and La Fuente allowed students previously excluded from extracurricular activities to participate, and girls responded to the opportunity at a higher rate than boys. The vast majority of both sexes had been indifferent—or frankly opposed—to extracurricular activities. Only one-fifth of the girls interviewed and 14 percent of the boys spontaneously mentioned liking extracurricular activities at the comprehensive high school; these boys focused on sports, unavailable at the continuation schools, while the girls said they missed social activities like dances and rallies. Students who eventually dropped out in the national High School and Beyond survey likewise reported lower levels of participation in most extracurricular activities, especially in athletics (Ekstrom et al., 1986: 56).

To participate in voluntary school activities, defined by adults and dominated by high-status peers, seemed to many Beacon and La Fuente students like participating in their own oppression. Partly in reaction against schooling practices that excluded or labeled them as losers, many students developed outsider identities, which the transfer to the continuation school simply reinforced. To quote students, they felt "rebellious," "foreign," "straight out," "unique," "independent," "different" and like a "misfit," "oddball," "anarchist," "outcast," "stranger," "bad guy," and "weirdo."[8] Others—in-between the popular crowd and the nerds—did not feel like outsiders but still saw themselves as different from the jocks and the preps.

Stoners at both schools, particularly the boys, seemed to hate extracurricular activities with the most intensity:

> They wanted us to have school spirit, but some of the things they did for school spirit were kind of corny. They were really like the fifties. They're all, "Oh boy, let's just put on our big poodle skirts and whatnot. Hot dog. Big Elvis there." People'd be like, "Come on. Have some school spirit." We'd be like, "Get a life. Go somewhere." (Bernard, La Fuente)

These boys tended to consider most extracurricular activities feminine. Stan, a self-described headbanger at La Fuente, explained why he thought his experience in school would have been more positive if he had been born female: "Girls are more sociable and more, I don't know. It would have been better. I'm not saying I want to be a girl or anything [though]." As it happened, Stan wanted to prolong this interview so he

8. As strong as this language seems, students usually referred to themselves in positive or neutral terms in comparison with the labels they said others used to describe them and their continuation classmates: "losers," "stoners," "dropouts," "troublemakers," "gangsters," "druggies," "messups," "fuckups," "bad kids," "burnouts," "stupid kids," "dummies," and "rejects."

could avoid the awards assembly scheduled next period. "I'm really not into social things—it's just like it's not my group."

A number of studies have indicated that girls are more sociable than boys, lending support to Stan's observation. Simmons and Blyth (1987, citing Maccoby and Jacklin, 1974) reviewed this literature and observed that this finding depends on the aspect of sociability under study: "[Maccoby and Jacklin] suggest that girls form smaller, more intimate groups of friends (pp. 225–26), and that they rate themselves higher on social competence and interest in social activities (pp. 158–60; 214)" (Simmons and Blyth, 1987: 71).

Girls derived more status, particularly among other girls, from participating in extracurricular activities. Under the sponsorship of women teachers at Beacon and La Fuente, girls organized social activities on an ad hoc basis—an apparently common approach in continuation schools (Botts, 1972: 576). That women were in charge of student activities in both schools seemed significant. Students, mainly boys, sometimes justified their lack of participation by pointing to certain—mainly men—teachers' lack of enthusiasm (Beacon, field notes, 10/25/88; La Fuente, 9/20/88, 1/18/89). The few boys who participated did relatively little and sometimes were at pains to let others know that they mainly wanted to get out of class. La Fuente girls, who dominated student council, were more likely to work in the student store to raise funds for activities; they planned and organized the Halloween and Christmas parties as well as the talent show. At Beacon, only one boy was on the newspaper staff and none worked on the yearbook; girls again were the major planners and organizers of an ice cream social, Thanksgiving potluck and talent show, and Christmas party.

In response to some student grumbling about Beacon's few social activities, two women teachers had their classes write about their feelings. Although most essays were positive, a few students expressed what I heard informally. One wrote: "This is a school to help drop-outs. If I wanted to go to a talent show and pot luck I could just go back to my old high school. . . . Some students don't want to get involved with school activities, like me!" (field notes, 11/29/88). In student interviews, 11 percent of boys versus 6 percent of girls spontaneously expressed similar views.

PEER RELATIONS

Girls were more likely to report conflict with youth subcultures privileged by the traditional high school (cheerleaders, athletes, college prep students) who threatened their popularity and boyfriend and marriage prospects, and the continuation setting changed this dynamic. Rich, a Beacon student, summed up the change: "At a normal high school, the jocks weigh out on top; at this one, the misfits weigh out. I mean, there ain't no jocks at this school. Here, jocks are despised." When asked to describe the atmosphere at the continuation school, one-fifth of the girls but only 6 percent of the boys spontaneously mentioned that there were fewer cliques, one indicator that the informal social system of the traditional high school had been more problematic for girls.[9] Boys reported more conflict with bullies and students of different ethnic backgrounds; the continuation program lessened, but did not do away with, these sources of conflict.

Although the reasons for peer conflict differed somewhat by gender (see chapter 5), girls were just as likely to experience strained peer relations and consider it an important factor in the school engagement process. Girls were more likely to report a definite improvement once at the continuation school (47 versus 44 percent for boys, with an additional 9 percent of boys saying they were not sure).[10] Considering student-to-student relations as a whole, both schools succeeded in promoting relative harmony, Beacon even more than La Fuente.

At both schools, the social class and academic achievement spectrum among students was narrower than at the comprehensive schools. Five factors reinforced this relative equalizing of student status, associated with fewer oppositional subcultures emerging among students (Davies, 1984: 177): (1) the emphasis on credits over letter grades, (2) the emphasis on individual improvement versus competitive ranking; (3) fewer turf battles because students no longer attended their neighborhood school; (4) the lack of age-grading; and (5) higher school staff tolerance of diversity, including subcultural styles that featured unorthodox dress and language.

Five additional factors seemed to have improved peer relations at Beacon. First, students sat around tables instead of in rows (compare Metz, 1986: 179), and some teachers encouraged students to help each other with school work. Second, Beacon was smaller, with only two com-

---

9. Pregnant and parenting girls' changed circumstances also seemed to lessen their involvement with old friends who took drugs and engaged in other activities that made reengagement difficult (for example, Mandy, La Fuente). Students' parents, too, argued that a baby sometimes acted as a counterbalance to negative peer pressure: "I see too many things going on out in the streets. I don't want her out there," said the mother of Gloria, a La Fuente student.

10. One indication of this improvement in peer relations was student responses to a series of questions that asked them to compare how they were treated by their peers based on how they looked in the comprehensive versus continuation settings.

prehensive schools feeding into it. Third, the main form of instruction at Beacon was individualized, and students could not fail. Fourth, school staff paired new students with older ones, trained to orient newcomers to the school during their first week.

Fifth, the ethnic composition of Beacon's student body was balanced to reduce racial tension. The research of St. John (cited in Stanlaw and Peshkin, 1988: 222) has shown that between 15 and 40 percent of any one ethnic group is optimal: with too few, the minority feels threatened, with too many, the shrinking majority does. Daniel, for example, was only one of two African-American students when he entered Beacon. "This one white dude . . . said, 'Why do they have to bring black people in a white school anyway?' 'Trying to break up the family'—that's what they called it when I first came here." Over two years later, Beacon was more diverse ethnically, and Daniel himself described it as "kind of like a family. It's a small school, so everybody's kind of comfortable around each other, even though everybody at this school is different."

THE LIMITS TO REENGAGEMENT

At best, Beacon and La Fuente rekindled an interest in learning in some students. Other students, however, seemed to be turning around academically and behaviorally, only to return to old habits, many to eventually drop out altogether or, perhaps more aptly, fade out. Folk theories of why students "lapse," as one teacher put it, abounded in both schools and roughly correspond to the various levels of analysis used in this study.

Teachers, partly reflecting their training in educational psychology, favored an individual analysis. Traditionalists argued that these students were lazy, spoiled, and irresponsible. Developmentalists claimed that they "feared success."[11] Continuation students, as one teacher explained, could not "handle too much praise" because they have always been "bad kids," and this had become an integral part of their identity (Beacon, field notes, 12/12/88). Added another teacher, those unaccustomed to succeeding then saw themselves as "phonies" when adults remarked on their academic progress (Beacon, field notes, 2/13/89). "Discouraged learners have to be taught how to internalize responsibility for their successes," read an article handed to me by a La Fuente teacher (field notes, 1/12/

---

11. There is an interesting parallel between teachers identifying continuation students as fearing success and the work Matina Horner (1974) did on "fear-of-success" among women of high intellectual ability and academic achievement. Subsequent research has shown that this syndrome occurs as frequently among males as among females (Levine and Crumine, 1975, and Tresemer, 1976, both cited in Goetz, 1978).

89). "They tend to see [success] as the result of luck or easy work [rather than their own effort]" ("Teaching Discouraged Learners," 1988: 28).

Students, for their part, offered a variety of explanations for why they began to slip out of the system again, ranging from the individual (laziness, "getting a big head" and then ceasing to strive for further successes), to peer pressure, from the situational (being overwhelmed again by nonschool problems) to, occasionally, the structural (feeling that good job prospects would be bleak with or without a diploma). "That's the way it is now. You get your diploma [and realize], 'Oh, I can flip burgers now' " (Ed, Beacon).[12]

I sensed a certain truth in all these explanations and, of course, no one factor set limits on the reengagement process for all students. But I was struck, in analyzing student interviews and field notes, by the enormous influence of peers in shaping student responses to academic success for both boys and girls. Rather than fearing success, students feared losing friends, who offered alternative definitions of success. Some students had gained peer admiration and acceptance for rebelling. If being praised or honored by teachers and the school meant ridicule from friends, then accepting it, at least outwardly, was extremely difficult to do, especially given the ethnic and class backgrounds and experiences of most continuation students.

I recorded many examples of students resisting praise from school authorities. At a La Fuente awards ceremony, for instance, I observed Jenny, Linda, Mandy, and Bill sitting at a distance. They made a point to scratch themselves in inappropriate places on their way up to the podium to receive certificates for attending a conference. In addition, Jenny got an attractive plaque for academic improvement. She and her friends pretended to spit on it, marked it with finger prints, then turned it over on an empty seat beside them (field notes, 2/22/89).

Collins (1988: 308) argues convincingly that ethnic minority and working-class people form tight-knit groups of peers, with primary loyalty to family and community, "and are skeptical about the ethos of individual self-advancement touted by the middle-class school." Continuation students lacked reinforcing messages in and out of school that academic success was meaningful. And because the continuation school was stigmatized, students often devalued their success within that arena ("This is just a bonehead school") and still felt scholastically inadequate and out of place on the next rung up the educational ladder.

---

12. In a study of African-American students, Felice (1981: 420) found that dropouts were more likely to perceive the occupational structure as closed; this was the most important variable distinguishing dropouts from stayins.

Even Ingrid, by far and away the most academically engaged and prepared student at Beacon and clearly capable of succeeding at both district comprehensive schools, was full of self-doubt and reluctant to cross educational borders. Arguing that Beacon should make its curriculum more strict while retaining an alternative pedagogy, she noted:

> I think it would make it more to the point where when they [students who have dropped out] decide to go to school, they'd be closer to the levels of what your typical high school kid at that age would be [at]. That is the reason why I think I never went back [to the comprehensive school]: because I was afraid I was going to be too far behind.

She and a small group of self-identified anarchist punks had found a home at Beacon. Other students and school staff were relatively tolerant of the punks' multicolored hair, pierced body parts, and propensity for dressing all in black. Ingrid and the other punks formed the intellectual rebel core at Beacon. They did not reject academic success per se (they loved to read and learn), but they rejected "pointless" school rules that infringed on their individuality, competitive ranking, and social climbers. "School should be fun," argued Paul, "not where everyone is out to kick you out or screw you up."

This subculture succeeded at Beacon because its members could be the proverbial big fish in a small pond: taking school on their own terms, displaying intelligence when need be, yet maintaining a nonconformist image. Other students admired them, sometimes grudgingly, for questioning authority because they seemed to have the brains to succeed in the mainstream but chose not to. These rebels were an important symbol to other continuation students that they, too, were "all right."

Other students, less successful by any school-defined criterion, sought common ground with peers. Not surprisingly, they found a comfort level among students like themselves with relatively few opportunities to excel academically and socially and who had lowered their expectations accordingly. Their behavior and attitudes strikingly paralleled those of women in "low-mobility organizational situations" in the corporation studied by Kanter (1977). The continuation push-throughs and push-outs developed various subcultural styles around their common fate that supported: (1) their low aspirations, for example, obtaining a credential with minimal effort, (2) their limited commitment to the institution, indicated by their lack of participation in voluntary school activities and focus on leisure, consumption—including drugs—and relationships, and (3) alternative definitions of success including solidarity with those who validated these definitions and criticism of those who did not as "school boys or girls," "goody-goody," and "teacher's pet."

An example: a number of students at both schools argued that going on to college was not their idea of success. "I don't need to go to college. I just want money to support myself and put a little bit away for entertainment," said Kris (Beacon). "People go to college to be rich. . . . [and] people who are rich aren't full of love anyway." Louise, a La Fuente student, made a similar point, adding: "I wouldn't be happy being fake like that, just for material possessions and a place in society. I'd rather live poorly than like that" (1/12/89 group discussion). Louise's and Kris's comments resonate to the observation of Sennett and Cobb (1972: 22–25) that working-class people sometimes feel that the work of college-educated people is not quite "real" work and are therefore scornful of it. Kris went out of her way to add, however, that not going to college did not translate into a stunting of intellectual growth: "There is no end to learning. From day one to the day you die, you're going to be learning something new every day" (Beacon, 4/12/88 group discussion).

Rich linked his concern about college directly to his fear of losing his friends. Knowing I had been to college, he asked me whether my friends were "hippies" or "business types" (Beacon, field notes, 1/23/89). Because Rich generally associated college graduates with business types, he predicted that he would only be playing at being a business type—as Louise put it, a fake. Against this anticollege attitude ran the ideal of individualism, however, which gave license to buck the crowd and make the choice to pursue more schooling and a good-paying job. Carlos countered Louise: "You can be yourself. You can have things. Just do what you want; don't care what [other people] think" (La Fuente, 1/12/89 group discussion).

Few adolescents, though, are truly that unmindful of what their friends think. As Stan explained: "I think the biggest problem facing teenagers is loneliness, the stress of worrying about whether or not they fit in. Everything else, you can choose to do it or you can choose not to do, [like] drugs" (La Fuente). Stan's point was painfully in evidence among continuation students considered "goody-goody" or "nerds"; they were truly outcasts. I followed Noreen's progress at Beacon more carefully than most. At the beginning of the school year, she felt other students "scapegoated" her and called her "goody-goody" because she did not do drugs; she confided that peer pressure to do drugs was a problem. By spring quarter she fully identified with the stoners "because they've been through a lot of garbage like me and they're more grown up" (field notes, 4/4/89). Her friendships within this group, however, were tenuous and stormy, even after she started smoking marijuana. Noreen did not return to Beacon the next fall.

Students could not fit in simply by willing it so. They did things like experiment with drugs in the hopes that those choices would allow them to belong. In the more typical case of students who did belong somewhere, they nonetheless faced the problem of how to change friendship groups when they realized that their current one did not support reengagement. For example, most of the students who agreed to talk to junior high students about how they got off track said it was because they "hung with the wrong crowd." They advised the junior high students to "make your own crowd," yet when asked how this might be done, nobody knew. Dennis offered, "Be a loner" (Beacon, field notes, 5/9/89).

8

HIDDEN HIERARCHIES

I thought La Fuente was a losers' school, mainly because it was a continuation school.
—Stan, age sixteen, La Fuente student

This is a place for people between school and the street, or between school and no school.
—Ed, age eighteen, Beacon student

Continuation schools and the students they serve often find themselves at the bottom end of a number of hidden hierarchies. And where there are hidden hierarchies, we also find what feminist legal scholar Martha Minow terms "the dilemma of difference." Analyzing the cases of bilingual and special education, she concludes that to ignore the differences of subordinate groups "leaves in place a faulty neutrality, constructed so as to advance the dominant group and hinder those who are different." But attending to their differences can highlight their deviance from the norm. "The dilemma of difference is the risk of reiterating the stigma associated with assigned difference either by focusing on it or by ignoring it" (Minow, 1984: 159, 202).

In the hidden world of continuation schools and beyond, we have seen how differences based on curricular program, gender, ethnicity, social class, sexuality, age, and knowledge get constructed into hierarchies. At a time when the nation's president and state governors vow to slash the dropout rate in order to make the United States globally competitive, an aggressive search is on for alternatives in education aimed at retaining those "at risk." But for these alternatives really to yield positive change, they will have to at least soften, if not neutralize, stigmatizing hierarchies. In this chapter, I return to a few hidden hierarchies that I have already examined, particularly in the areas of gender, adult-child power relations, and the credentialing process. In seeking to add to our knowledge about how best to improve schools and the prospects of all students—dropouts, pushouts, or eventual graduates—who feel alienated by the current system, we need to attend to other hierarchies that I will discuss as well, those that define the relationship between researcher and researched.

THE CREDENTIAL HIERARCHY AND THE DILEMMA OF DIFFERENCE

Dorian Gray and His Portrait:
Mainstream and Alternative Schooling

Is it a realistic goal for schools to engage all students to a degree that enables them to pursue their fullest potential? If so, how can schools prepare all students to meet this goal, regardless of inequalities in background, without helping to assign them different futures based on gender, class, and ethnicity? Given the demands of employers, institutions of higher education, and others on schools to rank and sort students, programs that group young people together on the basis of shared problems usually end up unwittingly stigmatizing their participants and reinforcing disengagement. Such was the case with both Beacon and La Fuente. One could argue, and correctly so, that continuation schools vary in organizational structure, philosophy, and so forth. Some are more successful in graduating students than others. I selected Beacon and La Fuente to represent two ends of the spectrum, yet both were used as safety valves by their districts.

As safety valve, the continuation school cannot be fully understood outside the context of mainstream schooling. It indicates that the comprehensive high school is not serving a wide range of its population well. Like Wilde's *The Portrait of Dorian Gray*, the continuation school has been relatively hidden from public scrutiny but reflects the problems created or ignored by its mainstream counterpart. Meanwhile, the comprehensive school, a relatively unreformed Dorian Gray, is able to function, though with increasing difficulty.

One indication of this difficulty is the proliferation of education "options" for "at risk" students at the secondary level over the last ten years. Besides continuation high schools, these options include educational clinics, alternative education and work centers, community schools, concurrent enrollment in adult education, independent study programs, teenage parenting and pregnancy programs, and partnership academies. Most appear to represent a dual response to: (1) students' need for flexibility and personalization with the stated aim of "dropout prevention and recovery," and (2) conventional high schools' need for mechanisms to isolate students who pose discipline and other problems and to provide specialized services efficiently.

As an examination of the history of continuation education shows, however, offering options without major reforms both inside schools (for example, improving the material conditions of teaching, rethinking standardized curricula as well as traditional teaching and disciplinary strategies) and outside the educational system (for example, providing job programs, more and better child care, funded access to contraception and abortion services, improved housing, social and health services) can simply mean replicating the sorting process pioneered in traditional educational settings. As budgets constrict, continuation teachers and administrators come under pressure to demonstrate results or face elimination, and consequently some have themselves begun to screen out the most disengaged students, relegating them to other optional programs further down the credential hierarchy.

In Ontario, California, for example, continuation administrators have argued: "Many students referred to the program have no positive academic intentions and are simply attempting to continue 'game-playing' and take up space in the program." As a solution, the district has begun a pre-continuation independent study program, which administrators feel has "enhanced" the continuation program because "non-attenders" and "non-productive" students are "redirected without enrollment," thus improving average daily attendance figures and the "academic setting" (Bratta, 1990: 8). In Milpitas, California, the continuation school requires students to improve their attendance at the comprehensive school as a condition of enrollment. Not coincidentally, its district uses temporary placement on independent study as a disciplinary threat, reserving the continuation school as a "privilege" (Freedberg, 1985). I have not surveyed the many alternative programs across the country and therefore can make no claim that these instances are representative. Both, however, were publicized through the California Continuation Education Association (CCEA), the Ontario case in the CCEA newsletter and the Milpitas example at a regional CCEA meeting I attended, suggesting a possible trend in the making.

The continuation school does succeed in reengaging some students; its claim to be a safety net rather than a safety valve is tenuous, however, given that so many fall through gaping holes in its weave: more than half of its students drop out or get pushed out. Its teachers worry that they are connecting with only a tenth of their students academically, and many of its students perceive themselves as losers, and this perception shifts only marginally as a result of their participation in the alternative setting.

What of incorporating some of the positive aspects of educational options—flexible scheduling, small class and school size, personalized attention, brokerage of social services—into mainstream high schools? This reform strategy holds promise, yet there are reasons to be skeptical that it will be widely implemented. First is the imbalance of power and resources that shapes the politics of schooling, particularly in large urban districts that draw on a dwindling property and industry tax base for funding. In times of fiscal constraint, programs that attempt to redirect resources to those most disadvantaged by the current system are politically vulnerable and likely to be eliminated.

Second, if the competitive academic curriculum retains its position of central importance and the comparative and selective functions of schools remain unchallenged, alternatives are liable to get pushed to the margins and devalued, as was the case historically when continuation programs were offered on-site with conventional high schools. Groups of teachers, administrators, and students tended to clash over academic and behavior standards, a dynamic that often led central office administrators to establish alternatives apart from the mainstream.

The tension between addressing students' "special needs" and separating and stigmatizing them exemplifies the dilemma of difference. Joan Scott proposes that the way out of the difference dilemma involves, first of all, challenging the meaning of difference as "fixed binary opposition" (1990: 145–46). Recall, for example, that continuation schools first claimed to serve vocationally, then socially "maladjusted" students, and later "divergent" youth or "outsiders." The schools, in the evolving terminology, provided "part-time," "life adjustment," and "alternative" programs. In each case, the students and schools were defined in binary opposition to the full-time, comprehensive ("conventional," "regular," "traditional," "normal") high school students and institutions and found lacking.

To disrupt the "operations of categorical difference," Scott argues, entails pursuing equality, but not equality in the sense of sameness. Rather, depending on the purpose and context, "Equality might well be defined as deliberate indifference to specified differences" (ibid.: 142). Certain advocates of alternative education have implicitly recognized this principle over the years. They have argued that to address students in all their diversity without recreating stigma would mean "diversifying the whole of public education into a system of optional alternative schools and programs serving all youth" (Barr, 1981: 571). Many students, not just potential dropouts and pushouts, could benefit from a system that provided a variety of learning strategies, flexibility in scheduling and the pace of learning, a range in the amount and types of support for students, and so forth.

Another vision that seeks to disrupt stigmatizing differences can be found in the movement to "detrack" schools, the objective of which is "to provide diverse groups of students with access to a common body of knowledge" (Oakes, 1992: 17). As Oakes makes clear, efforts to eliminate ability grouping, tracking, and other forms of curriculum differentiation challenge some deeply held values embedded in current school practices. If one assumes that the measured ability differences among students are partly a product of the schooling system's failure to counter the role that social class, ethnicity, and gender play in creating these differences, then the attempt to equalize learning opportunities would also involve reducing privileged groups' current comparative advantage. Further, the common curriculum itself would have to be made more democratic, that is responsive to the lives of working-class and ethnic minority girls and boys. Were our present system of schooling to change to the degree envisioned by either the detracking movement or the alternative schools movement, the category of "special needs" would likely disappear.

A Second-Best Solution

In light of the present level of funding for and structure of mainstream high schools, it is difficult to foresee much support for such radical change. Therefore, continuation schools and other second-chance programs appear to be the second-best solution. Continuation proponents argue persuasively that were we simply to eliminate these programs without restructuring mainstream high schools, students most in need of an advocate and extra help would suffer. Yet as second-chance programs have expanded at the margins of mainstream schools, problems of communication, coordination, and accountability have increased and so, therefore, have the possibilities that students will slip between the cracks.

In the short-run, states could increase accountability for retaining and engaging students throughout the educational system by requiring schools to track individuals from entry into kindergarten through to age eighteen or high school graduation and to calculate longitudinal dropout rates by ethnic group and sex. More commonly, schools report an annual dropout rate; this estimates the number of students who drop out or are pushed out during the school year. A longitudinal rate provides a more accurate and complete picture by estimating the percentage of students in a particular class who drop out or are pushed out between the time they enter and graduation. It also conveys more information about the timing of disengagement. Based on the interviews with Beacon and La Fuente students, for example, one would expect that boys, particularly Mexican-Americans, might disengage from school earlier than girls.

The longitudinal rate, and monitoring system needed to calculate it, could help administrators prevent students from slipping out of the system. At present, students who drop out between school years or in transition from one school or program to another, even within the same district, are sometimes not counted as dropouts. Or if they are counted, it is often by alternative programs such as continuation or adult education rather than the students' neighborhood comprehensive school; this accounting practice makes the mainstream school's record of retaining and engaging students seem better than it actually is.

Both the comprehensive high school and the options connected to it should take responsibility for students, regardless of where they are within the educational system. At the same time, policymakers should recognize that dropout prevention and recovery programs such as continuation schools will have a higher dropout rate because they serve many students who have already left once and tend to be severely behind on credit. Given the extra resources needed to provide these students with a better chance of academic success, funding formulas should provide greater financial incentives for retrieving and retaining dropouts and pushouts.

At a time when choice is being offered as a panacea to school administrators grappling with cultural diversity, with white and affluent flight, and with the needs of low-income people, the context of the debate needs to be broadened. Three lessons can be gleaned from this examination of the continuation education program. First, schooling options should be based on students' needs, not those of the educational system; change should proceed from the bottom up. Second, students and parents should be fully informed about the consequences of the choices open to them within the system. Third, a central forum of accountability within the system must be in place to allow for monitoring of who is shifting back and forth between various schooling programs so that one option does not become a safety valve for another and thus a point of final exit.

THE GENDER HIERARCHY

Gender hierarchy refers to the process whereby certain qualities and experiences come to be associated with males and are defined as superior while other qualities and experiences are associated with females and are deemed inferior. Discussed here are some research and policy implications of the gender hierarchy in three areas: teenage pregnancy, power relations between boys and girls, and the curriculum.

Teenage Pregnancy and Parenthood

Pregnant and mothering girls are doubly different. First, they have, according to prevailing attitudes, claimed adult status too early. Second, because pregnancy is defined as a "special need" and one that only females potentially have, pregnant girls also deviate from the male norm. Although it is no longer legal to deny pregnant and mothering girls access to schooling, it is still common to segregate them, sometimes coercively (Snider, 1989) and in ways not always in their best interest. In this study, for example, some pregnant and mothering girls had been college preparatory students. Although they ostensibly could choose whether to attend the remedially oriented La Fuente, the offer was linked to free prenatal and child care and special transportation only provided at the continuation school. So for those without other sources of support, the choice to attend La Fuente was constrained at best.

The question of whether pregnant and mothering girls would be best served in mainstream or alternative settings is an open one. The debate is currently shaped by how prevalent and accepted teenage pregnancy and parenthood is in a particular community, which in turn affects the cost of providing services in a centralized or decentralized manner. Proponents of providing services in a separate facility typically cite one or more of the following reasons: (1) the difficulty of guaranteeing the safety of pregnant students; (2) the difficulty in a large setting of controlling negative comments from peers and school staff members that can damage pregnant girls' self-esteem; and (3) avoidance of community controversy—and perhaps increased teenage pregnancy—by minimizing other students' contact with pregnant and mothering teens. In contrast, proponents of mainstreaming argue that their approach: (1) avoids the difficult transition to and from an alternative facility; (2) allows pregnant and mothering students to remain close to established friends; (3) allows access to a more diverse, usually more academically challenging curriculum; and (4) does not add further to the stigma already attached to teenage pregnancy by shunting students off to a separate facility.

The alternative approach often focuses on the "special" needs of pregnant and mothering girls and risks stigmatizing them, while the mainstream approach often fails to fully support students and risks losing them. Again, meeting their diverse needs without separation and stigma would involve reorganizing schools so that these needs were no longer considered "special." This might include, for example, providing a school-based health clinic, on-site child care for students as well as school adults, flexible scheduling, and a curriculum that fosters nurturance in all students, female and male.

Neither the alternative nor the mainstream approach addresses the issue of involving boys in the process. Boys who father children are rarely required or encouraged to participate in teen parenting programs, even when they are present in a school that offers one; such was the case at La Fuente. In addition, being in an alternative setting such as La Fuente did not prevent boys from ridiculing pregnant girls, underscoring teachers' resolve to limit discussions of sexuality to single-sex classes. Such meetings may be important, say, for building girls' confidence. Yet this approach fails to challenge prevailing gender relations and provides no sustained opportunity for dialogue between boys and girls.

Nurturance, long considered a female quality and concern and excluded from education's primary goals, is taught to girls in such elective classes as Family Living. This approach replicates "within the curriculum the split between the productive and reproductive processes of society," argues Jane Roland Martin (1985: 197–98; emphasis in original):

> If education links nurturing capacities and the 3 Cs [caring, concern, and connection] only to subjects such as home economics that arise out of the reproductive processes, we will lose sight of the *general* moral, social, and political significance of these traits. So long as rationality and autonomous judgment are linked exclusively with the productive processes of society, the reproductive ones will continue to be devalued.

One promising program, "Boys for Babies" in Toronto, Canada, has made nurturance a particular educational goal for boys. The course is aimed at fifth- and sixth-grade boys and

> attempts to break down male stereotypes about sex-appropriate behaviour and activities. Boys are withdrawn from their regular school programme and are given an opportunity to care for, learn about, and bond with infants who are brought in from the community. At the beginning most boys express the stereotyped belief that infant care is "women's work." Over the course of a month, however, the boys begin to change their own notions about whether care-giving should be restricted to one sex. In this environment the nurturing, caring, and sensitive behaviour of the boys is encouraged. At the end of four two-hour sessions most young men have had a positive experience and have re-

flected on the ways in which care-giving can be satisfying and positive. (Gaskell, McLaren, and Novogrodsky, 1989: 56–57)

Power Relations between Boys and Girls

We need more research that closely attends to the power relations between boys and girls rather than simply comparing the two sexes. The continuation girls in this study were more likely than the boys to have got off track academically because of romantic relationships. Further, they reported feeling marginal to, and sometimes subordinate within, largely male-dominated subcultures. Under certain circumstances, girls resisted male domination as individuals and in groups: the female-led student council coup at La Fuente was a striking example. A deeper understanding of these dynamics as they vary across contexts would help elucidate how adolescents learn gender—as well as class and ethnicity—from peers and might provide school practitioners with insights into how best to challenge prevailing power relations.

In the 1970s feminist scholars documented sex discrimination and stereotyping in schools and pressed for equality of treatment. In the 1980s, increasingly aware that girls may learn differently and that they are sometimes dominated by boys inside and outside the classroom, some feminists began to ask whether it would be better to educate girls in separate schools. I reject this solution because I believe public schools should reflect the diversity found in the wider community and that learning to communicate across divisions such as gender, ethnicity, and social class should be an overarching educational goal. How to set up classrooms and schools in ways that encourage boys and girls, for example, to talk to each other about controversial topics, to learn from each other, and to try to resolve conflicts then becomes key. We must start with a realization that, as Arnot (1983: 88) has observed in England, comprehensive public schools have not to date been charged with the task of restructuring the relations between male and female students (and teachers) to reduce the gender hierarchy. "Their historical role so far has been to facilitate different 'interests' and 'needs' without taking on the reform of those 'needs' and 'interests.' "

Many girls and some boys in this study tended to perceive that females were culturally devalued, although they could not always fully articulate these perceptions. This provides an opening for teachers and administrators to challenge attitudes and practices that keep girls subordinate. At the same time, it is not enough to encourage girls to adopt male traits currently associated with classroom success such as assertiveness because there are certain to be boys (and others) who will characterize such girls negatively. Susan, for example, was unafraid to speak her mind, and consequently many boys, and some girls, shunned her. Dennis, for instance, complained that she was "too loud. I don't like that." Witnessing such negative characterizations of forceful females can reinforce a girl's decision to remain silent in school contexts.

In thinking about how to encourage more positive interaction between boys and girls, researchers and practitioners might attend to contexts where cross-gender relations are comparatively friendly. Thorne (1986: 179–80), in an ethnographic study of nine- to eleven-year-olds, found relatively "relaxed cross-sex interactions": (1) in situations "organized around an absorbing task," (2) when adults, not children, were "responsible for the formation of the group," (3) where "principles of grouping other than gender were explicitly invoked," for example a mutual interest, and (4) "in less public and crowded settings" such as neighborhoods. Goodenough's (1987) kindergarten study highlighted the length of previous association in nursery school and the chance to build a sense of community as a major factor reducing sexist encounters.

Curriculum

In the progressive era, when continuation high schools first came into being, many school administrators believed that different curricula should be offered to meet the needs of different types of students, and they argued that girls and boys should be educated for different futures. Formally, we have moved from providing such a gender-bound curriculum to a relatively gender-blind one. The problem with ignoring gender, however, is that, like ethnicity, it continues to shape classroom interaction unofficially in ways that we sometimes miss or unwittingly reinforce. For example, as chapter 6 showed, few teachers prompted students to reconsider the gendered cultural beliefs they brought with them to school or produced in peer groups. A disproportionate number of girls disengaged from school through a withdrawal strategy, but teachers often either did not perceive this or attributed it to family or cultural values and left the strategy unchallenged.

Instead of a falsely gender-blind approach, Martin calls for a "gender-sensitive," situational curriculum strategy:

> It takes gender into account when gender makes a difference, as, for example, research shows it does in the way teachers respond to male and female students, and in the amount of space the liberal curriculum devotes to the deeds and works of men and women respectively. It ignores gender when, as in relation to the question, "Who in the United States should be educated for citizenship?" it does not. (Martin, 1990: 22)

How to take gender into account when it makes a difference, however, is far from easy.

In highlighting differences based on gender, we run the risk of reinforcing stereotypes. Consider a real example drawn from my field notes. Sandra (Beacon) was a bottle-of-bourbon-every-two-days alcoholic at age fifteen. Her polite demeanor and clean-cut looks blinded family members and teachers to this reality and the pain it masked, and she resented that these preconceptions had prevented those around her from seeing and acting: "I don't think there is enough help, at least from parents, school." Fewer girls than boys in this study had serious drug and alcohol problems. Will this finding simply confirm in people's minds what they already thought to be the case, putting off help and support for girls like Sandra?

This issue returns us to the question feminist theorists have been grappling with: "Can we think of difference without putting it against a norm? Can we recognize difference, but not in terms of hierarchy?" (Mascia-Lees, Sharpe, and Cohen, 1989: 29). This is a difficult question and one that deserves further attention. In laying out various differences in the ways girls and boys perceive and experience school, I have tried to emphasize that these differences are never absolute and are always bounded by certain historical and social conditions (Alcoff, 1988).

In attending to gender relations, feminist teachers will also run up against resistance from students, school people, and parents. In seeking to transform the curriculum, teachers will need to prepare students to cope emotionally and intellectually with conflict that is sure to arise in, say, discussions of institutional sexism and racism. Part of this preparation might include workshops in conflict resolution. Carrington and Troyna (1988) recommend approaching controversial issues holistically, helping students to identify the specific nature of racial, gender, and class inequalities, while at the same time connecting these with students' own experiences of inequality in an effort to create empathy. Fine (1991: 262) suggests constructing students' participation in social problems curricula around "small, pre-planned victories" in order to avoid perpetuating a "sense of hopelessness." In addition, the more teachers can collaborate with parents, community-based organizations (such as the battered women's shelter that La Fuente's Ms. Wilson contacted), and others, the more legitimacy will be lent to these curricular goals.

THE ADULT-CHILD HIERARCHY

On the surface of schools, there is nothing hidden about the age hierarchy: adults run schools, and children comply. But too much educational theory and practice is based on this simple model which ignores the power of peers and the fact that adult-child relations are never so neatly top-down. This study began to document, for example, how gender and the use of sexuality by students and teachers alike created opportunities for engagement and disengagement in the classroom.

Recent school reform proposals reflect some movement away from the notion of teaching as something done by adults to children, but they focus more on teacher-to-teacher relations—reforms such as teacher participation in school decision making and team teaching. By the same token, the latest reforms either ignore relations on the bottom end of the adult-child hierarchy—that is, students' relations with each other— or press for change without carefully considering the political relations within children's social groups.

For example, cooperative learning strategies have become increasingly popular, with the stated goal often to increase learning effectiveness and sometimes to foster friendships, not to remake gender relations. Not surprisingly, then, the limited research to date suggests "that, by itself, the implementation of cooperative learning groups does not necessarily lead to a more equitable and effective learning environment for females" (Sadker, Sadker, and Klein, 1991: 307). Likewise, continuation schools typically give students greater freedom to organize their own learning, leaving them with more time to interact in small groups, often informally segregated by subcultural style and gender. This approach helps keep some students in school but often because it makes it easier for them to devote more energy to the strong pull of a romantic relationship—not necessarily encouraging them to pursue further education.

The influence of peers on persistence in school deserves more attention. With adult family members spending more and more time working outside the home, children spend increasing unstructured and structured time with people their own age. The strategies individuals work out—often in interaction with close friends—to cope with school, and later the transition to work, can bring them into conflict with peers, parents, teachers, and other adults. These groups, in turn, can disagree among themselves about the best course of action, thus adding to the soap opera of high school.

Subcultural conflict looms particularly large in teenage lives because, however consciously, high school students are struggling for status. Most are not unaware that the results will have profound implications for how much schooling and the type of work they obtain, who they will marry, and how they will live as adults. This study showed that subcultural conflict was a major factor pushing some students out of school.

Future research needs to examine, for example, how and why the organization and governance of schooling promotes or lessens such conflict.

THE KNOWLEDGE HIERARCHY

What are the implications of the hidden hierarchies of gender, ethnicity, class, age and so forth for the production of knowledge? In a period when reformers call for gender-sensitive curricula, we lack a good research base that illuminates gender similarities and differences among students marginalized by current school practices. Feminist and other scholars have drawn attention to the need to incorporate gender, class, and ethnic considerations into research design and analysis (Grant and Sleeter, 1986). I took this call seriously, but the qualitative and exploratory nature of the study made me wary of interpreting, say, ethnic differences within a gender or class group given the small numbers of students in any one such category. One solution would be research teams made up of people of diverse backgrounds; at the same time, this would no doubt increase rapport with informants and deepen the researchers' understanding of the scene under study.

A more difficult challenge lies in the development of theoretical frameworks that address the ways gender, ethnicity, and class relations interweave across a variety of sites, including schools. The dichotomous categories that theorists often use to describe social structures do not adequately capture the way people construct their own worlds. Gender, ethnicity, and class operate differently depending on the context. Being male or female, for example, counts enormously in some situations and not much in others.

Feminist and other scholars have also argued that the relationship between researcher and researched is unequal, and some have proposed to reconstruct it. In this study, I tried to reduce the knowledge hierarchy by collaborating with teachers and students. I discovered that participatory research is a fruitful approach but one that falls short of a true collaboration, at least in an arena such as the school, which itself is hierarchically structured.

Participatory research prompts researchers to concern themselves with multiple perspectives as well as the implications of theoretically framed research questions for educational practice. This approach to research necessarily drew me into the soap opera of high school because it forced me to see the institution through students' eyes, meet all the characters, understand their motivations and how they affected each other. I also came to understand better the day-to-day dynamics that often support, but sometimes confound, broader organizational and structural analysis. In an era when the concept of academic objectivity is being rethought, I acknowledge that in the end these multiple perspectives were being filtered through my lens. I attempted to achieve a reflective stance by observing from the wings as well as switching between roles (uninitiated outsider, quasi-student, quasi-teacher, unofficial school aide). The challenge for the qualitative researcher, once immersed in the studied scene, will always lie in the tension between telling the story richly and becoming too much of a character in the soap opera itself.

Participatory research also creates some practical and ethical concerns. This type of inquiry is time-consuming. Researchers based outside of schools need to budget time in the collaborative project to offer help in areas not always directly related to the research problem at hand. This is only fair given the extra effort being expected of school people as part of the collaborative process. For example, I helped teachers with student activities and tutored students, and, in turn, teachers gave up prep periods to discuss hypotheses, suggested ways of seeking out and interviewing the most disengaged students, and read over preliminary analyses of the data. At the same time, I confronted traditional attitudes toward the research process that limited participation. For example, I tried to incorporate student views on how to make schools better into some project proposals, which prompted Joan to comment, "I feel like I'm writing this myself." She resisted my effort to involve her fully and indicated that the collaboration was more my responsibility than hers.

Joan's reluctance was not misplaced. While students tended to be the most forthcoming, they also had the least power and were therefore the most vulnerable. Those with the most experience in exercising power tended to be the most guarded. Researchers, particularly those with a base of support outside of schools, cannot avoid the fact of their own power. Typically, they have more control than other participants in how the research gets defined and communicated. Even if I had wanted to equalize relations among participants in the collaborative search for understanding, conflicts arose between students and teachers, teachers and administrators, within groups, and even within individuals over time that would have confounded this goal. I agree with Judith Stacey (1988), who argues that participatory, qualitative methods may expose people involved in research "to greater risk of exploitation, betrayal, and abandonment" than traditional methods.

I question whether a collaboration truly exists between unequal partners, as when I tried to involve students in the research process at Beacon and La Fuente. Collaboration can provide a way for students to feel that someone is listening to them and thinks what they have to say is important—maybe even important enough to prompt action. But as unequal partners, they do not have enough power to participate in the definition of the goals of schooling or the means to achieve those goals.

The collaborative approach can, however, yield deeper understanding. For example, in the initial talks with the advisory group at Beacon, female students urged me to include questions about boyfriends and whether girls were cutting school to spend time with them. This indeed became an important gender issue. I remember feeling that students would consider such a question too direct and prying—and no doubt a few did—and that I would let students raise the issue only if they so desired. And yet to have left this issue to chance was also problematic. Sandra, who had been battered by an ex-boyfriend, argued, and other girls agreed, that boyfriend-girlfriend issues deserved an explicit place on the research agenda. The boys, perhaps because of their own experiences and structural position, were indifferent. Thus, I was torn between wanting to understand the perspectives of students, including the boys', without imposing my definitions and concerns and possibly damaging rapport and, as a feminist, wanting the research to be useful to the girls.

The high school students gave me the most time. They generally wanted to see the school itself adapt to fit their attitudes and needs. But the collaborative projects we worked on together, shaped by what those with more power would allow us to do, aimed at encouraging the students themselves to change. None of the collaboration was geared, really, to allowing the high school students to have a direct impact on changing the institution—and that is probably what they would have wanted most.

Students in my advisory group wanted the opportunity to return to the comprehensive high schools, for example, to tell an assembly of their peers what the alternative school was "really like, cuz then we could get rid of all these rumors" (Pete)—to play up its appealing and distinctive organizational features. But they were justifiably skeptical that they would be given the chance because, as John put it, mainstream school administrators "don't want people to think that you can succeed at Beacon." Students felt that the districtwide dropout rate would decline if all young people received the personalized attention they now did, absent the stigma (if "we could get rid of all these rumors"). Yet students knew, too, that, in Kyle's words, "they don't have the capacity right now" to "tailor regular high schools so teachers will listen more."

Taken as a whole, the students' analysis of existing problems and tentative articulation of solutions reflected their double consciousness as continuation students with extensive experience in conventional schools.

Sandra conceded that most teachers wanted students "to become responsible adults, to graduate and be able to make it," but, she went on, "they have the wrong way to go about it." Kris agreed. And to her there was nothing hidden about the hierarchical realities that had helped make her, as she put it, a character in a soap opera:

> Schools separate people; they put people in different categories.
> Why can't they pat you on the back whenever you're good? . . .
> When you're down and you do something wrong, you need
> somebody there to tell you, "It's cool. You're a person, too. You
> can make it if you really want." [Instead] when you mess up,
> they put you in with the trash.

Appendix

ROUTES THROUGH
THE HIDDEN WORLD:
STUDENT FLOWS INTO AND OUT OF
BEACON AND LA FUENTE

The routes through high school and beyond have grown increasingly complex over the past quarter century. This has helped complicate the search for meaningful, reliable rates for dropouts and pushouts. Using the continuation school as a hub, student flows in and out provide a map for understanding the myriad checkpoints on the way to a high school credential. Not all students, of course, reach this destination. Although the dropout rate is only one measure of a school's effectiveness, it provides the major focus of the analysis to follow.

In California, 45 percent of those enrolled in continuation programs at some time during the 1986–87 school year left without graduating (28.5 percent transferred elsewhere, 16.5 percent dropped out, at least for the time being); 11 percent obtained a diploma or the equivalent, and 44 percent remained enrolled in continuation programs (CSDE, 1988: 21, 26). Although continuation school advocates interpret these numbers favorably, my case studies indicate far higher dropout rates.

This appendix contains three sets of flow charts. In the first and second, I charted one year's progress through Beacon and La Fuente, respectively, from fall 1988–89 to fall 1989–90. In the third, I tracked a cohort of students longitudinally, from the time they entered ninth grade through the end of five years. Each set includes information on the type of school, if any, that students attended (continuation, other alternative, or comprehensive high school) and on students' school status (still enrolled, graduated, dropped out or been pushed out) by the end of the period charted. Also included are the official reasons Beacon and La Fuente gave for students leaving without graduating or enrolling elsewhere, although most were sketchy at best.

Beacon's record keeping system was more trustworthy than La Fuente's, mainly because the same staff person had been at the job almost from the school's opening. At La Fuente, records were not kept consistently. So although I was able to verify that students who said they were transferring to a comprehensive school within the district actually did so, the same was not true for those who claimed to transfer outside of the district or to an alternative setting such as adult education. Given this, it was difficult for me, or the school for that matter, to know for sure what became of some students. But based on the information available, I constructed flow chart 1, part B.

One of the most common destinations for those leaving La Fuente and Beacon was the independent studies program, located on-site at La Fuente and off-site at the adult education center in Beacon's district. To enroll in ISP, both districts required students to read at a seventh-grade level or better. At the first meeting, a teacher determined how many credits each student needed and in what areas; together they agreed on a contract. During the course of the week, students read and wrote on their own and would subsequently meet with the teacher for an hour to discuss their progress and obtain new assignments. Students who missed appointments or completed less than half of their assignments tended to get referred back to their home school.

Throughout the year of intensive field work at Beacon and La Fuente, significant portions of continuation students dropped out or were pushed out of the continuation schools. More than one-half (52 percent) of those enrolled some time during 1988–89 at La Fuente left the educational system without graduating (49 percent of girls, 55 percent of boys; see flow chart 1); about one-third (32 percent of girls, 35 percent of boys) left Beacon without graduating (see flow chart 2). These figures for dropouts and pushouts are higher than annual rates reported to the state because I was able to verify that certain students who had supposedly transferred to adult education or independent studies programs either had never actually enrolled or had dropped out after a short time.

Fewer students graduated. Of all students enrolled during 1988–89, 10 percent had passed the CHSPE or GED or graduated from La Fuente (13 percent of girls, 7 percent of boys; see flow chart 1) and one-fifth had received a diploma from Beacon (24 percent of girls, 17 percent of boys; see flow chart 2).

These graduation rates were much lower than those of nearby comprehensive high schools, as expected given the "at risk" status of their student bodies, particularly the low credit standing of most pupils as they enter. The lack of close correspondence between a student's age and his or her actual grade level as well as the open-entry/open-exit feature of the program (students enroll or leave almost daily) further complicate measurement as well as interpretation of both graduation and dropout rates.

To clarify this, I examined the transcripts of students who entered Beacon (because its smaller size made the task more manageable) from September 1986 through May 1989 and selected those who had entered the ninth grade in 1985–86. The resulting 131 students (58 girls, 73 boys) comprised the should-be class of 1989 who ever enrolled at Beacon (see flow chart 3). I tracked these students through to the end of their fifth high school year, after which time few continue. My extensive search shows no similar research tracking a cohort through continuation school to dropout or diploma.

By July of 1990, 58 percent had dropped out (two-thirds of this number from Beacon directly, another one-third from other schools, mainly adult education), 30 percent had graduated, 11 percent were last enrolled in another school (current status unknown); only one student remained at Beacon. Across ethnic groups, girls were less likely to have dropped out than boys (45 versus 68 percent) and more likely to have graduated (36 versus 25 percent) or possibly to be enrolled in another school (19 versus 7 percent).

The continuation schools had ways of pushing out, or disengaging from, students seen as "troublemakers" or "nonstudents"—including girls, but more often boys. Students who did not demonstrate a certain amount of success—measured formally at Beacon and informally at La Fuente by attendance, productivity, and punctuality—were routinely transferred to other alternative programs one rung down the credential ladder. Of 350 dropouts and pushouts from La Fuente, for example, 16 percent were transferred to the district's independent studies program; almost one-third of those never showed up at all, whereas the rest stayed a couple of weeks or longer before leaving the schooling system altogether (see flow chart 1).

At Beacon, truant or nonproductive students were routinely enrolled in the district's adult education program, which in turn was not required to report them as dropouts if they subsequently left. Of the seventy eventual dropouts and pushouts who were enrolled at Beacon during 1988–89, Beacon referred 64 percent to adult education after several months, and most of these students—78 percent of such referrals—never actually enrolled; three-fifths of the adult education no-shows were male, two-fifths female (see flow chart 2). Explained one teacher: "There is no monitoring once they are at adult ed. It's really the end. They leave saying they'll make it there, but 99 percent won't. We say, 'Yeah, good luck'—sending them out feeling good. But we know they won't make it" (Beacon, field notes, 4/7/88).

APPENDIX

FLOW CHART I

One Year's Progress through Continuation High School:
Those Who Ever Enrolled at La Fuente, September 6, 1988, through June
15, 1989, Status as of October 25, 1989

Ever Enrolled in SAM Program, Total: 117		Never Enrolled in SAM Program, Total: 557	
Am. Indian girls:	4	Am. Indian boys:	9
Asian girls:	4	Am. Indian girls:	6
Black girls:	18	Asian boys:	15
Filipino girls:	2	Asian girls:	2
Latino girls:	64	Black boys:	53
Samoan girls:	1	Black girls:	20
White girls:	22	Filipino boys:	15
Race ? girls:	2	Filipino girls:	5
		Latino boys:	196
		Latino girls:	103
		Samoan boys:	10
		Samoan girls:	8
		White boys:	68
		White girls:	42
		Race ? boys:	4
		Race ? girls:	1

Those Who Ever Enrolled at La Fuente during 1988–89, Total: 674
18 entered as should-be freshmen, 125 as sophomores, 295 as juniors,
203 as seniors, 31 as fifth-year seniors, and 2 as sixth-year seniors

Transferred to Another School or Program, Total: 94	La Fuente Was Last School Ever Attended, through Oct. 1989, Total: 495	Referred to Independent Studies Program, Total: 85
See Flow Chart 1, Part B	See Flow Chart 1 Part A	See Flow Chart 1, Part C

FLOW CHART I, PART A

Those Whose Last School Ever Attended Was La Fuente

La Fuente was Last School Ever Attended through Oct. 1989, Total: 495	
Am. Indian boys:	6
Am. Indian girls:	7
Asian boys:	7
Asian girls:	6
Black boys:	40
Black girls:	33
Filipino boys:	7
Filipino girls:	4
Latino boys:	152
Latino girls:	130
Samoan boys:	9
Samoan girls:	5
White boys:	41
White girls:	46
Race ? boys:	2

Dropped Out of La Fuente, Total: 281

Am. Indian boys:	4
Am. Indian girls:	2
Asian boys:	3
Asian girls:	4
Black boys:	22
Black girls:	18
Filipino boys:	4
Filipino girls:	2
Latino boys:	97
Latino girls:	65
Samoan boys:	5
Samoan girls:	2
White boys:	26
White girls:	27

(see also: no shows at ISP)

Still Enrolled, Total: 164

Am. Indian boys:	2
Am. Indian girls	4
Asian boys:	3
Asian girls:	2
Black boys:	16
Black girls:	11
Filipino boys:	2
Latino boys:	43
Latino girls:	51
Samoan boys:	4
Samoan girls:	2
White boys:	11
White girls:	11
Race ? boys:	2

Graduated from La Fuente, Total: 50

Diploma:

Am. Indian girls:	1
Asian boys:	1
Black boys:	2
Black girls:	4
Filipino boys:	1
Filipino girls:	2
Latino boys:	12
Latino girls:	13
Samoan girls:	1
White boys:	3
White girls:	8

CHSPE/GED:

Latino girls:	1
White boys:	1

Official Reasons for Dropout or Pushout, Total: 281

Expelled, Subtotal: 1

Latino boys: 1

Left, under age 18 (truant), Subtotal: 217

Am. Indian boys:	3
Asian boys:	2
Asian girls:	2
Black boys:	15
Black girls:	15
Filipino boys:	1
Filipino girls:	2
Latino boys:	77
Latino girls:	53
Samoan boys:	4
Samoan girls:	2
White boys:	21
White girls:	20

Left, age 18 or over, Subtotal: 6

Filipino boys:	1
Latino boys:	2
Latino girls:	2
White girls:	1

Military, Subtotal: 1

Black boys: 1

Moved, no transcript requested, Subtotal: 11

Am. Indian girls:	2
Black boys:	1
Black girls:	1
Latino boys:	2
Latino girls:	2
Samoan boys:	1
White boys:	1
White girls:	1

No show for new term, Subtotal: 45

Am. Indian boys:	1
Asian boys:	1
Asian girls:	2
Black boys:	5
Black girls:	2
Filipino boys:	2
Latino boys:	15
Latino girls:	8
White boys:	4
White girls:	5

Those Who Transferred to Another School or Program from La Fuente

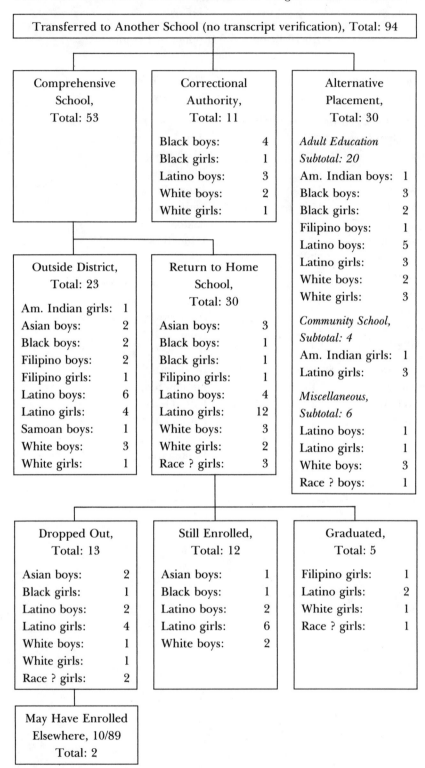

Transferred to Another School (no transcript verification), Total: 94

Comprehensive School, Total: 53

Correctional Authority, Total: 11

Black boys:	4
Black girls:	1
Latino boys:	3
White boys:	2
White girls:	1

Alternative Placement, Total: 30

Adult Education Subtotal: 20

Am. Indian boys:	1
Black boys:	3
Black girls:	2
Filipino boys:	1
Latino boys:	5
Latino girls:	3
White boys:	2
White girls:	3

Community School, Subtotal: 4

Am. Indian girls:	1
Latino girls:	3

Miscellaneous, Subtotal: 6

Latino boys:	1
Latino girls:	1
White boys:	3
Race ? boys:	1

Outside District, Total: 23

Am. Indian girls:	1
Asian boys:	2
Black boys:	2
Filipino boys:	2
Filipino girls:	1
Latino boys:	6
Latino girls:	4
Samoan boys:	1
White boys:	3
White girls:	1

Return to Home School, Total: 30

Asian boys:	3
Black boys:	1
Black girls:	1
Filipino girls:	1
Latino boys:	4
Latino girls:	12
White boys:	3
White girls:	2
Race ? girls:	3

Dropped Out, Total: 13

Asian boys:	2
Black girls:	1
Latino boys:	2
Latino girls:	4
White boys:	1
White girls:	1
Race ? girls:	2

Still Enrolled, Total: 12

Asian boys:	1
Black boys:	1
Latino boys:	2
Latino girls:	6
White boys:	2

Graduated, Total: 5

Filipino girls:	1
Latino girls:	2
White girls:	1
Race ? girls:	1

May Have Enrolled Elsewhere, 10/89 Total: 2

FLOW CHART I, PART C
Those Who Were Referred to Independent Studies Program by La Fuente

---

Referred to Independent Studies Program (ISP), including GED,
Total: 85

Never Showed Up,
Total: 17

Asian boys:	1
Black boys:	1
Black girls:	1
Latino boys:	4
Latino girls:	6
White boys:	3
White girls:	1

Ever Enrolled,
Total: 68

Am. Indian boys:	2
Am. Indian girls:	1
Asian boys:	2
Black boys:	2
Filipino boys:	5
Filipino girls:	1
Latino boys:	21
Latino girls:	8
Samoan girls:	4
White boys:	11
White girls:	10
Race? boys:	1

Dropped Out,
Total: 40

Moved:
White girls:	1

No show for new term:
Latino boys:	5
Latino girls:	2
White boys:	1

Left, under 18:
Am. Indian boys:	1
Am. Indian girls:	1
Asian boys:	1
Filipino boys:	1
Latino boys:	11
Latino girls:	4
Samoan girls:	1
White boys:	6
White girls:	4
Race ? boys:	1

Still Enrolled,
Total: 18

Asian boys:	1
Black boys:	2
Filipino boys:	1
Filipino girls:	1
Latino boys:	4
Latino girls:	2
Samoan girls:	2
White boys:	2
White girls:	3

Graduated or
Passed CHSPE or
GED,
Total: 10

Diploma:
Filipino boys:	2
White girls:	2

CHSPE/GED:
Am. Indian boys:	1
Filipino boys:	1
Latino boys:	1
Samoan girls:	1
White boys:	2

FLOW CHART 2
One Year's Progress through Continuation High School: Those Who Ever
Enrolled at Beacon, September 6, 1988, through June 15, 1989, Status as
of October 25, 1989

Entered from Alternative Programs, Total: 27	Entered from Comprehensive High Schools, Total: 148	Entered as Walk-ons (out of School), Total: 32
Black girls: 1	Am. Indian boys: 3	Asian girls: 1
Latino boys: 6	Asian boys: 6	Filipino girls: 1
Latino girls: 1	Black boys: 4	Latino boys: 5
White boys: 12	Black girls: 1	Latino girls: 7
White girls: 7	Filipino boys: 4	White boys: 7
	Filipino girls: 2	White girls: 11
	Latino boys: 32	
	Latino girls: 19	(63 percent of the
	White boys: 40	walk-ons had
	White girls: 36	been enrolled
	Other boys: 1	in the district
		before)

Those Who Ever Enrolled at Beacon During 1988–89, Total: 207
4 entered as should-be freshmen, 46 as sophomores, 74 as juniors,
67 as seniors, 15 as fifth-year seniors, 1 as sixth-year senior

Transferred to Another School, Total: 19	Beacon Was Last School Ever Attended, through Oct. 1989, Total: 137	Referred to Adult Education, Total: 51
See Flow Chart 2, Part B	See Flow Chart 2, Part A	See Flow Chart 2, Part C

FLOW CHART 2, PART A

Those Whose Last School Ever Attended Was Beacon

Beacon Was Last School Ever Attended, through Oct. 1989, Total: 137

Dropped Out of Beacon, Total: 22	Still Enrolled, Total: 79	Graduated from Beacon, Total: 36
Asian boys: 1	Am. Indian boys: 2	Am. Indian boys: 1
Black girls: 1	Asian boys: 4	Black boys: 1
Latino boys: 6	Black girls: 1	Filipino boys: 2
Latino girls: 4	Filipino boys: 2	Latino boys: 3
White boys: 3	Filipino girls: 2	Latino girls: 6
White girls: 7	Latino boys: 16	White boys: 10
	Latino girls: 12	White girls: 13
(see also: no shows at adult education)	White boys: 21	
	White girls: 19	

Official Reasons for Dropout or Pushout, Total: 22

Moved, no transcript requested:
Black girls: 1
Latino boys: 2
Latino girls: 3
White girls: 5

Left, under age 18 (truant):
Asian boys: 1
Latino boys: 2
Latino girls: 1
White boys: 3

Left, age 18 or over:
Latino boys: 2

Pregnancy:
White girls: 1

Work:
White girls: 1

Those Who Transferred to Another School from Beacon

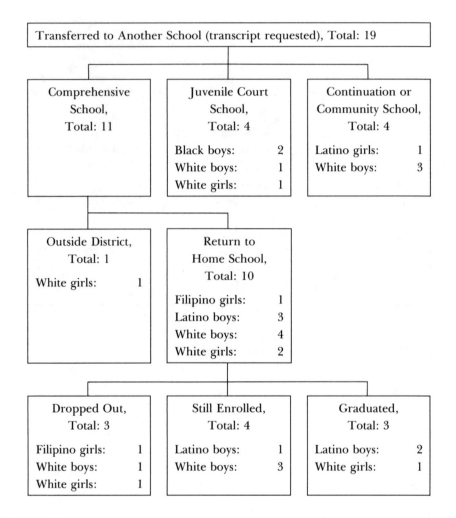

FLOW CHART 2, PART C

Those Who Were Referred to Adult Education by Beacon

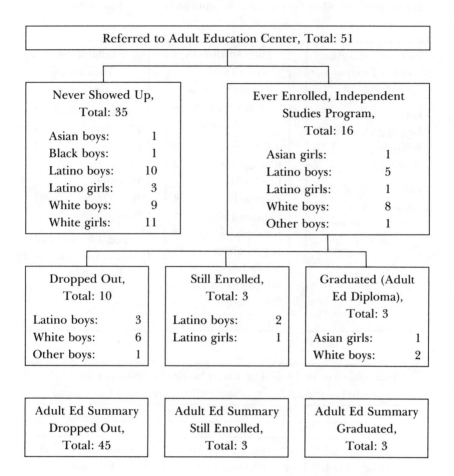

Referred to Adult Education Center, Total: 51

Never Showed Up, Total: 35		Ever Enrolled, Independent Studies Program, Total: 16	
Asian boys:	1		
Black boys:	1	Asian girls:	1
Latino boys:	10	Latino boys:	5
Latino girls:	3	Latino girls:	1
White boys:	9	White boys:	8
White girls:	11	Other boys:	1

Dropped Out, Total: 10		Still Enrolled, Total: 3		Graduated (Adult Ed Diploma), Total: 3	
Latino boys:	3	Latino boys:	2		
White boys:	6	Latino girls:	1	Asian girls:	1
Other boys:	1			White boys:	2

Adult Ed Summary Dropped Out, Total: 45	Adult Ed Summary Still Enrolled, Total: 3	Adult Ed Summary Graduated, Total: 3

FLOW CHART 3

A Longitudinal Tracking of a Continuation High School Class: Should-Be Class of 1989 Who Ever Enrolled at Beacon, Status as of June 1990

Entered from Alternative Programs Total: 19	Entered Directly from District's Comprehensive High Schools, Total: 86	Entered as Walk-ons, Total: 26
Latino boys: 4		Asian girls: 1
Latino girls: 2		Black boys: 1
White boys: 6	Asian boys: 1	Latino boys: 3
White girls: 7	Black boys: 2	Latino girls: 4
	Black girls: 2	White boys: 9
(more than half had been enrolled in the district before)	Filipino boys: 4	White girls: 7
	Filipino girls: 3	Race ? boys: 1
	Latino boys: 18	
	Latino girls: 13	(more than half had been enrolled in the district before)
	White boys: 21	
	White girls: 17	
	Race ? boys: 3	
	Race ? girls: 2	

Should-Be Class of 1989 Who Ever Enrolled at Beacon, Total: 131
39 entered as should-be sophomores, 79 as juniors, 13 as seniors

Transferred to Another School, Total: 17	Beacon Was Last School Ever Attended, through June 1990, Total: 45	Referred to Adult Education, Total: 69
See Flow Chart 3, Part B	See Flow Chart 3, Part A	See Flow Chart 3, Part C

FLOW CHART 3, PART A

Those Whose Last School Ever Attended Was Beacon

Beacon Was Last School Ever Attended, through June 1990, Total: 45

Black boys: 1; Filipino boys: 2; Latino boys: 8; White boys: 11;
Race ? boy: 1; Filipino girl: 2; Latino girls: 8, White girls: 12.

Dropped Out of Beacon, Total: 13	Still Enrolled, Total: 1	Graduated from Beacon, Total: 31
	Filipino girls: 1	
Black boys: 1		Filipino boys: 2
Latino boys: 5		Filipino girls: 1
Latino girls: 1		Latino boys: 3
White boys: 3		Latino girls: 7
White girls: 2		White boys: 8
Race ? boys: 1		White girls: 10
(see also: no shows at adult education)		74% in 1988–89; 26% in 1989–90.

Official Reasons for Dropout or Pushout,
Total: 13

Moved, no transcript requested:

Latino girls:	1
White girls:	2
Race ? boys:	1

Left, under age 18 (truant):

White boys:	2

Left, age 18 or over:

Black boys:	1
Latino boys:	3

No show after orientation:

Latino boys:	2
White boys:	1

FLOW CHART 3, Part B

Those Who Transferred to Another School from Beacon

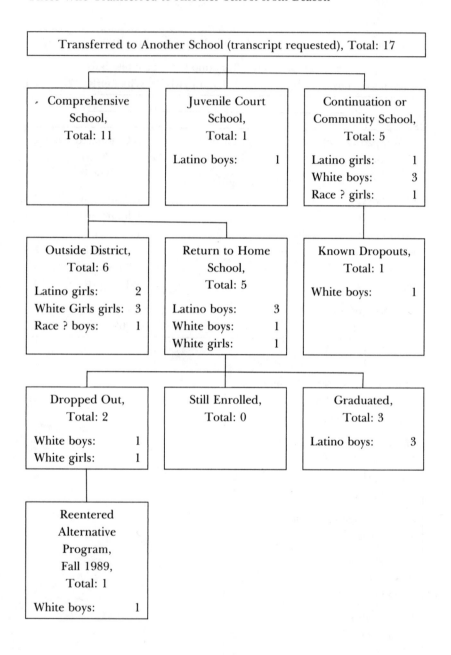

| Transferred to Another School (transcript requested), Total: 17 |

Those Who Were Referred to Adult Education by Beacon

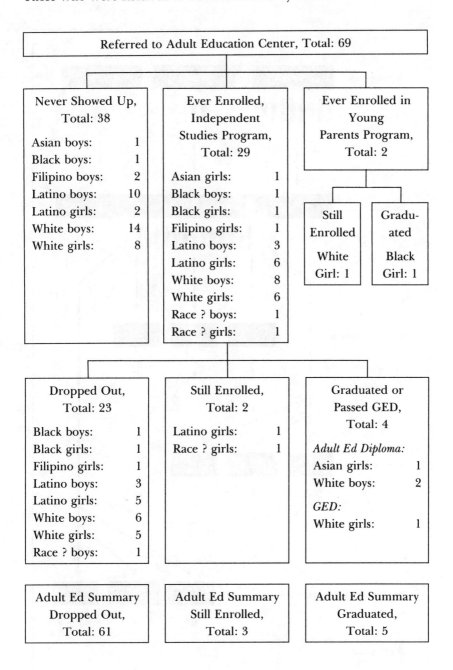

Referred to Adult Education Center, Total: 69

Never Showed Up, Total: 38

Asian boys:	1
Black boys:	1
Filipino boys:	2
Latino boys:	10
Latino girls:	2
White boys:	14
White girls:	8

Ever Enrolled, Independent Studies Program, Total: 29

Asian girls:	1
Black boys:	1
Black girls:	1
Filipino girls:	1
Latino boys:	3
Latino girls:	6
White boys:	8
White girls:	6
Race ? boys:	1
Race ? girls:	1

Ever Enrolled in Young Parents Program, Total: 2

Still Enrolled
White Girl: 1

Graduated
Black Girl: 1

Dropped Out, Total: 23

Black boys:	1
Black girls:	1
Filipino girls:	1
Latino boys:	3
Latino girls:	5
White boys:	6
White girls:	5
Race ? boys:	1

Still Enrolled, Total: 2

Latino girls:	1
Race ? girls:	1

Graduated or Passed GED, Total: 4

Adult Ed Diploma:
Asian girls:	1
White boys:	2

GED:
White girls:	1

Adult Ed Summary Dropped Out, Total: 61

Adult Ed Summary Still Enrolled, Total: 3

Adult Ed Summary Graduated, Total: 5

FLOW CHART 3, PART D

Shoul-Be Class of 1989 Who Ever Enrolled at Beacon, at a Glance

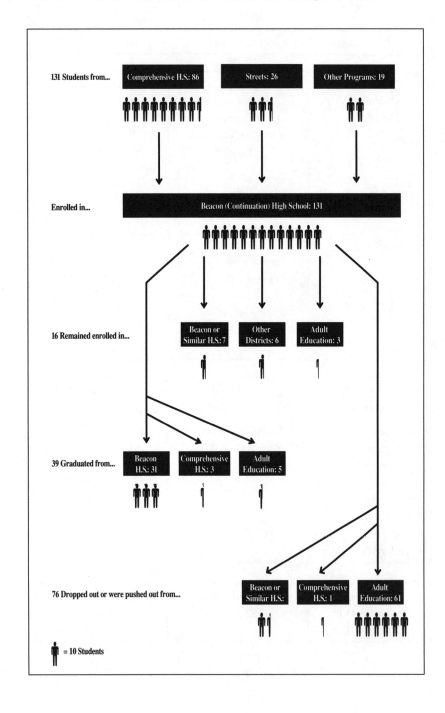

REFERENCES

Abrahamse, Allan F., Peter A. Morrison, and Linda J. Waite. *Beyond Stereotypes: Who Becomes a Teenage Mother?* Santa Monica: Rand Corporation, January 1988. ERIC ED 294 975.

Alcoff, Linda. "Cultural Feminism versus Post-Structuralism: The Identity Crisis in Feminist Theory." *Signs* 13, no. 3 (1988): 405–36.

Alvord, J. Barbara. "Male/Female Dynamics and Student Discipline." *NASSP Bulletin,* September 1979, 55–8.

Anyon, Jean. "Intersections of Gender and Class: Accommodation and Resistance by Working-Class and Affluent Females to Contradictory Sex-Role Ideologies." In *Gender, Class and Education,* edited by Stephen Walker and Len Barton, 19–37. London: Falmer Press, 1983.

Arnot, Madeleine. "Male Hegemony, Social Class and Women's Education." *Journal of Education* 164, no. 1 (1982): 64–89.

———. "A Cloud over Co-Education: An Analysis of the Forms of Transmission of Class and Gender Relations." In *Gender, Class and Education,* edited by Stephen Walker and Len Barton, 69–91. London: Falmer Press, 1983.

Arnove, Robert F., and Toby Strout. "Alternative Schools for Disruptive Youth." *Educational Forum* 44 (1980): 452–71.

Barr, Robert D. "The Growth of Alternative Public Schools: The 1975 ICOPE Report." *Changing Schools,* no. 12 (1975): 1–15. ERIC ED 106 898.

———. "Alternatives for the Eighties: A Second Decade of Development." *Phi Delta Kappan* 62, no. 8 (April 1981): 570–73.

Barro, Stephen M., and Andrew Kolstad. "Who Drops Out of High School? Findings from High School and Beyond." Unpublished research report, Washington, D.C., May 1987.

Bash, Carl E. "Continuation Group Seeks New Legislation." *California Journal of Secondary Education* 20, no. 2 (February 1945): 100–104.

REFERENCES

Becker, Howard. *Outsiders.* New York: Free Press, 1963.

Bill, Howard. "Dropouts: Prevention and Rehabilitation. Schools Rescue Potential Failures." In *Education U.S.A.* Washington, D.C.: National School Public Relations Association, 1972. ERIC ED 065 931.

Bogan, William J. "What Can Schools Teach in Eight Hours a Week?" *Chicago Schools Journal* 14 (January 1932): 193–94.

Boldenweck, Bill. "Comparing Past and Present." *San Francisco Examiner,* August 22, 1978, 4.

Born, Mary Ellen. "Never a Jungle: Observation of Socially Maladjusted Children at School." *California Journal of Secondary Education* 32, no. 5 (May 1957): 280–86.

Borus, Michael E., and Susan A. Carpenter. "A Note on the Return of Dropouts to High School." *Youth and Society* 14, no. 4 (June 1983): 501–7.

Borus, Michael E., and Richard Santos. "Youth Population." Chap. 1 in *Tomorrow's Workers,* edited by Michael E. Borus. Lexington, Mass.: D.C. Heath, 1983.

Botts, Robert E. "Will J. Reid: Profile of a Continuation High School." *Phi Delta Kappan* 53, no. 9 (May 1972): 574–76.

Bowles, Samuel, and Herbert Gintis. *Schooling in Capitalist America.* New York: Basic Books, 1976.

Bratta, John. "Independent Study and the Continuation Program." *California Continuation Education Association Newsletter,* March 1990, 8.

Brindis, Claire D., and Rita J. Jeremy. *Adolescent Pregnancy and Parenting in California: A Strategic Plan for Action.* San Francisco: Center for Population and Reproductive Health Policy, University of California, San Francisco, 1988.

Brophy, Jere. "Interactions of Male and Female Students with Male and Female Teachers." In *Gender Influences and Classroom Interaction,* edited by Louise Cherry Wilkinson and Cora B. Marrett, 115–42. Orlando, Fla.: Academic Press, 1985.

Bullock, Albert E., and Benjamin Weiss. "The Continuation Program in Los Angeles." *California Journal of Secondary Education* 20, no. 2 (February 1945): 86–91.

Burge, Penny L., and Steven M. Culver. "Sexism, Legislative Power, and Vocational Education." In *Gender in the Classroom,* edited by Susan L. Gabriel and Isaiah Smithson, 160–75. Urbana: University of Illinois Press, 1990.

Butler-Nalin, Paul, and Christine Padilla. "Dropouts: The Relationship to Student Characteristics, Behaviors, and Performance for Special Education Students." Annual Meeting of the American Educational Research Association, San Francisco, March 1989.

REFERENCES

Cagampang, Helen H., William H. Gerritz, and Gerald C. Hayward. *Pregnant and Parenting Minors and California Schools.* PC87–4–6-SOR. Berkeley: Policy Analysis for California Education, 1987.

California Commission for the Study of Educational Problems. *Report.* Sacramento: Calif. State Printing Office, 1931.

California Continuation Education Association. *CCEA District VIII Newsletter,* Fall 1975, 1–7.

——. *1987–88 State Directory.* Sacramento: CCEA, n.d.

California Legislature. Senate. *Report of the Senate Fact Finding Committee on Education.* Sacramento: Calif. State Printing Office, 1963.

——. Assembly Committee on Education. *Staff Report on House Resolution 330 (1964) by Assemblyman Beilenson.* Sacramento: Calif. State Printing Office, 1965.

——. Assembly Office of Research. *Dropping Out, Losing Out: The High Cost for California.* Sacramento: Joint Publications Office, 1985.

California State Board of Education. *Fourth Biennial Report, 1918–1920.* Sacramento: Calif. State Printing Office, 1921.

——. *Fifth Biennial Report, 1920–1922.* Sacramento: Calif. State Printing Office, 1923a.

——. *Vocational Education: Compulsory Part-Time Education.* Bulletin No. 23, P-T. E. Sacramento: Calif. State Printing Office, 1923b.

——. *Sixth Biennial Report, 1922–1924.* Sacramento: Calif. State Printing Office, 1924.

——. *Seventh Biennial Report, 1924–1926.* Sacramento: Calif. State Printing Office, 1926.

California State Dept. of Education. "Part-time Compulsory Education." *California Blue Bulletin* 5, no. 2 (June 1919): 3–4.

——. "The Best Way to Make Citizens of Aliens." *California Blue Bulletin* 6, no. 1 (March 1920): 19–21.

——. *Biennial Report, 1930–1932.* Sacramento: Calif. State Printing Office, 1932a.

——. *Continuation Education in California, 1931–32.* Bulletin No. 23. Sacramento: Calif. State Printing Office, 1932b.

——. *Handbook on Continuation Education in California.* By Emily G. Palmer. Bulletin No. 17. Sacramento: Calif. State Printing Office, 1932c.

——. *Continuation Education in California, 1932–33 and 1933–34.* Bulletin No. 17. Sacramento: Calif. State Printing Office, 1934.

——. "National Youth Administration Work Program and Compulsory Education." *California Schools* 7, no. 3 (March 1936): 92.

———. "Implementation Program to Follow CCC Educational Survey." *California Schools* 10, no. 7 (July 1939): 179–80.

———. "Cost of Continuation Programs." *Report for the Governor's Council,* January 27, 1946a, 13.

———. "Survey on Continuation Education." *Report for the Governor's Council,* May 27, 1946b, 12.

———. *Handbook on Continuation Education in California.* By Leo Jones. Bulletin XIX, No. 2. Sacramento: Calif. State Printing Office, 1950.

———. "Interviews with Students Who Drop Out of School." *Report for Governor's Council,* June 25, 1951: 6–8.

———. *Handbook on Continuation Education in California.* By the California Council for Continuation Education. Sacramento: Calif. State Printing Office, 1966.

———. *Handbook on Continuation Education in California.* By John R. Eales. Sacramento: Calif. State Printing Office, 1973.

———. *Biennial Report: Continuation Education Programs, 1983–1985.* Sacramento: California State Dept. of Education, 1985.

———. *Continuation Education Programs in California Public Schools.* By Robert E. Ehlers. Sacramento: Calif. State Printing Office, 1987.

———. *Continuation Education Programs: Biennial Report, 1985–1987.* By Mary Lou Hill. Sacramento: California State Dept. of Education, 1988.

———. *California Education Summit: Background Papers.* Sacramento: State Printing Office, 1990a.

———. *Focus on Excellence: Annual Performance Report for Vocational Education in California, 1988–89.* Sacramento: Calif. State Printing Office, 1990b.

Carnoy, Martin, and Henry M. Levin. *Schooling and Work in the Democratic State.* Stanford: Stanford University Press, 1985.

Carrington, Bruce, and Barry Troyna. "Combatting Racism through Political Education." In *Children and Controversial Issues: Strategies for the Early and Middle Years of Schooling,* edited by Bruce Carrington and Barry Troyna, 205–22. London: Falmer Press, 1988.

Carter, Susan B., and Mark Prus. "The Labor Market and the American High School Girl, 1890–1928." *Journal of Economic History* 62, no. 1 (March 1982): 163–71.

Children's Defense Fund. *Adolescent Pregnancy: An Anatomy of a Social Problem in Search of Comprehensive Solutions.* Washington, D.C.: Children's Defense Fund, 1987.

Ching, J. F. "Reasons Why Sixteen- and Seventeen-Year Old Pupils Leave Regular High Schools to Attend Continuation Trade Schools." *California Journal of Secondary Education* 10, no. 3 (February 1935): 188.

Clark, Burton R. *The Open-Door College.* New York: McGraw-Hill, 1960.

Cohen, Elizabeth G. "Expectation States and Interracial Interaction in School Settings." *Annual Review of Sociology* 8 (1982): 209–35.

Cohen, Ronald. "Ethnicity: Problem and Focus in Anthropology." *Annual Review of Anthropology* 7 (1978): 379–403.

Collins, James. "Language and Class in Minority Education." *Anthropology and Education Quarterly* 19, no. 4 (December 1988): 299–326.

Collins, Randall. "Some Comparative Principles of Educational Stratification." *Harvard Educational Review* 47 (February 1977): 1–27.

Connell, R. W. *Teachers' Work.* Sydney: George Allen & Unwin, 1985.

———. *Gender and Power.* Stanford: Stanford University Press, 1987.

Cremin, Lawrence. *The Transformation of the School: Progressivism in American Education, 1876–1957.* New York: Vintage Books, 1964.

Davies, Lynn. *Pupil Power: Deviance and Gender in School.* London: Falmer Press, 1984.

Deal, Terrence E., and Robert R. Nolan. "An Overview of Alternative Schools." Chap. 1 in *Alternative Schools: Ideologies, Realities, Guidelines,* edited by Terrence E. Deal and Robert R. Nolan, 1–17. Chicago: Nelson-Hall, 1978.

de Beauvoir, Simone. *The Second Sex.* New York: Alfred A. Knopf, 1953.

Douglas, Paul H. *American Apprenticeship and Industrial Education.* New York: Columbia University Press, 1921.

Duke, Daniel L. "Who Misbehaves?—A High School Studies Its Discipline Problems." *Educational Administration Quarterly* 12, no. 3 (Fall 1976): 65–85.

———. "Why Don't Girls Misbehave More Than Boys in School?" *Journal of Youth and Adolescence* 7, no. 2 (June 1978): 141–57.

Duke, Daniel L., and Irene Muzio. "How Effective Are Alternative Schools: A Review of Recent Evaluations and Reports." *Teachers College Record* 79, no. 3 (February 1978): 461–83.

Earle, Janice, and Virginia Roach, with Katherine Fraser. *Female Dropouts: A New Perspective.* Alexandria, Va.: National Association of State Boards of Education, 1987.

Eder, Donna. "The Cycle of Popularity: Interpersonal Relations among Female Adolescents." *Sociology of Education* 58 (July 1985): 154–65.

Edwards, Linda Nasif. "School Retention of Teenagers over the Business Cycle." *Journal of Human Resources* 11, no. 2 (Spring 1976): 200–208.

Eisenhart, Margaret A., and Dorothy C. Holland. "Learning Gender from Peers: The Role of Peer Groups in the Cultural Transmission of Gender." *Human Organization* 42, no. 4 (1983): 321–32.

Ekstrom, Ruth B., Margaret E. Goertz, Judith M. Pollack, and Donald A. Rock. "Who Drops Out of High School and Why? Findings from a National Study." *Teachers College Record* 87, no. 3 (Spring 1986): 356–73.

Elam, Stanley, ed. *The Gallup Polls of Attitudes toward Education 1969–1973.* Bloomington, Ind.: Phi Delta Kappa, 1973.

Elder, Glen H., Jr. "The Schooling of Outsiders." *Sociology of Education* 39, no. 4 (Fall 1966): 324–43.

———. "Continuation Schools and Educational Pluralism: A Vision of the Future." *California Journal of Secondary Education* 44, no. 7 (November 1969a): 324–8.

———. "Graduates of a Continuation High School: Their Life Patterns and Educational Attitudes." *California Journal of Secondary Education* 44, no. 7 (November 1969b): 329–33.

Evraiff, William. "Characteristics of Continuation School Students in Selected California Communities." Ph.D. diss., Stanford University, 1954.

Felice, Lawrence G. "Black Student Dropout Behavior: Disengagement from School Rejection and Racial Discrimination." *Journal of Negro Education* 50 (1981): 415–24.

Fine, Michelle. "Why Urban Adolescents Drop into and out of Public High School." *Teachers College Record* 87, no. 3 (Spring 1986): 393–409.

———. *Framing Dropouts: Notes on the Politics of an Urban High School.* Albany: State University of New York Press, 1991.

Fine, Michelle, and Pearl Rosenberg. "Dropping out of High School: The Ideology of School and Work." *Journal of Education* 165, no. 3 (1983): 257–72.

Fine, Michelle, and Nancie Zane. "Bein' Wrapped Too Tight: When Low-Income Women Drop out of High School." In *Dropouts from School,* edited by Lois Weis, Eleanor Farrar, and Hugh G. Petrie, 23–53. Albany: State University of New York Press, 1989.

Fishman, Pamela M. "Interaction: The Work Women Do." *Social Problems* 25, no. 4 (April 1978): 397–406.

Foley, Eileen M., and Susan B. McConnaughy. *Towards School Improvement: Lessons from Alternative High Schools.* New York: Public Education Association, 1982. ERIC ED 253 596.

Fordham, Signithia, and John Ogbu. "Black Students' School Success: Coping with the Burden of 'Acting White.'" *Urban Review* 18, no. 3 (1986): 1–31.

Freedberg, Louis. "Teaching Success—One School District Where Suspensions Have Been Suspended." *Pacific News Service,* October 31, 1985, 4–5.

Galas, Georgianna K., and Sadie V. Winans. "Credits and Grades in a Continuation High School." *California Journal of Secondary Education* 44, no. 7 (November 1969): 318–23.

Gaskell, Jane. "Course Enrollment in the High School: The Perspective of

Working-Class Females." *Sociology of Education* 58, no. 1 (January 1985): 48–59.

Gaskell, Jane, Arlene McLaren, and Myra Novogrodsky. *Claiming an Education: Feminism and Canadian Schools.* Toronto: Our Schools/Our Selves Education Foundation, 1989.

Giddens, Anthony. *Central Problems in Social Theory.* London: MacMillan, 1979.

Gilligan, Carol. *In a Different Voice: Psychological Theory and Women's Development.* Cambridge: Harvard University Press, 1982.

Goetz, Judith Preissle. "Theoretical Approaches to the Study of Sex-Role Culture in Schools." *Anthropology and Education Quarterly* 9, no. 1 (1978): 3–21.

Goffman, Erving. *Stigma: Notes on the Management of Spoiled Identity.* Englewood Cliffs, N.J.: Prentice-Hall, 1963.

Goldberger, Anthony M. *Variability in Continuation School Populations: A Study of the Significance of Differences in the Proportions of Child Workers.* Contributions to Education No. 454. New York: Teachers College, Columbia University, 1931.

Goodenough, Ruth Gallagher. "Small Group Culture and the Emergence of Sexist Behavior: A Comparative Study of Four Children's Groups." In *Interpretive Ethnography of Education,* edited by George Spindler and Louise Spindler, 409–46. Hillsdale, N.J.: Lawrence Erlbaum Associates, Publishers, 1987.

Goodsell, Willystine. *The Education of Women: Its Social Background and Its Problems.* New York: MacMillan , 1923.

Grant, Carl A., and Christine E. Sleeter. *After the School Bell Rings.* Philadelphia: Falmer Press, 1986.

Greene, Leonard. "State Students More Ambitious But Less Prepared, Study Says." *San Francisco Chronicle,* March 14, 1990, A-6.

Grissom, J. B., and L. A. Shepard. "Repeating and Dropping Out of School." In *Flunking Grades: Research and Policies on Retention,* edited by L. A. Shepard and M. L. Smith, 64–78. London: Falmer Press, 1989.

Haro, Carlos M. "Truant and Low-Achieving Chicano Student Perceptions in the High School Social System." *Aztlan: International Journal of Chicano Studies Research* 8 (1979): 99–131.

Hart, Ann Weaver. "Leader Succession and Socialization: A Synthesis." *Review of Educational Research* 61, no. 1 (Winter 1991): 451–74.

Hartmann, Heidi. "Capitalism, Patriarchy, and Job Segregation by Sex." In *Women and the Workplace: The Implications of Occupational Segregation,* edited by Martha Blaxall and Barbara Reagan, 137–69. Chicago: University of Chicago Press, 1976.

REFERENCES

Hendrick, Harry. " 'A Race of Intelligent Unskilled Labourers': The Adolescent Worker and the Debate on Compulsory Part-Time Day Continuation Schools, 1900–1922." *History of Education* 9, no. 2 (1980): 159–73.

Hendrick, Irving G. "The Impact of the Great Depression on Public School Support in California." *Southern California Quarterly* 54, no. 2 (Summer 1972): 25–40.

———. "California's Response to the 'New Education' in the 1930s." *California Historical Quarterly* 53 (Spring 1974): 25–40.

Hess, G. Alfred, Jr., Emily Wells, Carol Prindle, Paul Liffman, and Beatrice Kaplan. *"Where's Room 185?" How Schools Can Reduce Their Dropout Problem: An Ethnographic Investigation of Four Matched Pairs of Urban High Schools.* Chicago: Chicago Panel on Public School Policy and Finance, 1986.

Hicks, Robert S. "Continuation Pupils Are Our Forgotten Youth." *California Journal of Secondary Education* 20, no. 2 (February 1945): 75–78.

Hill, Mary Lou. Telephone conversation. State Department of Education, Sacramento, Calif., June 15, 1988.

Hirano-Nakanishi, Marsha. "The Extent and Relevance of Pre–High School Attrition and Delayed Education for Hispanics." *Hispanic Journal of Behavioral Sciences* 8, no. 1 (1986): 61–76.

Horner, Matina S. "Toward an Understanding of Achievement-Related Conflicts in Women." In *And Jill Came Tumbling After: Sexism in American Education,* edited by Judith Stacey, Susan Bereaud, and Joan Daniels, 43–63. New York: Dell Publishing, 1974.

Hunt, Dennis. " 'Thrash' Group Makes 'Mainstream' Metal Seem Tame: Dancing with Mr. Megadeth." *Los Angeles Times,* March 9, 1988.

Imber, Michael. "Part-Time Compulsory Education for Young Workers: The Continuation School, 1909–1935." Unpublished paper, Stanford University, 1978.

Irvine, Jacqueline J. "Teacher Communication Patterns as Related to the Race and Sex of the Student." *Journal of Educational Research* 78 (1985): 338–45.

Jacobs, J. Smith. "An Outsider Looks at California Continuation Schools." *California Journal of Secondary Education* 26, no. 7 (November 1951): 430–35.

———, ed. "Symposium: Problems of Current School-Leaving Age Requirements." *California Journal of Secondary Education* 33, no. 2 (February 1958): 93–128.

Johnson, Norris Brock. *West Haven: Classroom Culture and Society in a Rural Elementary School.* Chapel Hill: The University of North Carolina Press, 1985.

Jones, Arthur J. *The Continuation School in the United States.* U.S. Dept. of the Interior. U.S. Bureau of Education. Bulletin No. 1. Washington, D.C.: GPO, 1907.

Kanter, Rosabeth Moss. *Men and Women of the Corporation.* New York: Basic Books, 1977.

Kantor, Harvey. "Vocationalism in American Education: The Economic and Political Context, 1880–1930." In *Work, Youth, and Schooling: Historical Perspectives on Vocationalism in American Education,* edited by Harvey Kantor and David Tyack, 14–44. Stanford: Stanford University Press, 1982.

Kantor, Harvey, and David Tyack, eds. *Work, Youth, and Schooling: Historical Perspectives on Vocationalism in American Education.* Stanford: Stanford University Press, 1982.

Karabel, Jerome. "Community Colleges and Social Stratification." *Harvard Educational Review* 42, no. 4 (November 1972): 53–94.

Karweit, Nancy. "Time-on-Task Reconsidered: A Synthesis of Research on Time and Learning." *Educational Leadership* 41 (1984): 33–35.

Katznelson, Ira, and Margaret Weir. *Schooling for All: Class, Race, and the Decline of the Democratic Ideal.* New York: Basic Books, 1985.

Kelly, Gail P., and Ann S. Nihlen. "Schooling and the Reproduction of Patriarchy: Unequal Workloads, Unequal Rewards." In *Cultural and Economic Reproduction in Education: Essays on Class, Ideology and the State,* edited by Michael W. Apple, 162–80. London and Boston: Routledge & Kegan Paul, 1982.

Kessler, Sandra, Dean J. Ashenden, Robert W. Connell, and Gary W. Dowsett. "Gender Relations in Secondary School." *Sociology of Education* 58, no. 1 (January 1985): 34–48.

Kett, Joseph F. "The Adolescence of Vocational Education." In *Work, Youth, and Schooling: Historical Perspectives on Vocationalism in American Education,* edited by Harvey Kantor and David Tyack, 78–109. Stanford: Stanford University Press, 1982.

Kirp, David. *Just Schools: The Idea of Racial Equality in American Education.* Berkeley: University of California Press, 1982.

Knoeppel, Janet W. "The Students Served in Continuation Education." *California Journal of Secondary Education* 44, no. 7 (November 1969): 298–301.

Kolstad, Andrew J., and Phillip Kaufman. "Dropouts Who Complete High School with a Diploma or GED." Annual Meeting of the American Educational Research Association, San Francisco, March 1989.

Kolstad, Andrew J., and Jeffrey A. Owings. "High School Dropouts Who Change Their Minds about School." Annual Meeting of the American Educational Research Association, San Francisco, April 1986.

Lahaderne, Henriette, and Philip Jackson. "Withdrawal in the Classroom:

A Note on Some Educational Correlates of Social Desirability among School Children." *Journal of Educational Psychology* 61, no. 2 (1970): 97–101.

Landon, Eliot F., and Katherine Cox. "Continuation Education in San Diego." *California Journal of Secondary Education* 20, no. 2 (February 1945): 95–99.

Larson, Katherine A. "Early Secondary School Adjustment for At-Risk and Highest-Risk Students." Annual Meeting of the American Educational Research Association, San Francisco, March 1989.

Leedom, Elizabeth. "Continuation High Schools vs. Military: 'Second-Class' Diplomas Hurting Some Graduates." *San Francisco Examiner*, February 21, 1988, B-1, B-6.

Lightfoot, A. B. "How One Continuation School Carries On." *School and Society* 38, no. 966 (July 1933): 17–18.

Lockheed, Marlaine E., and Susan S. Klein. "Sex Equity in Classroom Organization and Climate." In *Handbook for Achieving Sex Equity through Education*, edited by Susan S. Klein, 189–217. Baltimore: Johns Hopkins University Press, 1985.

Los Angeles Public Schools. *Los Angeles Public Schools, Annual Report of the Board of Education and Superintendent: 1906–1907.* Los Angeles: Los Angeles Public Schools, 1907.

Lubeck, Sally. "Nested Contexts." In *Class, Race, and Gender in American Education*, edited by Lois Weis, 43–62. Albany: State University of New York Press, 1988.

Luxton, Meg. "Two Hands for the Clock: Changing Patterns in the Gendered Division of Labour in the Home." In *Through the Kitchen Window: The Politics of Home and Family*, edited by Meg Luxton, Harriet Rosenberg, and Sedef Arat Koc, 39–55. Toronto: Garamond Press, 1990.

McCormick, William J. "Continuation High School Effectiveness Multivarate [sic] Analysis of 441 School Outcomes." Unpublished paper, California State Department of Education, Office of Program Evaluation and Research, July 1990.

McDade, Laurie. "Sex, Pregnancy, and Schooling: Obstacles to a Critical Teaching of the Body." *Journal of Education* 169, no. 3 (Fall 1987): 58–79.

McDonough, E. M. "Organization and Administration of a Continuation School." *Industrial-Arts Magazine*, March 1921, 203–55.

McGowan, William N. "What's Happening in California Secondary Schools." *California Journal of Secondary Education* 34, no. 8 (December 1959): 485–89.

McLaren, Peter L. *Schooling as a Ritual Performance*. London: Routledge & Kegan Paul, 1986.

McRobbie, Angela. "Working Class Girls and the Culture of Femininity."

In *Women Take Issue,* edited by Women's Studies Group, Centre for Contemporary Cultural Studies, 96–106. London: Hutchinson, 1978.

Markey, James P. "The Labor Market Problems of Today's High School Dropouts." *Monthly Labor Review* 111, no. 6 (1988): 36–43.

Markey, Kathryn. "This Continuation School Has Room for All." *California Journal of Secondary Education* 15, no. 3 (March 1940): 160–63.

Martin, Jane Roland. *Reclaiming a Conversation: The Ideal of the Educated Woman.* New Haven: Yale University Press, 1985.

———. "The Contradiction of the Educated Woman." In *Changing Education: Women as Radicals and Conservators,* edited by Joyce Antler and Sari Knopp Biklen, 13–31. Albany: State University of New York Press, 1990.

Mascia-Lees, Frances E., Patricia Sharpe, and Colleen Ballerino Cohen. "The Postmodernist Turn in Anthropology: Cautions from a Feminist Perspective." *Signs* 15, no. 1 (1989): 7–33.

Matute-Bianchi, Maria Eugenia. "Ethnic Identities and Patterns of School Success and Failure among Mexican-Descent and Japanese-American Students in a California High School: An Ethnographic Analysis." *American Journal of Education* 95 (November 1986): 233–55.

Mayman, J. Edward. "The Evolution of the Continuation School in New York City." *School Review* 41, no. 3 (March 1933): 193–205.

Mehan, Hugh, Alma Hertweck, and J. Lee Meihls. *Handicapping the Handicapped.* Stanford, Calif.: Stanford University Press, 1986.

Metz, Mary Haywood. *Different by Design: The Context and Character of Three Magnet Schools.* New York: Routledge & Kegan Paul, 1986.

Minow, Martha. "Learning to Live with the Dilemma of Difference: Bilingual and Special Education." *Law and Contemporary Problems* 48, no. 2 (1984): 157–211.

Moore, Kristen A. "Government Policies related to Teenage Family Formation and Functioning: An Inventory." In *Teenage Pregnancy in a Family Context,* edited by T. Ooms. Philadelphia: Temple University Press, 1981.

Morena, James Charles. "Characteristics of Boys in a Metropolitan Continuation High School." Ph.D. diss., Stanford University, 1953.

"New Dyslexia Studies Say Many Girls Are Afflicted." *New York Times,* August 22, 1990, 1.

New York State Teachers' Association. Special issue on continuation schools. *New York State Education* 17, no. 4 (Dec. 1929): 291–328.

Nielsen, Francois, and Roberto M. Fernandez. *Achievement of Hispanic Students in American High Schools.* Washington, D.C.: GPO, 1981.

Nine-to-Five [9to5]. National Association of Working Women. *Profile of Working Women.* Cleveland: 9to5, National Association of Working Women, 1989.

Oakes, Jeannie. *Keeping Track: How Schools Structure Inequality.* New Haven: Yale University Press, 1985.

————. "Can Tracking Research Inform Practice? Technical, Normative, and Political Considerations." *Educational Researcher* 21, no. 4 (May 1992): 12–21.

Offe, Claus. "Notes on the Laws of Motion of Reformist State Policies." Unpublished paper, 1976.

Olsen, Laurie, with Rebekah Edwards. *Push Out, Step Out: A Report on California's Public School Dropouts.* Oakland: Citizens Policy Center, 1982.

Olson, Alden G. "How Richmond Provides for Continuation Youth." *California Journal of Secondary Education* 20, no. 2 (February 1945): 92–94.

Osborne, Janet K., and Deborah A. Byrnes. "Gifted, Disaffected, Disruptive Youths and the Alternative High School." *Gifted Child Today* 13, no. 3 (May/June 1990): 45–48.

Page, Reba. "Lower-Track Classes at a College-Preparatory High School: A Caricature of Educational Encounters." In *Interpretive Ethnography of Education: At Home and Abroad,* edited by George Spindler and Louise Spindler, 447–72. Hillsdale, N.J.: Lawrence Erlbaum Associates, Publishers, 1987.

Peng, Samuel S., and Ricky T. Takai. "High School Dropouts: Descriptive Information from High School and Beyond." *National Center for Education Statistics Bulletin,* November 1983, 1–10. ERIC ED 236 366.

Petchesky, Rosalind Pollack. "Reproduction and Class Divisions among Women." In *Class, Race, and Sex: The Dynamics of Control,* edited by Amy Swerdlow and Hanna Lessinger, 221–41. Boston: G. K. Hall, 1983.

Polit, Denise F., and Janet R. Kahn. "Teenage Pregnancy and the Role of the Schools." *Urban Education* 22, no. 2 (July 1987): 131–53.

Poole, Millicent E., and B. C. Low. "Who Stays? Who Leaves? An Examination of Sex Differences in Staying and Leaving." *Journal of Youth and Adolescence* 11, no. 1 (1982): 49–63.

Raywid, Mary Anne. *The Current Status of Schools of Choice in Public Secondary Education: Alternatives, Options, Magnets.* Hempstead, N.Y.: Hofstra University, Project on Alternatives in Education, 1982. ERIC ED 242 055.

Reed, Donald R. "The Nature and Function of Continuation Education: An Overview of an Exciting and Expanding Field of Education." *California Journal of Secondary Education* 44, no. 7 (November 1969): 292–97.

Reskin, Barbara, and Heidi Hartmann, eds. *Women's Work, Men's Work: Sex Segregation on the Job.* Washington, D.C.: National Academy Press, 1986.

Rios, Isnoel Mendez. "An Ethnographic Study of Intracultural Variation among High School Students of Mexican Descent." Ph.D. diss., Stanford University, 1989.

Robertson, Heather-jane. "Teacher Development and Gender Equity." In

Understanding Teacher Development, edited by Andy Hargreaves and Michael G. Fullan, 43–61. New York: Teachers College Press, 1992.

Rose, Mike. *Lives on the Boundary: The Struggles and Achievements of America's Underprepared.* New York: Free Press, 1989.

Rosenberg Foundation. "Continuation Schools Statewide Study," No. 238 (1953–59) and "U.C. Berkeley, Institute of Human Development, Continuation Schools Study," No. 457 (1964–66). Unpublished files, San Francisco.

Rothman, David J. *Conscience and Convenience: The Asylum and Its Alternatives in Progressive America.* Boston: Little, Brown & Co., 1980.

Rubin, Lillian. *Worlds of Pain.* New York: Basic Books, 1976.

Rumberger, Russell W. "Dropping Out of High School: The Influence of Race, Sex, and Family Background." *American Educational Research Journal* 20, no. 2 (Summer 1983): 199–220.

———. "High School Dropouts: A Review of Issues and Evidence." *Review of Educational Research* 57, no. 2 (Summer 1987): 101–21.

———. "Chicano Dropouts: A Review of Research and Policy Issues." Chap. 2 in *Chicano School Failure and Success: Research and Policy Agendas for the 1990s,* edited by Richard R. Valencia. Forthcoming.

Rury, John L. "Urban School Enrollment at the Turn of the Century: Gender as an Intervening Variable." *Urban Education* 23, no. 1 (April 1988): 68–88.

Sadker, Myra, David Sadker, and Susan Klein. "The Issue of Gender in Elementary and Secondary Education." *Review of Research in Education* 17 (1991): 269–334.

Schmidt, Leo, Calvin C. Nelson, Louis S. Barber, and Clyde D. Powell. "Continuation School Objectives: The Student Viewpoint." *Thrust for Educational Leadership* 4, no. 4 (March 1975): 23–24.

Schur, Edwin M. *The Politics of Deviance: Stigma Contests and the Uses of Power.* Englewood Cliffs, N.J.: Prentice-Hall, 1980.

Schwartz, Frances. "Supporting or Subverting Learning: Peer Group Patterns in Four Tracked Schools." *Anthropology and Education Quarterly* 12, no. 2 (1981): 99–121.

Scott, Joan W. "Gender: A Useful Category of Historical Analysis." *American Historical Review* 91, no. 5 (December 1986): 1053–75.

———. "Deconstructing Equality-Versus-Difference: Or, the Uses of Poststructuralist Theory for Feminism." In *Conflicts in Feminism,* edited by Marianne Hirsch and Evelyn Fox Keller, 134–48. New York: Routledge, 1990.

Sedlak, Michael W. "Young Women and the City: Adolescent Deviance and the Transformation of Educational Policy 1870–1960." *History of Education Quarterly* 23, no. 1 (Spring 1983): 1–28.

Sennett, Richard, and Jonathan Cobb. *The Hidden Injuries of Class.* New York: Alfred A. Knopf, 1972.

Shaffer, E. Evan. *A Study of Continuation Education in California.* California State Department of Education. Sacramento: Calif. State Printing Office, 1955.

Silver, Harold. "Ideology and the Factory Child: Attitudes to Half-Time Education." In *Education as History*, 35–59. London: Methuen & Co., 1983.

Silverman, Hirsch Lazaar. "Educational 'Unadaptives' and the Schools." *Bulletin of the National Association of Secondary-School Principals* 42, no. 240 (October 1958): 129–33.

Simmons, Roberta G., and Dale A. Blyth. *Moving into Adolescence: The Impact of Pubertal Change and School Context.* New York: Aldine de Gruyter, 1987.

Smith, William C. "The Saturday Continuation School." *California Journal of Secondary Education* 20, no. 2 (February 1945): 79–81.

Smithies, Elsie M. *Case Studies of Normal Adolescent Girls.* New York: D. Appleton and Company, 1933.

Snider, William. "Study: Schools Violating Rights of Pregnant Girls." *Education Week*, May 17, 1989, 5.

Stacey, Judith. "Can There Be a Feminist Ethnography?" *Women's Studies International Forum* 11, no. 1 (1988): 21–27.

———. *Brave New Families.* New York: Basic Books, 1990.

Stanlaw, James, and Alan Peshkin. "Black Visibility in a Multi-Ethnic High School." In *Class, Race, and Gender in American Education*, edited by Lois Weis, 209–29. Albany: State University of New York Press, 1988.

Stern, David, James Catterall, Charlotte Alhadeff, and Maureen Ash. *Reducing the High School Dropout Rate in California.* Berkeley: School of Education, University of California, Berkeley, 1985.

Stern, David, E. Gareth Hoachlander, Susan Choy, and Charles Benson. *One Million Hours a Day: Vocational Education in California Public Secondary Schools.* Policy Paper No. PP86–3–2. Berkeley: Policy Analysis for California Education, 1986.

Stinchcombe, Arthur. *Rebellion in a High School.* Chicago: Quadrangle, 1964.

———. "Social Structure and Organizations." In *Handbook of Organizations*, edited by James G. March, 142–93. Chicago: Rand-McNally, 1965.

Stolzman, James, and Herbert Gamberg. "Marxist Class Analysis versus Stratification Analysis as General Approaches to Social Inequality." *Berkeley Journal of Sociology* 18 (1973–74): 105–25.

Swidler, Ann. *Organization without Authority: Dilemmas of Social Control in Free Schools.* Cambridge: Harvard University Press, 1979.

REFERENCES

———. "Culture in Action: Symbols and Strategies." *American Sociological Review* 51 (April 1986): 273–86.

"Teaching Discouraged Learners: A Round-Table Discussion." *Instructor Secondary Edition,* Fall 1988, 27–30.

Thorne, Barrie. "Girls and Boys Together . . . But Mostly Apart: Gender Arrangements in Elementary Schools." In *Relationships and Development,* edited by Willard W. Hartup and Zick Rubin, 167–84. Hillsdale, N.J.: Lawrence Erlbaum Associates, Publishers, 1986.

———. "Children and Gender: Constructions of Difference." In *Theoretical Perspectives on Sexual Difference,* edited by Deborah L. Rhode, 100–113. New Haven: Yale University Press, 1990.

Tibbitts, F. Lyman. "Functions of Co-ordination." *Industrial Arts and Vocational Education* 24, nos. 7, 9, 10 (July, September, October 1935): 199–290.

Tronto, Joan C. "Beyond Gender Difference to a Theory of Care." *Signs* 12, no. 4 (Summer 1987): 644–63.

Trout, Robert G. "The Ills of Continuation in California." *California Journal of Secondary Education* 12, no. 3 (March 1937): 181–82.

Tyack, David. *The One Best System: A History of American Urban Education.* Cambridge: Harvard University Press, 1974.

———. "The History of Secondary Schools in Delivering Social Services." Unpublished paper, Stanford University, 1978.

Tyack, David, and Michael Berkowitz. "The Man Nobody Liked: Toward a Social History of the Truant Officer, 1840–1940." *American Quarterly* 26 (Spring 1977): 31–54.

Tyack, David, and Elisabeth Hansot. *Managers of Virtue: Public School Leadership in America, 1820–1980.* New York: Basic Books, 1982.

———. *Learning Together: A History of Coeducation in American Public Schools.* New Haven: Yale University Press, 1990.

Tyack, David, Robert Lowe, and Elisabeth Hansot. *Public Schools in Hard Times.* Cambridge: Harvard University Press, 1984.

U.S. Bureau of the Census. *Historical Statistics of the United States: Colonial Times to 1970, Part 1.* Washington, D.C.: GPO, 1978.

———. *Current Population Reports* Series P-60, No. 175. *Poverty in the United States: 1990.* Washington, D.C.: GPO, 1991.

U.S. Dept. of Education, Center for Education Statistics, OERI. *Digest of Education Statistics.* Washington, D.C.: GPO, 1987.

U.S. Dept. of Health, Education and Welfare, Federal Board for Vocational Education. *Digest of Annual Reports of State Boards for Vocational Education to the Office of Education.* [Title varies]. Washington, D.C.: GPO, 1917–1965.

U.S. General Accounting Office. *School Dropouts.* GAO/HRD-86–106BR. Washington, D.C.: GPO, 1986.

Valli, Linda. "Becoming Clerical Workers: Business Education and the Culture of Femininity." In *Ideology and Practice of Schooling,* edited by Michael W. Apple and Lois Weis, 213–34. Philadelphia: Temple University Press, 1982.

Voss, John W. "Current Materials and Events in Continuation Education." *California Journal of Secondary Education* 30, no. 8 (December 1955): 465–68.

———. "Current Events and Materials in Continuation Education." *California Journal of Secondary Education* 33, no. 3 (March 1958): 151–55.

Warner, Gordon. "A History of the Continuation Education Program in California." Ph.D. diss., University of California, Berkeley, 1954.

Wax, Rosalie. "The Warrior Dropouts." In *Education: Readings in the Processes of Cultural Transmission,* edited by H. Lindquist, 207–17. Boston: Houghton Mifflin, 1970.

Weber, Edward J. "Dropouts Who Go to School." *Phi Delta Kappan* 53, no. 9 (May 1972): 572–73.

Wehlage, Gary G., and Robert A. Rutter. "Dropping Out: How Much Do Schools Contribute to the Problem?" *Teachers College Record* 87, no. 3 (Spring 1986): 374–92.

Wehlage, Gary G., Robert A. Rutter, Gerald R. Smith, Nancy Lesko, and Ricardo R. Fernandez. *Reducing the Risk: Schools as Communities.* London: Falmer Press, 1989.

Weiler, Kathleen. *Women Teaching for Change: Gender, Class and Power.* South Hadley, Mass.: Bergin & Garvey, 1988.

Weis, Lois. "High School Girls in a De-Industrializing Economy." In *Class, Race, and Gender in American Education,* edited by Lois Weis, 183–208. Albany: State University of New York Press, 1988.

White, Lawrence B. "Continuation Education for Disadvantaged Youth in California." *California Journal of Secondary Education* 37, no. 87 (December 1962): 399–406.

Willis, Paul. *Learning to Labour: How Working Class Kids Get Working Class Jobs.* Farnborough, Eng.: Saxon House, 1977.

Wolpe, AnnMarie. *Within School Walls: The Role of Discipline, Sexuality and the Curriculum.* London: Routledge & Kegan Paul, 1988.

Yllo, Kersti, and Michele Bograd, eds. *Feminist Perspectives on Wife Abuse.* Newbury Park, Calif.: Sage Publications, 1988.

Young, Timothy. *Public Alternative Education.* New York: Teachers College Press, 1990.

REFERENCES

Zane, Nancie. *In Their Own Voices: Young Women Talk about Dropping Out.* Washington, D.C.: NOW Legal Defense and Education Fund, 1988.

Zober, Edith. *A Demonstration of Reorientation of Illegitimately Pregnant Teenage Girls Living in Rural Areas.* Washington, D.C.: Children's Bureau, U.S. Department of Health, Education and Welfare, 1967. ERIC ED 025 798.

INDEX

Ability grouping. *See* Tracking

Abortion, 154, 184

Absenteeism. *See* Attendance

Academic achievement, 4, 141–42, 204–5

Academics: disengagement from, 30, 126, 128, 210, 211; reengagement in, 202–6, 212. *See also* Teacher-student relations

Academic status: and gender, 103, 129–30, 137–38, 163–64, 204–5; and peer relations, 105, 135; and teacher bias, 105, 140n.7

Adjustment education, 35, 48–57, 59. *See also* Prosser, Charles

Administrators, 51, 73–74, 178–79. *See also* Principals

Adoption, 154

Adult-child hierarchy, 225–27. *See also* Teacher-student relations

Adult education: diploma, 84; as safety valve, 88–89, 99–101, 220, 232, 233–34, 243, 247, 248

Adults as continuation students, 35, 44, 45

African-American students, 27–28, 59, 129, 153n.11, 163, 210, 211n.12

Alienation from comprehensive school, 4, 59–60, 127, 130–31, 135–36, 167–68, 206–7

Alternative schools: in California, 60–61; continuation as form of, 35, 59–61; enrollment in, 1–2; expansion of, 94, 216–17;

nationwide, xvi, 61; in New York, 2n.1, 61; as reform strategy, xv–xvi, 218; as safety valve, 2–3, 216, 219–20; in Washington, 2, 61. *See also* Adult education; Continuation education; Continuation high schools; Independent studies programs; School-age mothers programs

Arnot, Madeleine, 171, 223

Arnove, Robert F., 2

Asian-American students, 28, 70, 129, 200n.1

Attendance, 81, 82–83, 98–102. *See also* Compulsory school attendance laws; Truancy

Barr, Robert D., 218

"Beacon" continuation high school: curriculum at, 168, 208; dropout and graduation rates at, 200; features of, 12, 13–14, 15–16, 70–71; history and reputation of, 10, 13–14, 15–16, 33–34, 65, 70–73, 80–81; and pushouts, 98–100; students, 15–16, 28; suspensions at, 108–9, 112

Becker, Howard, 69

Black students. *See* African-American students

Bowles, Samuel, 7, 31

Boyfriends: as alternative to academic success, 98, 102, 143, 144; as alternative to work, 192–93, 198;

267